D0953281

The World of Gerard Mercator

The World of

GERARD MERCATOR

The Mapmaker Who
Revolutionized Geography

Andrew Taylor

WALKER & COMPANY
New York

First published in the United States of America in 2004 by
Walker Publishing Company, Inc.

Published simultaneously in Canada by Fitzhenry and Whiteside,
Markham, Ontario L3R 4T8

For information about permission to reproduce selections from this book, write to Permissions, Walker & Company, 104 Fifth Avenue, New York, New York 10011.

Art Credits: Pages i, xi, and 95 used by permission of the National Maritime Museum, Greenwich, England. Pages ii–iii, xii, and 97 used by permission of the Bibliothèque Royale Albert I, Brussels. Pages 3, 28, 49, 61, 122, 126, 211, 214, and 231 used by permission of the Science Photo Library, London. Pages 10, 46, 70, 109, and 154 used by permission of the British Library, London, Rare Books and Maps Collections. Page 18 used by permission of the Hereford Cathedral Library, Hereford, England. Pages 34–35 used by permission of the Library of Congress, Washington, D.C. Page 42 used by permission of Museo del Prado. Pages 52–53, 62–63, and 136–37 courtesy of Historic Cities Research Project http://historic-cities.huji.ac.il The Jewish National and University Library of The Hebrew University of Jerusalem. Page 75 used by permission of the National Gallery, London. Pages 84–85 and 202–203 used by permission of the Bibliothèque National de France. Page 88 used by permission of the New York Public Library, Rare Books Division. Pages 237 and 250 used by permission of the Royal Geographical Society, London. Page 252 used by permission of the Bodleian Library, Oxford, England.

Library of Congress Cataloging-in-Publication Data

Taylor, Andrew, 1951–
    The world of Gerard Mercator / Andrew Taylor.
        p.   cm.
    Includes bibliographical references (p.   ).
    ISBN 0-8027-1377-7 (hardcover : alk. paper)
        1. Mercator, Gerard, 1512–1594.   2. Cartographers—Netherlands—
    Biography.   3. Cartography—History—16th century.   I. Title.
    GA923.M37T39 2004
    526'.092—dc22
    [B]

                                        2004043068

Book design by Ralph L. Fowler

Visit Walker & Company's Web site at www.walkerbooks.com

Printed in the United States of America

10 9 8 7 6 5 4 3 2 1

For Sam, Abi, and Bec,

and all the years they have to come.

CONTENTS

ACKNOWLEDGMENTS

This book started with a journey to Hereford in England, where one of the great treasures of medieval Europe is on permanent display in the cathedral's New Library Building. The Hereford *mappamundi* sparked my initial interest in maps as a way of glimpsing the past, and my first thanks should go to the dean and chapter of the cathedral. They have custody of an irreplaceable treasure which belongs to all of us, and they make it available to anyone who cares to see it. Without that first visit, I would never have found my way to Mercator of Rupelmonde.

Because my grasp of foreign languages falls far short of Mercator's, I relied on several individuals to help me read letters and documents. Mark Riley, professor of classics at the California State University, Sacramento, was not only generous enough to translate Mercator's letters into English but also kind enough not to laugh outright at my own rusty Latin. Patrick Roberts of London similarly helped me with a number of French documents, and the late Dr. Dik ter Haar of Magdalen College, Oxford, welcomed me into his home and patiently guided me through many pages of Flemish. Any mistakes are mine; to all of them, my thanks.

In London and Oxford, the staffs of the British Library, the London Library, and the Bodleian Library were unfailingly helpful. Peter Barber, of the British Library's Maps Department, was particularly generous with his time in discussing Mercator's map of Britain with me. I had unstinting help, too, from the Plantin-Moretus Museum in Antwerp, where it was a privilege to walk through Christopher Plantin's old workshops; from Duisburg's Kultur und Stadthistorisches Museum; the

Mercator Museum in Sint Niklaas, Belgium; and the Cathedral of St. Jan, 's Hertogenbosch. A moment I shall never forget came in the Bibliothèque Nationale, Paris, when I first saw the map that is at the heart of the book: Mercator's world map of 1569.

Toby Eady and Mike Fishwick in London gave me the benefit of their professional help and advice in too many ways to list, and in New York, I had the good fortune to work with George Gibson. Every book needs the creative destruction of a good editor, and this volume had one of the best.

Friends helped in various ways. Tony and Jean Conyers lent me books from their library and must have wondered if they would ever see them again; Alison Roberts joined me on the trip to see Mercator's map in Paris; Grenville Byford shared his experiences as an ocean sailor to help me understand the minutiae of navigation; and Julian Bene, who spent many late nights and lengthy e-mails discussing Mercator and his life, may well recognize some of his conclusions in the book. Penny Berry came with me on that first visit to Hereford and not only tolerated an interest that changed into an obsession, but shared in it wholeheartedly, in England, Belgium, and Germany. The book that resulted is hers as much as mine.

But none of these people will object to the observation that the greatest thanks of all are due to Dr. Tim Littlewood and his National Health Service team in the Hematology Department at Oxford's John Radcliffe Hospital. I owe them everything, and I don't forget.

The World of Gerard Mercator

Introduction

ONE OF MY earliest memories is of myself as a small boy sitting on a wide window ledge, with my whole world laid out around me. As I turned my head, I took in the comfortable, familiar room behind me, the door into the kitchen, and the wooden sideboard up against the wall, while outside I could see down the yard toward the joiner's shop, which I knew was filled with sawdust and sharp blades. I could also see the familiar stone steps up to my front door, and another house across the way, where an old man used to sit in the doorway for hours on end, dozing.

That was about as far as my world stretched. I was aware, of course, of other worlds beyond, worlds I had heard about, half understood, or imagined for myself. Scattered among them were a few familiar islands that I had visited and knew fairly well—the stone-flagged floor of the greengrocer's on the corner, for instance, the high wall on top of which I could walk up to the church, or the little vegetable garden where I used to watch my father as he worked—but for all intents and purposes, they were surrounded by darkness. Good things occasionally came in from those shadows outside—bars of chocolate brought by a kindly aunt, perhaps, or my mother's shopping—but they were on the whole mysterious and unwelcoming, and if I occasionally peopled them with monsters, that was no more than any child does.

The story of discovery and mapmaking is one of pushing back shadows. The great explorers brought back undreamed-of riches and stories of unknown lands and peoples that were barely believable—the discovery of America, for instance, has been described as the greatest surprise in history—but their claims and discoveries had to be evaluated, laid out on paper, before they could form a coherent picture of the world. Much of that work was carried out by unknown figures, whose maps are lost, forgotten, or remembered only by passing mentions in ancient documents. Some were sailors or traders themselves, trying to prepare reliable charts for their own use and for those who came after them, but many were scholars who never went to sea. A few became famous and produced individual maps that stand out as landmarks in the history of the understanding of the planet. But none, in the last two thousand years, achieved as much as Gerard Mercator in extending the boundaries of what could be comprehended.

Mercator saw himself as a scholar in the ancient tradition, an *uomo universale* in the mold of the Renaissance—a seeker of truth to whom the whole of knowledge was a single book to be opened. His achievement was nothing less than to revolutionize the study of geography and redraw the map of the world.

Born near Antwerp in 1512, he lived through almost the entire turbulent sixteenth century—an age in which the known world grew year by year as new voyages made new discoveries, but one which also saw the Catholic Church and Europe itself torn apart by Martin Luther and the Protestant reformers. The sacking of cities, the smashing of statues by reformist zealots, and the religious savagery of Church authorities were all part of the temper of the times. This was the age of the Inquisition, whose power, as Mercator was to discover firsthand, extended across the Low Countries: The judicial torture and burning of the unfaithful were commonplace. But it was also an age of intellectual upheaval. Almost halfway through the century, the Polish astronomer Nicolaus Copernicus published his revolutionary theory that the Earth revolved around the Sun— an idea that was confirmed some sixty-five years later by the observations of Galileo Galilei through his telescope. The Church, still clinging to the old idea of the Earth at the center of the universe, could make Galileo recant, but it could not erase the new thinking.

By the time Mercator was born, the printing press had made books readily available across Europe, but the language of religion and intellec-

Gerard Mercator

tual debate was the same as it had been in the days of the medieval copy-ists toiling over manuscripts in the monasteries. Not just the Bible but also scientific, medical, and philosophical texts were written in Latin. At the University of Leuven and later in Duisburg, Mercator's conversation and correspondence were also in Latin. However, by 1594, the year he died, Bibles in the daily language of the people were commonplace. Galileo's writings appeared in clear and lucid Italian. This signified more than a change of vocabulary or language; scientists, by the turn of the century, were gaining the confidence to rely on observation, measurement, and reasoning rather than looking into the past for inspiration.

Mercator's own life reflected the era of change in which he lived, being full of apparent contradictions and opportunism, and extending over one of civilization's major crossroads. In many ways a child of the past, he was born into poverty and owed his first chances in life to the wealth of the traditional Catholic Church; yet his surviving letters are those of a tolerant reformist with Protestant leanings, who kept his religious views to himself. Like the artists of the Italian Renaissance, he relied on the favor of princes, dukes, and high dignitaries of the Church, but he also built a commercial business which depended on the new prosperous middle class that economic growth had created.

Mercator studied and created maps with a passionate attention to detail that would have been familiar to any of the scholars or artists of the Italian Renaissance. In his studies, he showed unswerving respect for the authority of Claudius Ptolemy of ancient Alexandria, who had proposed his own map projections—ways in which the Earth might be flattened out onto a sheet of paper. At the same time, Mercator did more than any other geographer of his day to demonstrate that Ptolemy's classical ideas of the world were outdated, misleading, and often simply wrong. As a cartographer, Mercator spent his lifetime collecting, collating, and assessing the latest reports from explorers whose discoveries rendered Ptolemy's ideas inadequate to describe the new world that was emerging; as a mathematician, he answered the problem of projection with his own solution, which has lasted for more than four hundred years.

There are few reliable contemporary descriptions of Mercator, few clues to the personality of the scholar who did more than anyone in the last two thousand years to turn mapmaking into a precise science. Moreover, many of his letters are lost. A number of the letters that do survive are appeals to dukes and princes of the German city-states, to dignitaries of the Catholic Church, even to the Holy Roman Emperor Charles V himself for support and sponsorship, for Mercator well understood the advantages of influential backing. Throughout his life, he was a driven man: Long hours at his desk as a student gave way to long hours at his workbench as he built the business that was to make his fortune, and the habit of study never left him. In the infirm years before his death, he would urge his children to carry him, chair and all, to his books.

Fear is an overpowering emotion in those of his letters that do survive—fear of death and damnation, fear of not completing the work he had begun, fear of failure. Orphaned at an early age, sent off to the harsh rigors of a monastic school, he knew little of maternal love or family stability, and his difficult childhood left him cautious and circumspect. In his business life, he was assiduous in appealing for official copyright protection for his maps and globes, and the careful investment of his profits in property and forestland showed his awareness of the importance of security.

He was also aware, as he had to be, of the value of silence. In the religious conflicts of his time, his principles were those of a reformer, but his arrest and imprisonment at the hands of the Inquisition clearly reinforced his instinct for caution. Even after he moved from Leuven to the more relaxed environment of Duisburg, in Germany, he avoided any involvement in religious argument. Rather than the perils of theological disputation, he enjoyed his reputation in the town as a good host and dinner guest. The handful of contemporary accounts speak of him as a witty and entertaining conversationalist, and gifts of food and wine from the city authorities suggest a man who was known to enjoy good company and a well-stocked table.

But more than anything else, he was a scholar. Though he never traveled beyond the well-known towns of northern Europe, never, so far as we know, even boarded a ship, his work, together with that of sea captains and explorers, allowed people of the sixteenth century and the generations who followed them accurately to imagine the world beyond the horizon.

He created his projection almost in passing and showed few signs of appreciating the importance of what he had done—and yet it has defined the shape of the world in the modern age. There is no doubt that it produced a distorted image, as any flat map of the spherical world must. As a result, Mercator himself has often been accused in the last few years of racism, because his projection makes the continent of Africa seem smaller than it really is, or of imperialism, because it appears to exaggerate the size and importance of Europe—accusations that a scholar of the sixteenth century would not even have understood. The challenge of spreading the globe out flat on a desk, of presenting the known world in a way that could readily be seen and comprehended, was one with which philosophers, travelers, and geographers had been struggling for thousands of years. By Mercator's day, the time was ripe for a solution.

Chapter One

Pushing Back Shadows

MERCATOR WAS BORN barely twenty years after Christopher Columbus first crossed the Atlantic. Yet even though the fifteenth and sixteenth centuries are considered the great age of discoveries, an astonishing amount was known, or at least rumored, about North, South, East, and West before any of the memorable voyages of exploration ever left port.

Nearly two thousand years earlier, the Greek historian Herodotus was told of Phoenician sailors who claimed to have sailed around the southern tip of Africa.* A hundred years or so after his death, during the fourth century BC, another Greek explorer, Pytheas of Massilia, sailed into the far northern seas, to a country he called Thule, where he said the Sun went to sleep.† Still farther north, he said, land, sea, and air coalesced into a mixture on which people could neither walk nor sail. Ancient Norse sagas spoke of journeys to "a new land, extremely fertile

---

*According to the story Herodotus was told, the Phoenician fleet left the Red Sea and claimed to have spent three years sailing around Africa and back to the Mediterranean. One of the crew described how the Sun was on their right hand as they sailed west around the southern tip of Africa—a detail that Herodotus, for whom the Sun was always on the left hand on a westerly journey, took as proof that the account should not be trusted. In fact, it seems to demonstrate that the expedition had indeed reached the Southern Hemisphere.

†Strabo, one of the Greek chroniclers who reported Pytheas's journey, called him a liar, but later scholars believe that he probably sailed right around Britain and returned to Massilia (Marseilles) after visiting the continental North Sea coast and even the Baltic.

and even having vines" that lay far to the west, beyond the setting Sun.[1] Claudius Ptolemy, the Alexandrian librarian and scholar of the first century AD, had heard about the island of Taprobane, or modern Sri Lanka.[2]

Commercial ambition drove travelers on over new horizons. From as early as 500 BC, trading caravans from China made their way along a variety of routes through central Asia, bringing bales of fine silk to be bartered for Persian warhorses or Arabian spices, frankincense, and myrrh. Lines of heavily laden camels followed secret and well-guarded tracks through the deserts of Arabia, carrying gold, ivory, rare woods, and the spices of Yemen to the trading centers of the Mediterranean. Elsewhere, Phoenician ships journeyed beyond the Pillars of Hercules at the mouth of the Mediterranean to the very edges of the known world, bringing back tin from the Scilly Isles off the southwest coast of Britain. The prophet Ezekiel described the goods carried by the Phoenician traders, and the towns to which they traveled. "Tarshish *was* thy merchant, by reason of the multitude of all kind of riches, with silver, iron, tin, and lead, they traded in thy fairs. Javan, Tubal, and Meshech, they *were* thy merchants: they traded the persons of men and vessels of brass in thy market. They of the house of Togarmah traded in thy fairs with horses and horsemen and mules."[3]

The Phoenician capital Tyre, on the coast of what is now Lebanon, had trading links that extended through the entire eastern Mediterranean and far beyond. The places Ezekiel named in these verses as the Phoenicians' trading partners in the sixth century BC were in central Asia, southern Arabia, Armenia, and the coast of Spain, and his list of the merchandise—slaves, animals, manufactures, luxuries, and other goods— that appeared in their marketplaces lasted for more than twenty biblical verses. Travel and its commercial benefits were common enough; from the earliest times, explorers and adventurers had returned with exotic cargoes, but the stories they brought back were confused and unreliable. The island of Taprobane that Ptolemy described was said to dwarf the Indian peninsula that lay to its north, while the great medieval map of the world, dating from the late thirteenth century and still on display at Hereford in England, shows two distinct Niles, one running into the eastern Mediterranean, the other snaking across almost the whole width of the African continent. The accounts of the early adventurers were neither more nor less believable than the grotesque creatures with which ancient Greek and Roman authors loved to people the unknown places. There was no agreed view of the world; anything was possible. Travelers had no reliable or accurate way to record what they had found, to set it out for people to see. To become part of a shared image of the world, their stories had to be written down, described, and mapped.

Today, the oldest so-called maps look like little more than a few carved scratches, their meaning lost with the civilizations that created them. About four thousand years ago, craftsmen near the present-day village of Bedolina, some ten thousand feet high in the Italian Alps, set about carving the rock with rough bronze or iron tools. They drew pictures of animals, daggers, and suns, much as their cavemen ancestors elsewhere in Europe had done ten thousand years earlier. But the artists of Bedolina also produced one of the first known maps. The *Mappa di*

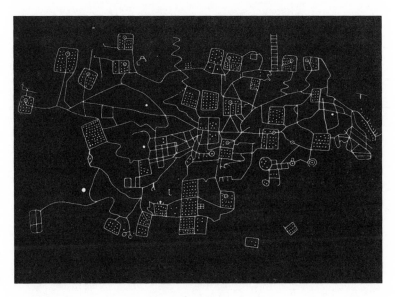

The Mappa di Bedolina *in Italy.*

Bedolina is approximately four yards wide and six yards high, an ambitious patchwork of carved lines and symbols, with a series of crudely drawn rectangles, most of them filled with carefully spaced dots and linked with snaking irregular lines. They seem to represent fields with paths, rivers, or irrigation canals running between them—a graphic illustration of a cultivated landscape in the Valley of Valcamonica below. Their carvings could have had some religious or magical purpose, but after four millennia, we can only guess at what it might have been. Armed figures, huts, and shapes like ladders were added to the map hundreds of years afterward, maybe adapting it for new mystical or ceremonial rites in a mixture of religious faith and straightforward observation that was to characterize mapmaking through the ages.

Centuries later, merchants and travelers who were pushing farther and farther afield in the search for new markets brought back garbled reports of the mighty Rivers Don and Nile running south out of Asia and

A T-O map from Etymologiarum *by Isidore of Seville*

north out of Africa to form a *T*-shape with the well-traveled waters of the Mediterranean. The waters of the ocean were then thought to surround the world in a gigantic *O*, leading to the creation of the so-called T-O maps, which represented for ancient Greek, Roman, and even Arab seamen an agreed image of the outline of the world.

THAT WAS THE WORLDVIEW Claudius Ptolemy inherited as he worked in the great library of Alexandria around the middle of the second century AD. His name appropriately linked the Greek-Egyptian Ptolemy with the Latin Claudius, for Alexandria was a cosmopolitan place, more than five hundred miles from Greece, under Roman rule, and yet at the heart of Greek civilization. The city, with its port and its great lighthouse, was a triumphal expression of Greek civilization and Roman power. Like Antwerp in Mercator's day, it was one of the world's great cultural and commercial crossroads, with mineral ores and spices ferried down the Nile from the depths of Africa and along an elaborate network of canals, then traded along the waterfront with the day-to-day cargoes that had been brought into harbor from the busy eastern Mediterranean. Sailors and merchants brought with them tales of distant lands like Taprobane, half-digested stories that might conceal a thin vein of truth for scholars trying to extend their grasp of the unknown world. Busy ports have always been the mines of geographers; travelers' gossip was the unsmelted ore of exploration for Ptolemy, as it was to be for Mercator.

The merchants brought wealth to Alexandria as well. In the days of its greatness, the story went, the buildings contained so much glistening marble that a tailor could thread his needle by the reflected light of the Moon. The library where Ptolemy worked, with its collection of some seven hundred thousand manuscripts in Hebrew, Greek, and Egyptian, was one of the most obvious expressions of that wealth. Just as the merchants in the port haggled and bargained over the commerce of the mightiest empire the world had ever seen, so Alexandria's scholars swapped ideas and theories in the library and the museum associated with it.

There are no surviving original manuscripts of Ptolemy's work, and hardly any facts known about his life, but it would be hard to exaggerate the effect of his books on the generations that followed him. For centuries after his death, they were largely forgotten in the West, but to Mercator, the writings of Ptolemy represented the fount of ancient knowledge, the standard by which new discoveries and theories should be measured. Apart from the eight books of the *Geographia,* the *Almagest* set out Ptolemy's views on astronomy and the place of the Earth at the center of the universe, while his various other writings encompassed mathematics, music, and history.

Other writers had concentrated on stories of the wonders that lay at the farthest reaches of knowledge, but Ptolemy's main interest lay in establishing a reliable and coherent system for showing the spherical Earth on a flat sheet of paper. Philosophers could only suggest what form the Earth took, while travelers either by land or by sea could do little more than estimate distances—in both cases, their contributions were merely elegant guesswork. The generally accepted image of the land surrounded and limited by the ebbing and flowing waters of the sea suggested a comfortingly finite world. Ptolemy raised the possibility of a world beyond those boundaries, basing his conclusions not just on the arguments of the philosophers and on the reports of travelers but also on exact astronomical measurements.

Ptolemy saw geography as a mathematical enterprise, a matter of measurement and calculation rather than the simple telling of stories. Like Mercator some fourteen centuries after him, he designed and made instruments for measuring angles and altitudes in the heavens; his *Geographia* includes descriptions of a brass astrolabe and a quadrant for calculating the height of the Sun in the sky.

Ptolemy knew the true location of a place could be fixed by taking precise sightings of the stars. The *Geographia* therefore included a catalog of some eight thousand place-names, rivers, mountains, and peninsulas, each of them with its position defined by degrees of latitude and longitude. It is a work of staggering ambition and exactitude—the first time anyone had attempted to use coordinates in such a precise way. Many of the observations Ptolemy needed to make the calculations had already been taken, but to place cities in remote or unexplored parts of the world, he had no choice but to rely on traditional accounts and the estimates of travelers. In such a case, he said, the mapmaker should use his judgment as to what figures to use, "deciding what is credible and what is incredible."[4]

It is impossible to know whether Ptolemy drew any maps to go with his *Geographia*. The illustrations that adorned medieval versions of his books were additions by later copyists working to his descriptions and coordinates, but in them his worldview, with the traditional three continents of Europe, Asia, and part of Africa, can clearly be recognized. Taprobane is grotesquely out of proportion in comparison with the half-formed India that lies to its north, and the coastline of the Far East is clearly drawn largely from imagination, but the Arabian peninsula and the whole of the Mediterranean basin are presented in some detail.

Perhaps most important of all, though, Ptolemy left open the possibility that there were more lands to be discovered beyond the extent of his own knowledge. Where the Romans and Greeks who came before him had been content to keep their studies inside the limits of the habitable world, his interest was in the Earth as a whole, and geography, for him, was no more or less than the art of making maps. "It is the prerogative of Geography," he said, "to show the known habitable earth as a unit in itself, how it is situated and what is its nature; and it deals with those features likely to be mentioned in a general description of the earth, such as larger towns and great cities, the mountain ranges and the principal rivers."[5]

The circle of seas that surrounded the Earth in the early T-O maps was one way of suggesting a round world, but Ptolemy's was the first serious attempt to deal with the problem of projection. He described two possible solutions, based on a simple rectangular grid that ancient Greek philosophers had already devised, but adapting it to take account of the fact that the Earth was curved, not flat.* The systems he suggested were, as they had to be, a compromise, and one which worked satisfactorily enough within the limits of the known world. Even in the sixteenth century, most maps were still produced on grids that were simple adapta-

---

*This knowledge that the Earth was round was commonplace by Ptolemy's day. The idea that this was somehow forgotten in the following centuries is a modern myth. Columbus himself, writing to Ferdinand and Isabella on his third voyage, mentioned in passing, "I have always read that the world, both land and water, was spherical," although he actually went on to suggest that it might actually be pear-shaped. Modern historians of science have found no evidence for the supposition that educated people in the Middle Ages believed in a flat Earth.

tions of Ptolemy's projections. Mercator's greatest achievement would lie in rethinking these fifteen-hundred-year-old proposals.

Ptolemy's geographic writings are filled with errors of fact, many of them, as he engagingly admitted himself, due to a lack of basic information. Some, such as the "great southern continent" that he believed must balance the world on its axis, would endure, like the fabulous creatures described by Herodotus and other Greek writers, for centuries after Mercator.

For all its shortcomings, though, the rediscovery and publication of the *Geographia* in the West laid the foundations for the work of the great cartographers of the sixteenth century. The book traveled with Columbus to the New World; when Mercator compiled his great world map of 1569, he began with Ptolemy's calculation of the position of Alexandria. The *Geographia* was still being treated as the ultimate authority fourteen hundred years after its author's death. It shows a man trying to apply scientific methods to achieve a precise, objective representation of the world in a way that was unique in his time, and remained so until Mercator's day.

IN THE EAST, the scanty records and remains of the work of the Chinese suggest that they had their own impressive tradition. Around the third century AD, a government minister of works named Phei Hsiu set out official principles for the making of maps under the Chin Dynasty. The most important of these was that they should be constructed on a rectangular grid in order to create a consistent scale and locate places accurately. There is no evidence that Ptolemy's thinking had reached the Far East—a grid system had been introduced in China some two hundred years before Phei Hsiu by Ptolemy's near-contemporary Chang Heng, an astronomer royal of the Han Dynasty.* He wrote of a spherical world suspended in infinity, like a yolk in an egg, and the system he in-

*Chang Heng was an inventor and philosopher as well as a cartographer. His greatest triumph was the creation in AD 132 of an ornate machine for predicting earthquakes—an early seismograph that, when vibrated, would release a ball from a carved dragon's head attached to the edge of a bowl.

troduced of building up a map by equal squares—"casting a net over the Earth," in a contemporary phrase—was the basis of Chinese cartography for centuries.

Chang Heng's grid made no allowance for the curvature of the Earth, and it is hard to know from what is left of ancient Eastern cartography whether his image of a spherical world had any effect on current thought. There are no indications that early Chinese mapmakers realized the world was a sphere, that the lands they were mapping were consequently curved, nor whether the challenge, which still fascinates cartographers, of representing such a three-dimensional world on a flat surface had even occurred to them as a problem.

In the Islamic world, Arab mapmakers drew on the ideas of Ptolemy and the Greeks to develop their own traditions. By the eighth century, they were compiling maps for overland diplomatic missions to China, military campaigns, and trading expeditions; the tales of Sindbad the Sailor, dating from some two hundred years earlier, are ample evidence of their seafaring traditions. Unlike the work produced by medieval monks in Europe, their maps seem to have been designed for use as much as for study, but they were still based mainly on copies of older European originals. There are early versions of the T-O maps, with south at the top and Mount Sinai in the center and, slightly later, more distinctively Arab interpretations in which a disk-shaped world, surrounded by water, is pierced from the east by the Arabian Gulf and the Red Sea, and from the west by the waters of the Mediterranean.

Later mapmakers of the tenth and eleventh centuries were often slave dealers or traders, making their way north to the shores of the Caspian Sea and up the Volga River deep into the heart of Asia. Asian tribesmen, Russians, Norsemen, and Arabs would meet on one of the medieval world's great trading routes, exchanging goods, knowledge, and ideas.

One account, by the writer Ibn Haukal, author of *The Book of Roads and Kingdoms*, which contained a map of the Islamic world as it was then known, described a meeting toward the end of the tenth century with the great Arab cartographer al-Istakhri. "He showed me the geographical maps in his work, and, when I had commented on them, he gave me his work with the words, 'I can see that you were born under a lucky star, therefore take my work and make such improvements as you think fit.' I took it, altered it in several particulars, and returned it to him."[6]

There was cooperation not just between individuals but between cultures. One of the greatest of all the Arab cartographers, Muhammed al-Idrisi, was born in Morocco, studied at Cordoba in Islamic Spain, and worked at the twelfth-century court of the Christian king Roger of Sicily. There, he produced several world maps that drew directly both on Ptolemy and on the observations of Arab travelers, and which were still being used as models by Islamic cartographers four hundred years later. Among them were a large rectangular map in seventy sheets, and a smaller, circular map, similar to the T-O maps of the West, but incorporating curved parallels, which suggest that al-Idrisi was aware of the spherical shape of the world. The maps and sources that he used are lost, but the geographic detail he provided was far in advance of anything that was being produced by the copyists in Europe's monasteries. Al-Idrisi's representation of Spain, for example, with the northern coast of Africa, the Straits of Gibraltar, and Bay of Biscay all clearly discernible, is far more detailed than the stylized version presented around the same time by European mapmakers. When Al-Idrisi described Britain as "a great island, shaped like the head of an ostrich," and the peninsula of Cornwall as "like a bird's beak,"[7] he had evidently been studying more accurate maps than anything available in Europe.

DESPITE ITS ULTIMATE INFLUENCE in Europe, for hundreds of years after publication of the *Geographia*, Christian scholars turned their backs on Ptolemy's knowledge. With the fall of the Roman Empire, the original manuscripts that Ptolemy had written in the second century were lost and forgotten. For the medieval scribes of the early Church, the old T-O maps compiled in the centuries before Ptolemy had the great advantage that they could easily be adapted to place the holy city of Jerusalem at the center of the world, as the Bible itself decreed.[8] For them, as for the Greek philosophers, the sea was a fitting symbol to represent the mysteries that bounded man's little area of knowledge on every side. What had not been established by exploration was supplied by imagination or faith; the maps that the medieval Christian scholars drew were therefore inaccurate, impressionistic expressions of belief, not descriptions of fact.

Some of these great *mappaemundi,* the medieval pictures of the world, were also works of art of staggering beauty. Most of them are lost, but in the English cathedral city of Hereford, it is still possible to glimpse the vision of the world that was in men's minds on the eve of the age of discoveries. The great Hereford *mappamundi* dates from the last years of the thirteenth century.[9] Even after a visitor to the cathedral has puzzled out the fact that, as on almost all early maps, east is to the top, and has spotted the outline of the Mediterranean Sea that divides the world down the middle, the coastlines and landforms are almost unrecognizable. There is no mistaking the traditional *T*-shape of great waters surrounded by the *O* of the ocean, although the lands are threaded with rivers. The British Isles clutch grimly to the perimeter of Europe, twisted and misshapen; instead of the familiar boot shape of Italy, there is a bloated peninsula, dotted with apparently random cities and ribbed with unknown rivers. The names of Europe and Africa are transposed, probably a mistake by the copyist. Indeed, the map as a whole seems to be sketched more in hope than in conviction. Any modern classroom could produce a dozen more realistic views of the world. Ptolemy would have scoffed.

Yet the Hereford *mappamundi* has its own confidence, as befits the only complete wall map of the world known to have survived from the Middle Ages. It speaks the language of another age. What were once its bright colors are faded and browned into a dull ochre that challenges the eyes, while the drawings that crowd the map seem almost to jostle each other aside; it takes a while to focus on them individually, to see the delicacy and precision with which they are sketched in. Carefully drawn towers and turrets mark some of the cities of which the mapmaker had heard: The familiar names of the Bible are clustered around Jerusalem, and, closer to home, Paris, Ghent, and even Hereford itself are marked. But it is a work to be interpreted, rather than simply consulted; a statement of belief.

Medieval library catalogs show that there were few monasteries or noble palaces without such maps in their stores of manuscripts. Charlemagne, at the end of the eighth century, had plans of Rome and Constantinople engraved on silver tablets among a comprehensive collection, and most great libraries would have included maps of the Holy Land as well as the great *mappaemundi*—triumphs and baubles for the rich and mighty, and reminders for the humble poor of their place in the great scheme of being. Few survived. A sister-map of the Hereford *mappamundi*, the Ebsdorf map, was rediscovered in a Benedictine monastery in the German town whose name it bears after being lost for six hundred

The Hereford mappamundi

years, only to be destroyed by Allied bombing during World War II. Now it survives only in modern copies and photographs. The history of cartography is the tantalizing study of what has been left behind.

The worldview of the *mappaemundi* encompassed the soul as well as time and space. The Hereford map, for example, shows not only the towns of the Holy Land but also the expulsion of Adam and Eve from Eden and Noah riding on the waters of the Flood. It admits no conflict between geographic accuracy and religious faith: The holy city of Jerusalem stands unchallenged at the center of the world, while Paradise itself is shown far away in the apparently unreachable East, a round island circled by flames that warn the importunate traveler not to dare too much.

The *mappaemundi* may have been used for planning journeys from town to town across Europe—marks over the great central city of Paris on the Hereford map suggest that fingernails may have traced a route through it at various times—but it mattered little to the mapmaker that the shape of the coastlines should be so inaccurate, or that the whole map should have been shoehorned so ruthlessly into an all-embracing circle of ocean. Much more important, from his standpoint, God had to be shown overseeing the whole of his kingdom, and the fabulous creatures described by the ancients, such as the *bonnacan*, with its bull's head, horse's mane, and ram's horns, the screaming mandrake plant, and the death-dealing cockatrice, needed to be faithfully represented to demonstrate the awesome variety of his Creation.

The Hereford *mappamundi* laid out a world at once mysterious and threatening, where the only hope of safety was to be found in the majestic figure of Christ that dominates the map. To criticize it for inaccuracy would be as foolish as to find fault with Picasso's famous painting as a street guide to Guernica. Yet for the rapidly growing world of the fifteenth and sixteenth centuries, the *mappaemundi* were quickly proved inadequate. A new geography was needed to enable sailors to plot a reliable course across the oceans and to represent the world they were revealing.

Three events in the half century or so before Mercator's birth made his achievement as a cartographer both possible and necessary. The first was the rediscovery of the geographic writings of Ptolemy, brought back into Europe after hundreds of years; the second was the development of printing, which meant that Ptolemy's ideas could be spread more quickly and efficiently than the monks who had copied them by hand could ever have dreamed; and the third was the voyage of Christopher Columbus, who, looking for Asia, discovered America.

Other explorers had made great discoveries around the coast of Africa and in Asia about lands that were already dimly known about, but Columbus's voyage proved that there really was a world elsewhere. The looming shadows that had marked the boundaries of geographic knowledge ever since man first looked about him were beginning to part, to reveal a reality far different from anything the ancient scholars had imagined.

Chapter Two

Forgotten Wisdom

OR THE SCHOLARS of fifteenth- and sixteenth-century Europe, who
looked on the past with reverence, the rediscovery of Ptolemy's
writing in the early fifteenth century was a revelation and an inspiration. The task of translating the *Geographia* into Latin from an original
Greek manuscript in Byzantium was begun by the Byzantine scholar
Manuel Chrysoloras and finished in 1406 by his pupil Jacobus Angelus
in Tuscany.

In the Arab world, the *Almagest* and the *Geographia* had both been
known by then for some five hundred years, and practically every Islamic
cartographer either mentioned, quoted, or silently borrowed from what
they called the *Kitab gagrafiya* (Book of Geography). However, not until
the fall of Byzantium to the Turks in 1453 did refugees bring the manuscripts to the West in any numbers. Monks in Florence translated them
from Greek into Latin and wrote them out painstakingly by hand,
making copies available over the following years, first without maps,
then with regional maps, and finally with world maps drawn according
to Ptolemy's recommendations. At the time of Mercator's birth, they
were still fresh and exciting—a philosophical framework into which
the new discoveries about the extent and shape of the world could be incorporated.

Ptolemy's books had been copied and copied again in the Arab world
for centuries prior to the time they resurfaced in Europe; by then, they
almost certainly included the additions and amendments of generations
of nameless and unknown thinkers. Nonetheless, however much or lit-

tle of them had actually been written by Ptolemy himself, they were a virtual synthesis of classical scientific knowledge.

The *Geographia* concentrated on the arts and skills of mapmaking, discussing the comparative merits of flat maps and globes, and arguing through the mathematics of how a map should be constructed and how the world could be divided into the three continents of Europe, Asia, and northern Africa. The great undiscovered continent that Ptolemy believed lay to the south turned the Indian Ocean into an inland sea, and in the East, the known world petered out in the unexplored lands beyond the Ganges. West of the Pillars of Hercules, at the mouth of the Mediterranean, of course, he described nothing but sea and a few scattered islands.

Fresh versions appeared year by year, with cartographers adapting and expanding Ptolemy's work. An edition was printed in Cologne in 1475 without maps; only two years later, the interest and the technology existed to prepare a version in Bologna that included twenty-six copper engravings based on Ptolemy's text. By the time Mercator was working, the book's reputation was established among scholars, even though the great voyages of the fifteenth and sixteenth centuries were already demonstrating its limitations.

For all the dedicated work of the monastic copyists, it was the development of printing that allowed Ptolemy's work to be widely read in Europe. The impact of Johannes Gutenberg's first press with movable type in the 1450s is hard to exaggerate. In the Low Countries alone, more than four thousand different books were produced in the first decades of the sixteenth century; there were in excess of 130 printers there, half of them in the thriving city of Antwerp.

Ptolemy's *Geographia* was only one of a range of classical works that flooded off the new presses to feed the public's apparently insatiable appetite. As these books were shipped around the continent, they invigorated and inspired learning not just in the palaces, monasteries, and great houses that had always collected rare and expensive manuscripts, but also in the studies of poor students. Without the explosion of printing, Mercator would never even have seen many of the books that enthused him at

Leuven. He would certainly never have gathered around him the personal library in which he delighted in the German city of Duisburg.

However, for all the excitement that the rediscovery of Ptolemy's *Geographia* stirred up, his three continents soon could no more be accepted as they stood than could the old T-O maps or the *mappaemundi*. There had been rumors for centuries of scattered islands far away to the west, but no one had any idea of the vast extent of the newly discovered land. Just twenty years before Mercator was born, the discovery of America had revealed a new world of which Ptolemy and his predecessors never dreamed, confounding the ancient view that the Earth was limited to the three continents of Europe, Asia, and the strange and mysterious Africa.

While the actual extent of the world would have astonished the ancients, its round shape had been known since well before Ptolemy's time. Various early Greek philosophers had produced detailed arguments to prove that the Earth was cylindrical, disk-shaped, or rectangular, that it was cushioned in compressed air, or that it was floating on water. Yet by 250 BC, Eratosthenes of Cyrene, one of the scholars who devised a rudimentary grid of latitude and longitude, had not only accepted the idea of a spherical world but had studied the stars to calculate its circumference.[1]

Strabo, another Greek geographer and historian, who worked before Ptolemy in the library of Alexandria in the last century BC, had a severely practical turn of mind. The world could be represented on a globe, he declared, but the globe would have to be ten feet across to show all the necessary detail. The work of Ptolemy himself a century or so later in devising projections shows that he had no doubts either about the curvature of the Earth. For accuracy, he concluded, there was no substitute for a globe.

Ptolemy had described in great detail how it should be done, with the globe suspended between two poles connected by a semicircle, which should almost touch its surface. Such an arrangement, he wrote, had advantages and disadvantages when compared to his own efforts at working out a way of projecting a map onto a flat surface: "It preserves the world's shape, and avoids the need for any adjustment of it, but it hardly provides the size needed for containing most of the things that must be marked on it, nor can it allow the entire map to be shown from one vantage point."[2]

Like his books, Ptolemy's endorsement of the globe was lost to Europeans in the Middle Ages. There are tantalizing mentions in classical literature of various globes, including small representations of the Earth enclosed within glass spheres which showed the constellations, like the pair Charles V, the Holy Roman Emperor, would later demand from Mercator. But if the Greeks or Romans ever made large detailed models of the spherical Earth, in line with the recommendations of Ptolemy and Strabo, none of them survived. European craftsmen produced armillary spheres in which concentric metal rings would demonstrate the supposed motion of the planets around the Earth, but they showed no interest in the idea of a terrestrial globe.

The Arabs, on the other hand, turned Ptolemy's words into reality. Many of them used his *Almagest* rather than the *Geographia* and showed the stars, not the Earth, in their work. In Florence's Museum of the History of Science, there is an engraved metal sphere about eight inches in diameter, with 1,015 stars marked on it according to Ptolemy's descriptions, made by Ibrahim ibn Said al-Sahli al Wazzan with his son Muhammed in Valencia, in Moorish Spain, in the late eleventh century.

Such magnificent celestial globes were often carved on brass or silver, intended for a study rather than the navigator's desk, but the Arabs must have made terrestrial globes as well. None survives today, but Christopher Columbus said in his ship's log that he had seen globes of the world on which the island of Cipangu, or Japan, was marked.

The Arab globes were also studied by Martin Behaim, a Nuremberg traveler and adventurer who set out to copy the technique and manufacture a globe of his own toward the end of the fifteenth century. Behaim claimed to have sailed the coasts of Africa with the Portuguese explorers, and to have seen the globes at the Royal Observatory, which had been established in about 1420 by Portugal's Prince Henry the Navigator at the southern port of Sagres.[3]

One advantage that neither Strabo, Ptolemy, nor their Arab imitators had mentioned was that the globe offers a dramatic way of demonstrating the circularity of the Earth to a layman—an investor, for instance, who might be persuaded to put money into an expedition. The Portuguese had demonstrated that there were riches to be won in the East, and in order to show the wealthy financiers of Germany how easily the Indies could be reached by sailing west, Behaim constructed the first modern globe known to have been produced in Europe. It was intended not for scholars or sailors but for bankers.

Behaim, the son of a German nobleman, had been packed off to Portugal as a young man to gain experience as a businessman, but had spent more time there among the sailors and navigators around the docks than in import and export. He had a healthy disrespect for authority—in his youth, he was said to have served a month in prison for dancing at a Jew's wedding during Lent—but he also had a shrewd commercial eye. He was fascinated not only by what he had seen of the voyages of discovery but also by Prince Henry's Arab globes.

None of those globes is known to have survived, but the Arabs had proved that Ptolemy's theory worked. A globe to show how the western ocean lay between the continents of Europe and Asia was clearly the way to impress a skeptical audience with the practicality of sailing west to reach the Spice Islands in the East. The Portuguese controlled the passage around the southern coast of Africa, and huge costs were involved in the ancient overland trails from Asia through Arabia to the Mediterranean. The globe—which Behaim called his *erdapfel*, his earth-apple—was a striking demonstration of another route.

Today, Behaim's brainchild is the most famous exhibit in Nuremberg's Germanisches Nationalmuseum,[4] darkened by age and scarred by the attentions of well-meaning "restorers" in the nineteenth century—the oldest terrestrial globe in the world. It was a scientific wonder, an artistic triumph representing the best thinking of Behaim's age about the shape of the world—and a commercial dead end. Unlike the globe manufacturers who followed him in the sixteenth century, Behaim could not profit from selling examples of his creation; his globe was, unavoidably, unique. He lived before the development of printing techniques enabled artisans and mapmakers to create limitless copies of their work, and his map had to be painted by hand onto sheets of thin, fine leather after they had been stuck to a twenty-inch papier-mâché shell and mounted on an elegant wooden stand. It was never designed for navigation. Apart from the equator, a single meridian, and the Tropics of Cancer and Capricorn, there were no longitudes and latitudes marked on it, although Behaim did include the constellations of the zodiac and an array of forty-eight flags of European nations and noble families, fifteen coats of arms, and forty-eight portraits of kings and rulers. The globe was a tool of commerce, and to catch the interest of the Nuremberg merchants, Behaim incorporated lengthy descriptions of what merchandise could be purchased in the various islands of the Far East, and how trade should be conducted. For the artist Behaim paid to paint his globe, it was a miniature masterpiece. But however much the burghers of the town admired the piece, it could never be reproduced, except by starting from scratch with a new map.

BEHAIM'S TIMING, though, was unfortunate from an even more important point of view. As he was completing his model of the world, the world itself was changing beyond recognition. In Spain, the armies of Ferdinand and Isabella finally drove the Moors out of Grenada, breaking their last fingerhold in Europe and ending an Islamic presence that had lasted nearly eight centuries and enriched the country with art, literature, science, and trade. The king and queen had united the great kingdoms of Aragon and Castile with their marriage in 1469, starting an era of increasing royal prestige and power, and the departure twenty-three years later of Muhammad XI, or Boabdil, the last Moorish ruler on Spanish soil, reflected a new confidence for Christendom and the end of any lingering Arab dreams of further European conquest.

Some years later, a by then noted traveler of the day looked back to record the scene in Grenada as Boabdil left. "On the second day of the month of January, I saw the royal banner of Your Highnesses raised by force of arms on the towers of the Alhambra, which is the fortress of the said city, and saw the Moorish king come to the gates of the said city and kiss the royal hands of Your Highnesses."[5] He could tell that he was witnessing one of history's defining moments. This same traveler had several names during a seafaring life which took him from country to country in the west of Europe, seeking support and financial sponsorship to fulfill the dream that was to turn into the second great event of this annus mirabilis. To his Genoese parents, he was Cristoforo Colombo; to the Spanish who eventually supplied him with money and ships, he was Cristóbal Colón; and to English-speaking historians, he later became Christopher Columbus.

By comparison with the defeat of the Moors, his exploits in the Ocean Sea, the Atlantic, attracted little immediate attention; but they rendered Martin Behaim's globe out of date almost before its paint was dry. Behaim's masterpiece had not even been unveiled to the Nuremberg merchants in 1492, when on August 3 three small ships set sail from Palos de la Frontera in southern Spain on a secret mission to an unknown destination. Seventy days later, Columbus and the captains of his little fleet stood on the shore of an island he named San Salvador in honor of the Holy Savior he believed had blessed his voyage.

In theory, maintaining a course due west by keeping the Sun at a constant height in the sky was simple enough, but the voyage had tested contemporary seamanship and navigation to the limit. Columbus had found it impossible to record how far he was going, let alone log his course. In fact, the devious captain kept two logs, one to reassure the crew, by understating the distances the ship had traveled, and a second, secret one for his own use, which recorded how far he believed they had really gone.* Yet even his supposedly accurate private calculations of the expedition's position were often wrong. His observations of flotsam, the behavior of birds and fishes, and the seaweed in the Sargasso Sea all seemed to indicate that the ship was coming close to land, but the helmsman failed to find bottom first with one plumb line, then with two tied together. The flotilla was still in deep water, far out at sea.

Navigation devices were notoriously untrustworthy, and the traditional astrolabe with which Columbus tried to take sightings of the Sun above the horizon was almost impossible to use accurately on the pitching

---

*This practice was first noted on Sunday, September 9: "He made that day 15 leagues and decided to reckon less than he made, so that if the voyage were long the people would not be frightened and dismayed." Columbus wrote many similar notes during the rest of the voyage.

Christopher Columbus

and tossing deck of a ship. As the flotilla headed west into the unknown, even the compass seldom showed true north, and its increasing inaccuracy added considerably to the panic among his crew. "The pilots took the north, marking it, and they found that the needles declined north-west a full point, and the sailors were alarmed and depressed," Columbus noted in his journal on September 17.[6] Mariners had been aware for some time of the phenomenon of magnetic deviation—the way variations in the Earth's magnetic field cause the compass needle to diverge from true north depending on the position of a vessel on the Earth's surface—but they had no idea why or how it happened. The effect was much more pronounced as they headed west; even their instruments were betraying them. None of the old rules learned in years of sailing near to the coasts of Europe and Africa seemed to apply.

The areas in which Columbus had complete and unquestioning faith proved to be even more deceptive. He was sailing with all the preconceptions of a medieval Christian—the same preoccupations as the creators of the outdated *mappaemundi*. Many of the maps he had consulted as he planned his journey not only showed the lands that the cartographer believed existed, but also related them to the faith of the Catholic Church; the Bible was as much a source of geography as Ptolemy or the accounts of ancient travelers. Their reports were woven together with biblical tradition, so that, for example, the Rivers Ganges, Nile, Tigris, and Euphrates were identified as the four rivers said by Genesis to flow from Paradise. None of the maps Columbus consulted gave any hint of a vast new continent over the horizon.

Columbus, a devout Catholic who believed that he was on a special mission from God, never saw any reason to doubt the authority of the Bible. The medieval mapmakers, on the impeccable authority of St. Augustine, had placed the earthly Paradise in the farthest east of Asia, and when in 1498, on the third of the four voyages he made across the Atlantic, he found freshwater, not salt, out at sea off the northeast coast of South America where the Orinoco River pours into the ocean, his mind was made up. He declared that he was approaching the four heavenly rivers. "I say that if this river does not originate in the Terrestrial Paradise, it comes and flows from a land of infinite size to the south, of which we have no knowledge as yet. But I am completely persuaded in my own mind that the Terrestrial Paradise is the place I have described," he wrote to Ferdinand and Isabella.[7]

Such a huge outpouring of freshwater could only come from a vast area of land, and he was convinced by this time that he had reached a stretch of the mainland that had never before been discovered by Europeans. His argument was faultless, but his conclusion was wrong. The Bible had said nothing about a great and unknown continent to the west, and Columbus found it easier to believe that he was approaching the gates of Paradise than that he was standing at the threshold of a new world.

He had the same misconceptions about the world as Martin Behaim, although there is no evidence that they ever met or corresponded. "This is the island of Cipangu of which so many marvellous tales are told," Columbus declared confidently in his journal, as he sailed northwest from San Salvador to Cuba. "On the globes which I have seen, and on the drawings of *mappamondes*, it is in this region."[8] It is still there on Behaim's globe. Halfway across the great Ocean Sea is shown St. Brendan's Island,* the "Promised Land of the Saints" that fascinated generations of mapmakers, and about the same distance farther on, the island of Cipangu, or Japan, with its temples and palaces of gold. Between them the globe shows nothing but sea.

In planning his original voyage, Columbus relied heavily on the mistaken observations of Marco Polo, who had reached the court of Kublai khan by traveling overland through Asia more than two hundred years before, but had exaggerated the distance he had covered. Columbus's logic was faultless—the longer the journey by land to the east, the shorter the route by sea to the west—and it led him to underestimate the circumference of the world by about 25 percent.

Once he left the well-charted waters east of the Canary Islands, he had guidance, and probably a roughly drawn map, from a Florentine physician, astronomer, and geographer named Paolo Toscanelli dal Pozzo. Toscanelli, like Columbus, had studied the travels of Marco Polo, and had a thorough knowledge of the writings of Ptolemy. He had talked to European travelers to India and the Far East, and also to at least one ambassador from India who had visited Pope Eugenius in Rome. All his researches led him to the conclusion that the landmass of Europe and Asia spread across nearly two-thirds of the globe, so that the western route across the ocean to Asia could cover no more than 130 degrees of longitude. If Ptolemy's estimate of 500 miles for each degree was correct, the journey to the land of the great khan should have been no more than 6,500 miles.†

---

*St. Brendan's Island is mentioned in a ninth-century Latin manuscript titled *Navigatio Santi Brendani Abatis* (The Voyage of the Abbot St. Brendan). It describes a seven-year odyssey undertaken by Brendan in the sixth century that led ultimately to a beautiful and mystical island. Explorers tried in vain for centuries to find this island. There is a modern theory that Brendan could have landed on the coast of Newfoundland, more than four hundred years before any Viking expedition could possibly have reached it.

†The true distance is approximately 11,000 miles; but Toscanelli's map of the world, drawn some twenty years before Columbus set sail, made it seem temptingly close.

. . .

THE KNOWN WORLD was expanding in other directions as well in the years shortly before Mercator's birth. Four years before Columbus's first voyage, the Portuguese navigator Bartholomeu Dias had rounded the southern tip of the African continent, overturning the accepted Ptolemaic wisdom that the African mainland was connected to a great southern landmass. As the fifteenth century drew to a close, the new Portuguese king Emmanuel—Manuel o Venturoso, the Fortunate—called on Dias to help with the construction of a flotilla of three ships to open a new trade route to India. Leadership of the new expedition was to have been offered to a military commander and government official named Estevão da Gama, but he died before the preparations were complete. Emmanuel turned to Estevão's twenty-eight-year-old son, who had already distinguished himself in naval engagements with the French in the defense of Portuguese settlements on the coast of Guinea. Vasco da Gama was entrusted with the voyage, which the king hoped would establish Portuguese trading supremacy for generations.

If the magnitude of Columbus's discovery was initially unappreciated, news of da Gama's return to Lisbon in September 1499 from Calicut on the west coast of India, more than two years after he had embarked, shook the commercial houses of Europe to their foundations. The Italian merchants who had made fortunes out of their control of the overland trade routes into the eastern Mediterranean faced imminent disaster. "In this I clearly see the ruin of the City of Venice," declared the wealthy Venetian banker Girolamo Priuli in his diary,[9] and he was not mistaken: The prosperity of Venice, which had controlled the European end of the great caravan routes across Asia and Arabia, was one of the casualties of a series of discoveries that continued over the following decades.

The expeditions were driven partly by religion—by the desire to find more Christian communities to counterbalance the growing threat of militant Islam, whose soldiers still lined the southern and eastern borders of Christendom even after the expulsion of the Moors from Andalusia. But the prospect of trade, the quest for wealth, lay behind everything.

King Emmanuel himself, writing to Ferdinand and Isabella after Vasco da Gama's return, declared that the motive of the voyage had been "the service of the Lord our God, and our own advantage"—about nutmeg and the spice trade rather than knowledge.

For someone drawn to cartography, Mercator could hardly have been born at a more propitious moment in the history of geography and exploration. In the east, Dias and Vasco da Gama had shattered the old assumptions by sailing into a sea that should have been surrounded by land, while to the west, a new continent of undreamed-of size and wealth had been discovered, even if it was not yet appreciated.

For centuries, Europe had seemed, to Europeans at least, an oasis of certainty in a vast and unfriendly desert of ignorance. Following these voyages, the continent engaged in an unprecedentedly outward-looking period of exploration; where men had once dreamed of dragons and sea monsters, they found elephants and giraffes. A scramble for land, wealth, and influence that was to double the size of the known world within a few decades had begun.

Practically every voyage added more knowledge of new lands. Progress was faster to the east and in the Indian Ocean, where there was already a network of established trade routes and a ready supply of local guides and pilots, but along the coasts of America, too, the map began to take shape. In 1500, for instance, the Portuguese explorer Pedro Alvares Cabral set out to follow da Gama's route to India but, in pushing even farther west in search of good winds, became the first mariner to sight the coast of Brazil.[10]

Europe was buzzing with gossip and speculation about the new discoveries, but the maps drawn during the early sixteenth century show how gradually geographic knowledge accumulated. The German clergyman-cartographer Martin Waldseemüller produced a world map in 1507 in which the coastlines of Europe, Africa, and the Middle East are all instantly recognizable today—but to the east and west, those confident outlines faded into guesswork and supposition. Waldseemüller drew the Far East with little more accuracy than Ptolemy had managed fifteen hundred years earlier, and America clings to the map's left-hand edge, a long narrow strip of land that is evidently sketched in with only the skimpiest knowledge. For all the lack of detail and the unfamiliar outline, though, America is there—a separate continent, divided from Asia by the waters of the Pacific Ocean. Waldseemüller's map was the first to suggest that what had been shown before as a collection of islands off the coast of Asia was actually a single landmass.

Parts of the eastern coast of North America had been surveyed and mapped by the turn of the century, particularly by the Florentine explorer Amerigo Vespucci, and the title Waldseemüller chose for his map indicates the two sources on which he relied. It was drawn, he said, "secundum Ptolomei traditionem et Americi Vespucii aliorumque lustrationes" (according to the account of Ptolemy and the voyages of Amerigo Vespucci and others). By then, Vespucci had led several expeditions down the east coast of the vast new land, seeking financial backing wherever he could find it, and sailing sometimes under the Spanish flag, sometimes under that of Portugal. He had none of Columbus's obsessions with Cathay or the terrestrial Paradise, and declared that the lands far to the west were a discovery which "it is proper to call a New World."[11]

No European had yet seen the west coast of the Americas, and in this section of the map, Waldseemüller's guesswork was amazingly accurate. Not until 1513, six years after it was published, did the Spanish explorer Vasco Núñez de Balboa become the first European to set eyes on the Pacific Ocean from the famous "peak in Darien,"[12] and another nine years passed before Ferdinand Magellan's expedition arrived back in Spain after sailing across that ocean. The presence of the then-unknown Pacific on Waldseemüller's map is one of the great mysteries of cartographic history. Perhaps he had access to more information, now lost, from Vespucci's expeditions, or, more likely, perhaps he simply drew his conclusion from Vespucci's belief that America was a completely new world. Whatever his motive, Waldseemüller named the continent America on his map in Vespucci's honor. "I do not see why anyone should object to calling it after Americus the discoverer," he declared in the book that accompanied his map.[13] Waldseemüller sold more than a thousand copies of his map and his book—enough to establish the name

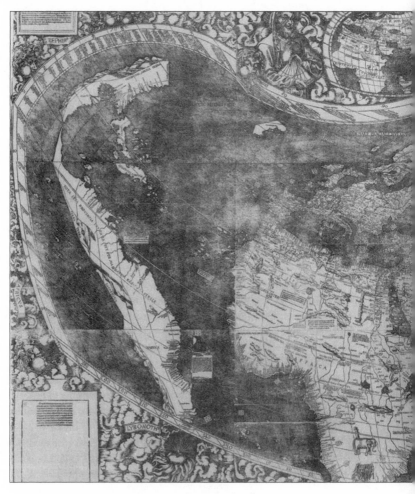

Martin Waldseemüller's World Map, 1507

America in people's minds, though when he realized his mistake a few years later, he tried to give Columbus the credit he deserved.*

*The only known surviving copy of the map—twelve sheets printed by woodcut, adding up to a total of thirty-six square feet—was rediscovered in 1901 in the sixteenth-century south German castle of the magnificently named Prince Johannes Waldburg-Wolfegg, and sold for $10 million to the U.S. Library of Congress a hundred years later—"America's birth certificate," according to the publicity at the time of the purchase.

Fifteen years after Waldseemüller's map, the first known circumnavigation of the globe was completed[14]—the crucial final proof, if any
were needed, that the world was round. Ferdinand Magellan left
Seville in late September 1519 with the commission of King Charles I—
later to be the emperor Charles V—and a ragtag and bobtail fleet of five
aging ships, crewed by the sweepings of the Spanish docks. As a young
man, according to some reports, he had been a pupil of Martin Behaim;

if so, the return of his expedition after a full three years at sea proved both the strengths and the shortcomings of his teacher's ideas. Behaim had been right about the shape of the world—but disastrously wrong about the lands that lay on its surface. Magellan had sailed around a continent that Behaim never dreamed existed. He died shortly afterward in a skirmish with natives on a Pacific island, but the return in 1522 of the *Victoria*, sole survivor of his flotilla, was the inspiration for a succession of Spanish probes up the western coast of South America.

WHEN MERCATOR was born in 1512, the known world was, thus, still surrounded by shadows. By the time he died eighty-two years later, merchants and bankers were making vast fortunes by bringing regular cargoes back from the East Indies by sea,* while the apparently limitless gold and silver† plundered from the ancient civilizations of the New World to the west had turned the economies of Spain and Europe upside down. During his lifetime, the traders, financiers, and businessmen of Europe took control of the new lands that had been revealed, and they did so because mariners gradually took control of the seas.

In the Middle Ages, there had been no sense that knowledge could be outdated, that the wisdom of the ancients could be challenged by experiment, observation, or reason. Religion, too, had been buttressed by that same sense of stability. Suddenly, such challenges seemed to be happening all the time. Reflecting the frenetic pace of discovery, George Beste, who sailed the northern seas later in the sixteenth century with the English explorer and sometime pirate Martin Frobisher, would write with a mixture of awe and excitement: "Within the memory of man, within these fourscore years, there hath been more new countries and regions discovered than in five thousand years before; yea, more than half the world hath been discovered by men that are yet (or may

---

*In the early 1600s, merchants reckoned that the value of a cargo of spices could increase more than tenfold between its purchase in the Indies and its sale in the Mediterranean.

†The value of the precious metals brought back to Europe grew rapidly throughout the sixteenth century, from around 195,000 ducats a year in the first decade to some 2.4 million a year in the '50s, and nearly 8.5 by the 1590s.

very well for their age be) alive."[15] Within eight decades, in other words, the size of the known world had doubled.

FOR MORE THAN two hundred years, European mariners had prepared sketch maps to show the coastlines and the approaches to ports in Europe. But the maps that were available were virtually useless for long-distance navigation. The so-called portolan[16] charts were often produced as an accompaniment to written descriptions of the coastal features, compiled by sailors for themselves or their close associates and based largely on their experience of the coasts that they illustrated. They were drawn by detailed observation and with careful reference to the mariner's compass, but they had generally no lines of latitude and longitude, no learned references or legends. They took no interest in interior features; river mouths or distinctive skylines visible from the sea might be noted, but cities, inland roads, even mountain ranges were almost always omitted. They were maps by seamen, for seamen—tools of the trade. Rough mapping was the stock-in-trade of any experienced mariner. The only surviving map drawn by Columbus himself, showing northwest Hispaniola, now the northern coast of Haiti, demonstrates how accurately a skilled seaman could make a running survey of an unknown coastline. But the sailors' rough sketches, like the portolan maps, made no allowance for the curvature of the Earth.

Even Waldseemüller's groundbreaking world map was constructed on a projection originally devised by Ptolemy in the second century AD. Mariners knew that any accuracy in following the traditional maps with which they were provided over great distances was impossible, and cartographers understood why. Michiel Coignet, a chartmaker of Antwerp, pointed out later in the century[17] that there was simply no point in laying off a course according to compass bearings as they appeared on a traditional map; the straight lines on the flat sheet of paper, transferred to the curved surface of the globe, would produce a series of spiral curves that would take a ship drastically off course.

The solution to this problem, navigators found, was a combination of dead reckoning—estimating their position by judging the distance the ship had sailed along a known compass bearing—and keeping as

much of their course as possible due east or west. By "sailing the latitudes," the parallel lines around the Earth's surface, they could avoid
the distorting effects of the curvature of the Earth. The traditional sailing directions for reaching the West Indies from Europe were "south
until the butter melts, then due west into the sunset."[18]

In practice, ships sailed miles out of their way, aiming far to the east
or west of their chosen destination in order to find the correct latitude.
The unreliability of navigational instruments, the difficulty of taking
sightings to check latitude on the rolling deck of a ship, and the need for
frequent tacking in contrary winds all made matters worse; but the un-
derlying problem was that neither sailors nor scholars had tackled the
problem of reproducing the curved surface of the spherical Earth on a
flat map. While voyages were short and close to land, the problem of
projection could be more or less ignored; following a line ruled straight
on a map would simply result in a small navigational error. As the ships
ranged farther from the well-known waters of the Mediterranean,
though, the effects of this failing became more dramatic. Men could sail
the seas of the world with greater confidence than ever before, but they
could not map them accurately.

A Small Town on the River Scheldt

THE RESEARCHES OF SCHOLARS and geographers, the work of printers and booksellers, and the discoveries of hard-bitten sailors and explorers had combined to make the early sixteenth century the most favorable time in which a man of Mercator's talents and interests could have been born. But the land in which he grew up was riven by political factions and smoldering with religious hatreds.

At the start of the new century, the birth in 1500 of the future Holy Roman Emperor Charles V in the ancient merchant city of Ghent in Flanders marked the climax of more than 150 years of schemes, machinations, and marriages among the ruling families of Europe. While the adventurers of Spain and Portugal were discovering new worlds abroad, in Europe the dukes of Burgundy had been busily laying their hands on as much of the old one as they could, marrying their way into a realm that eventually stretched across the prosperous financial heartland of northern Europe. They turned marriage from a sacrament to a strategy. During a century and a half of buying, inheriting, and most of all marrying into new possessions, they could have taught the rest of Europe a lesson, had anyone thought to heed it: War could be profitable, but well-planned matrimony was infinitely more so.

Philip, one of the dukes of Burgundy, was a member of the powerful Habsburg family, who had been building up their own lands in Germany with similar determination throughout the fifteenth century, and he married Joanna of Spain, the daughter of Ferdinand and Isabella, whose own marriage in 1469 had already united the Spanish kingdoms of Aragon and Castile. Charles was the son of Philip and Joanna's triumphal dynastic marriage, and he steadily inherited individual titles and honors throughout his childhood to make up a patchwork empire that would eventually stretch over more than half the known world.

He was shy and awkward, an unprepossessing figure with the long lower jaw and bulging eyes of the Habsburg line, but when his father died in 1506, he became ruler of the Netherlands and the rest of the Burgundian inheritance. He was just six years old, and his paternal aunt, Margaret of Austria, acted as regent. By the time he was sixteen, Charles's inherited lands stretched not just through Spain and parts of Italy but also across the apparently limitless Spanish possessions in the Americas. Three years later, in 1519, the death of his paternal grandfather, Maximilian, pushed the borders of his realm farther to the east, where his Habsburg ancestors were the most powerful dynasty in central Europe, ruling lands in Austria, Carinthia, Slovenia, and the Tyrol.*

The Habsburgs also held a virtually hereditary position in Germany as Holy Roman Emperors, but although they had occupied the imperial throne for nearly eighty years,† on his grandfather's death Charles still had to win the support of the seven electors, the German princes who formally approved the succession of the Holy Roman Empire. The successful but expensive campaign of bribery with which he secured the imperial crown left him crippled by debt throughout his reign,‡ and he faced a constant struggle to raise money to pay the massive armies on which his grandiose campaigns to maintain his authority depended.

---

*Charles's inheritances came in three strands. The Habsburg lands in Germany were inherited through his father's line; the duchy of Burgundy, which included the Low Countries, came through his paternal grandfather Maximilian's marriage to the daughter and heir of Duke Charles the Bold of Burgundy; the Spanish kingdoms of Aragon and Castile, along with their possessions in southern Italy and the Mediterranean and their New World empire, came to him through his mother, Joanna.

†The first Habsburg succeeded to the throne in 1273, but other families had intervened several times in the years up to 1440. After Charles, the unbroken Habsburg line continued until the mid–eighteenth century.

‡The Augsburg banker Jakob Fugger told him, with scant respect for his mighty office, "It is well known that Your Imperial Majesty could never have won the Imperial Crown without my help."

The empire was vast and unwieldy, and his possessions were too far-flung to be governed. When Charles traveled to his Spanish kingdom to secure the succession there in 1517, he was thought of as a foreign inter-loper surrounded by boorish Flemish advisers who trampled over the country's aristocracy, while in the Netherlands he was reviled as a lover of Spanish luxury with an intolerable train of arrogant Castilian grandees. Had they ever heard it, his Netherlands subjects would have been less than amused by his famous boast, "To God I speak Spanish, to women Italian, to men French, and to my horse, German." His native Flemish was not even on the list.

There was constant feuding in Spain, and near anarchy in Germany, where the great inheritance of the Holy Roman Empire was largely ruled by lawless and belligerent knights who accepted no authority but their own. The disparate duchies, counties, and cities of the Nether-lands were racked with ancient feuds. The Hoeks of Holland, the Ka-beljaws of Zeeland, and the Lichtenbergers and Lockhorsts of Utrecht wrangled in a constant round of shifting alliances, betrayals, victories, and defeats. In Guelderland the Heckerens fought the Bronkhorsts, and in Friesland the Schieringers were the sworn enemies of the Vetkoopers. The great free cities of Ghent, Bruges, Antwerp, and Brus-sels zealously guarded their ancient privileges against any attempt to impose central authority.

In addition to this internecine violence, over the next half century Charles would face recurrent international wars with the French, and with the armies and navies of the Ottoman emperor Suleiman the Magnificent, massed on the eastern and southern borders of his em-pire. His reign was an endless round of revolts, rebellions, wars, and betrayed alliances.

The imperial crown also involved him inextricably in the bloodlet-ting of the Reformation. Bitterness over corruption in the Catholic Church had existed for as long as anyone could remember; to the re-formists, the popes in Rome seemed more concerned with worldly show than piety. In the late 1470s and early 1480s, Sixtus IV built the Sistine Chapel; then Julius II and Leo X supported the work of Michelangelo and Raphael; in the following years, the supposedly celibate Alexander

Charles V by Titian

VI used bribery, corruption, and murder to advance the interests of his children, Lucrezia Borgia and Cesare Borgia. None of them seemed interested in the reforms for which many in the Church and among the laity were crying out. During Charles's reign, these demands developed into not only a religious challenge to the Church but also a political challenge to the Holy Roman Empire itself. Charles V—"God's standard bearer," as he grandly called himself—saw his duty as defending the Catholic faith not just from the Muslim Ottoman Empire across his borders but also from the reformists and Protestants within. In 1523, when Gerard Mercator was a boy of eleven, two young monks, Johann Esch and Heinrich Voes, were burned alive as heretics in the central square of Antwerp, the first of tens of thousands to go to the stake over the next half century as the Inquisition sought to root out heresy wherever it hid. The legacy of the complex genealogical maneuvering that had created Charles V's empire was one of political chaos and human misery across the Netherlands and the rest of Charles's domain.

IN THE YEAR 1512, the artisan Hubert de Cremer was one of Charles's struggling subjects. His was the misery of poverty: His father had made the journey east from his native Flanders to Gangelt, in the German duchy of Jülich, many years before, filled with hope and ambition for the future, but Hubert had become a cobbler scrabbling to find enough money to feed his wife and family. He already had five children, and his wife was expecting their sixth, but though he was willing to work, he had found few opportunities in Gangelt. His best hope of staving off poverty lay in returning to Rupelmonde, where his father's family still lived.

The port of Antwerp, just a few miles downriver from the town of Rupelmonde, was one of the most affluent centers in the Low Countries, one of the largest cities of its day, where eighty thousand people lived in houses that were the envy of the rest of Europe. Antwerp had been a busy port on the River Scheldt for centuries—its name comes from the Flemish *aan-de-werfen* (on the wharves)—but the bales and baskets piled high on the docks were not just a sign of its prosperity; they were tangible evidence that the world was growing faster than it had ever done before. The ships that maneuvered for position brought cargoes not only from the Baltic, England, Spain, and Germany but from farther afield as well, from lands that were so distant, so newly discovered, they still seemed almost mythological to the laborers who sweated to unload the merchandise.

Not many years before, the ports of Venice and the other Italian city-states had been crowded with cargo ships, linking with the ancient overland routes from the East to bring spices, precious stones, silks, and finery to Europe. For centuries, all roads really had led to Rome. But by 1512, ships could follow Vasco da Gama's route to India around the southern tip of Africa and bring their cargoes straight back to the north and west of Europe. The rapidly growing trade with the New World, too, could be carried out more easily from western Europe than from Italy. The pattern of commerce was shifting: More than 2,500 ships might be crowded into Antwerp's port at any one time, and 500 vessels would come and go in a single day.

With the cargoes came stories of new expeditions, and of the fresh discoveries that were being made in the New World and in the farthest reaches of Asia. Such talk, true and false alike, was devoured by the educated citizens; but the bales, bundles, and boxes were the real stimuli to anyone with imagination and curiosity about distant lands. The waters of the Scheldt flowed for hundreds of miles through a continent hungry for the goods that the ships had unloaded. Along the docks of Antwerp, the age of discoveries was a daily reality.

When he arrived there late in February 1512, Hubert had four sons, a daughter, a pregnant wife, and no real prospects of employment. His one advantage was an uncle in the Catholic Church. Several years before, in Gangelt, Hubert had named his firstborn child after his father's brother, and he turned to that same Uncle Gisbert, the chaplain of Rupelmonde's Hospice of St. Jean. Gisbert was not wealthy but comfortably off, and he used his influence to find Hubert and his family a place in the monastery guesthouse. It would have been a simple, even spartan home, but still a welcome shelter for a family on the brink of penury. There, at six o'clock in the morning on March 5, 1512, only a few days after she had arrived in Flanders, Hubert's wife, Emerance, gave birth to their sixth child, Gerard. The anxious cobbler made a precise note of the date and time, as he had done for the birth of his other children.

The town's tax records show Hubert, Emerance, and their six children lived on top of each other in a lodging half the size of the house his single uncle Gisbert kept for himself.* Gisbert, a busy, energetic priest, filled

---

*It is easy to miss the house now, an anonymous little end-of-terrace cottage of weathered brick beside the road that leads past the neatly fenced commuter homes into Rupelmonde's marketplace. There are lace curtains at the windows, a car parked in the road outside. Next door is a white-painted modern house; it takes a second glance to register the traces in the brickwork farther down the terrace where the main arched entrance into the hospice would have been, and to note the arched windows and the massive two-foot-thick walls. The street name, unchanged for centuries, is a clue as well: Kloosterstraet, or Cloister Street. This is a hidden remnant of Rupelmonde's medieval past. The

with ambition for himself and his family, was the key to whatever future they would have. For him as for many others, the Church had been a route to worldly security as well as to salvation, and his post as chaplain at the hospice gave him financial independence, respectability, and a degree of influence. Well educated himself, he determined to do what he could for the rest of his family. Within a few months, his nephew Hubert was using his skills to produce shoes for the hospice and steadily building up his business in the town, while the older boys, with Gisbert's encouragement and influence, had started on careers of their own in the Church. Rupelmonde's church records show that Hubert's second son, Dominic, eventually followed his great-uncle into the post of chaplain at the hospice, while the eldest boy, Gisbert, named in his great-uncle's honor, became a priest in the nearby village of St. Nicholas. There was no doubt that they and the other two boys would do well, while their sister, Barbe, was being carefully prepared for the marriage that would secure her future.

Gerard, like his brothers, received his education on the hard wooden benches of the local village school. The few hundred houses in Rupelmonde were huddled around the church, a short way from the river and the imposing black fort that glowered down upon it. Nearby was the ancient water mill where grain was brought from the surrounding fields, its great rough limestone grinders making the wooden structure groan and vibrate as they turned under the power of the rising and falling tides. Farmers brought their produce to a regular market on the riverbank, while barges would tie up to sell cheeses from Brussels, or herring, imported cloth, and ironware from the wharves of Antwerp. Bigger, seagoing ships often moored at the wharves, pausing on their journeys upriver to Brussels. Outside the village, the landscape stretched away for miles, flat and open.

---

old lady who comes to the door peers suspiciously at camera and notebook, wondering what the interest might be. Not many people come here, she says dubiously, shaking her head; the house's disguise works well. Elsewhere in Rupelmonde, a statue of the village's only famous son has dominated the marketplace since 1871, and there are Mercator-waffles for sale, as well as trinkets and T-shirts in the tourist shop; but only a simple, Flemish plaque—"Gerardus Mercator is hier geboren in 1512"—marks the house.

Rupelmonde

With its fields, mill, market, school, and church, the little town provided for every aspect of life, but the fort, with its high stone walls and
seventeen towers, overshadowed everything. Built by Norman invaders
in the eleventh century to overawe and terrify the local people, it was no
mere monument to past brutality. Behind its bleak walls there still languished criminals, dissidents, traitors, and forgotten men.

The young Gerard was apparently drawn to the sheer variety the
landscape offered, for he developed a love of nature that would stay
with him throughout his life. From his earliest days, at least according
to the stories that grew up around him later, the schoolmaster had little need to encourage his pupil to greater effort in the classroom.
Much of the work in the single schoolroom was learning by rote, the
children chanting the Latin of the Lord's Prayer or the Creed, or the
questions and answers of the catechism. Every lesson, every moral
precept, was based upon the Bible. At home, there was neither leisure

nor privacy in the crowded and hardworking household, but the young boy usually managed to find a place to hide away with his books. Often, he would be huddled with them long into the night, forgetting to eat or sleep, and his potential was clearly recognized by his uncle.

In 1526, Hubert de Cremer died suddenly, and the family was threatened with disaster once again. (There is no record of what killed him.) Emerance was able to survive on the little money he had saved, and five of their children were almost old enough to look after themselves. However, Gerard was just fourteen, and if he had had to work in order to earn his keep, his family's hopes for his future would have been dashed. An apprenticeship could have led only to a life of unremitting toil like his father's; there would have been no time for learning.

Once again, they had to rely on Gisbert. Three masses a week at the hospice brought him a regular income of some forty-three pounds a year—enough for him to have acquired two small farms as well as his own house, and enough, if he chose, to provide for the education of his great-nephew. The young boy was taken from his family and went to live with his great-uncle, who became not only his benefactor but also his adoptive father and his tutor. Yet if Gerard, like his two elder brothers, were to follow Gisbert into the Church, he would need more than a smattering of Latin grammar picked up at home and on the benches of Rupelmonde's school. The boy would have to be educated.

Chapter Four

Among the Brethren of
the Common Life

THE ARTIST ALBRECHT DÜRER, journeying through the Netherlands from his native Germany, described 's Hertogenbosch,
stranded on the windswept and unwelcoming plains some seventy-five
miles northeast of Antwerp, as "a fair city, with an extremely beautiful
church and a strong fortress. . . ."[1] The Gothic ramparts of the Cathedral of St. Jan might have impressed a traveler, but the town itself was a
bleak and forbidding place, a long way from the riverside idyll of Rupelmonde. Here, fifteen thousand people lived behind high stone walls,
which would surround the young Gerard for the next three years.

The town's name means "woods of the duke," and the harsh guttural
of the Flemish pronunciation reveals its sixteenth-century soul. It was already one of the oldest towns in the Low Countries when Gerard arrived—no balmy country retreat, but a fortress set up by Duke Henry I
of Brabant more than three centuries earlier to protect the remote northern borders of his dukedom. The grim stone walls could keep out foreign enemies, but inside them, 's Hertogenbosch seethed with religious
and political discontent that occasionally erupted in violence, as occurred in many Netherlands towns. 's Hertogenbosch, the Netherlands,
and most of Europe were in ferment. The trouble had been building for
decades.

Ten years earlier, when Gerard was still a young boy, stories had
begun filtering back from Germany of a young priest who had issued a

Martin Luther

direct challenge to the Catholic Church on the need for reform and an end to corruption. In nailing his list of ninety-five theses to the church door in Wittenburg, Martin Luther had ignited the first flames of a conflagration that would engulf much of Europe.

Only God, he declared, and not papal authority, could forgive sin; the selling of indulgences by which divine forgiveness could supposedly be guaranteed in return for the payment of cash was a corrupt and cruel deception. Luther called for reform rather than revolution. "If the Pope knew the exactions of the pardon-preachers, he would rather that St. Peter's church should go to ashes, than that it should be built up with the skin, flesh and bones of his sheep," he declared in one of his theses. Yet the whole of Christendom, not just the Catholic Church, threatened to go to ashes: Political dissatisfaction and growing national feeling in the Netherlands, Germany, and much of northern Europe had prepared the ground for a conflict that would tear the continent apart, leaving it split irrevocably between Catholics and Protestants.

Johannes Gutenberg's first presses produced massive runs of printed papal indulgences, but they also turned out seemingly unlimited editions of non-Latin Bibles on which the faithful could rely. Alongside them were other religious texts, mystical books, and lives of the saints, many of them written in the day-to-day language of the people, breaking forever the Catholic Church's monopoly on Holy Writ. The anxieties of kings, emperors, and the Church itself could do nothing to hold back the rapid spread of movable type.

Printed tracts showered from the new presses like sparks, lighting a thousand fires of heresy—fires that were fed among the German princes and nationalists in the Low Countries by resentment of the emperor's power. There was already bitterness over the harsh taxes with which Charles tried to claw back the massive debts he had incurred. Despite the treasure that was starting to flow into his coffers from the New World, he relied largely on the merchants of the Netherlands to finance his wars: For every hundred florins in gold and silver that fell into Charles's lap from the New World, four hundred were squeezed from the taxpayers of the Netherlands. The Venetian ambassador Antonio Soriano described the Low Countries as "the treasures of the King of Spain, his mines, his Indies which have sustained all the Emperor's enterprises." Others, more crudely, saw them as a cow to be milked to exhaustion.

The merchants' pockets were not bottomless, though, and their goodwill was easily exhausted. Every new demand for tax was met by angry resistance, which often mingled with religious dissent and spilled over into fighting on the streets of towns in the Netherlands.

In 's Hertogenbosch, angry crowds rampaged through the narrow streets while Gerard was at school; but the discontent was more often sullen and unspoken. The town had been home to the artist Hieronymus van Aken, better known today as Hieronymus Bosch.[2] His wild, tortured depictions of the sufferings of Hell were well known, apparently orthodox enough, and greatly appreciated by the Church authorities—Bosch had painted several altarpieces for the Cathedral of St. Jan in his hometown—but they had a subversive and less conventional secondary meaning.[3] Bosch was a reformist, possibly even an out-and-out heretic who saw the Catholic Church as Satan's embassy on Earth. The evidence is there in Bosch's works, a telling example of the double-edged, evasive atmosphere of the town where Gerard was growing up.

Many of the symbols in Bosch's paintings seem now to be consistent with heretical thinking, and his anger over the corruption and avarice of the Church is even clearer. His massive triptych, *The Haywain,*[4] shows a nun cradling the head of a sick or dying beggar in a conventional representation of the Church's Christian care for the poor. Elsewhere in the same painting, though, other nuns are sweeping the peasants' crop of hay into their own bags; in another vignette, one of them seems to be making sexual advances toward a musician. *The Ship of Fools*[5] shows a nun and a monk picking over a dish of cherries, a common image of sexual gratification. Seen together, the symbols are unmistakable, but individually they are subtle enough not to offend.

Bosch led a perilous double life, because he was also a leading member in 's Hertogenbosch of an orthodox and solemn religious fraternity, the Brotherhood of Our Lady. He was a respected figure in the town, as his father and grandfather had been before him, and even took the city's name for his own. He married a local woman, owned a house, and died. Little else is known about his life, but that is the point: He had avoided attracting attention.

The school Gisbert chose for his young charge in 's Hertogenbosch revealed the private thoughts behind his own daily life. Like Hieronymus Bosch, he had taken care not to provoke the Church authorities, but the hardworking Gisbert de Cremer had been leading something of a double life as well, building his career within the Church while discreetly supporting the agitation for reform. He handed Gerard over to a religious community known for their reformist zeal, the Brethren of the Common Life.

The Brethren had a long tradition as teachers, but they were not a comfortable institution. For themselves, they had renounced the possession of property and embraced a life of simple obedience; their rule was self-denying and ascetic, and they expected the boys in their care to abide by it as well. One famous former pupil gave a glimpse of the harsh life the pupils could expect: The humanist Erasmus of Rotterdam, who had written his own biting satires on Church corruption, *In Praise of Folly*

's Hertogenbosch, from Civitates Orbis Terrarum, *1572*

and *Colloquia,* spoke of beatings and bullying at the school by overzealous teachers who wanted to direct their young charges toward the priesthood. His own youthful love of learning had been thrashed out of him for a time by their merciless severity, he said; his time at the school was nothing more than two years lost from his life. "Their chief care, should they see any youth of unusually high spirit and quick disposition . . . is to break his spirit and humble him by blows, threats, scoldings, and other devices," he told a friend.[6]

The Brethren were not monks and took no vows, but they were loyal to the memory of their fourteenth-century founder, Geert Groete, who had drawn crowds with his impassioned preaching against lax ecclesiastical discipline and the corruption of the clergy. They observed a rule of sobriety and chastity that was at least as strict as that in many monasteries. More than a thousand pupils were housed in separate dormitories according to social rank and economic status, ranging from rich to poor. Gerard de Cremer was numbered straightaway among the poor students, making their way each day from the *domus pauperum* to the

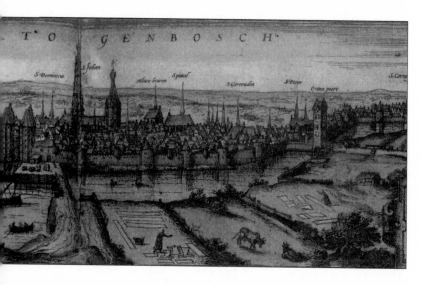

school beneath the twisted cathedral gargoyles that Hieronymus Bosch had known so well.

There he encountered the traditional three-branched humanist *trivium* of grammar, rhetoric, and logic, all of which looked resolutely back toward the certainties and inspiration of the past. Poetry and philosophy came from Homer, Ovid, Plato, Aristotle, and other pagan authors, and theology from Christian divines such as Augustine, Origen, and St. Jerome. Geography, too, came from the distant past: In an age when knowledge of the world was increasing faster than ever before, Gerard and his classmates were pointed sternly toward the learning of Ptolemy and Pliny. All of it was sandwiched between two, sometimes three, daily celebrations of the Mass, and all of it was in Latin. That, not the crudity of workaday Flemish, was the language of the churchman and the scholar.

Among Gerard's teachers was the grandly named author and playwright Georgius Macropedius—a man already with a dangerous reputation of his own for sympathizing with reformers. Macropedius's character fitted well with the stern philosophy of the school. In his plays, which were often performed by his pupils for the townsfolk, only the rod and the lash saved boys from willfulness, whoring, theft, and a shameful death on the gallows. To the general approval of the rest of the cast, recalcitrant pupils were soundly whipped until they screamed, and when their mothers tried to intervene, much the same treatment was meted out to them.

That would have been the regime in many schools, at least as far as the pupils were concerned. There was little room for sympathy or consolation. Thus, when news came that Gerard's mother had followed his father to the grave, the boy had to cope with it on his own. Her death, like that of her husband, did not merit any official record of its cause; death, like sickness, poverty, or disaster, was an ever-present threat. Within the space of two years, Gerard had lost both his parents, and Gisbert's generosity and his own talents were all he could rely on.

He had clearly fitted in during his time in the ascetic world of the Brethren. Unlike Erasmus, he never complained later in his life of their harshness, and the rules that the Brethren applied to their traditional task of transcribing manuscripts show how diligently he learned their lessons. "You ought to attend in your copying to these things: that you make the letters properly and perfectly, that you copy without error, that you understand the sense of what you are copying, and that you concentrate your wandering mind on the task," said their rulebook. The art of copying was virtually destroyed by the new flood of printed books by the time Gerard was studying at 's Hertogenbosch, but as an adult he would become known throughout Europe for the precision of his engraved lettering and his obsession with accuracy, as well as for the single-minded concentration with which he applied himself to his books. He thrived on the traditional emphasis on ancient learning. Ptolemy, introduced to him by the teachers in the cathedral, would remain his scholastic guide and mentor throughout his life.

Gerard also drew some lessons from his great-uncle and from his own earlier life: that the Church had always been a source of support and stability in the confusing world in which he was growing up, and that Gisbert's prosperity showed the material rewards that could come from not challenging the system openly. The Brethren were always careful to keep the sympathy for the reform movement which they had inherited from their founder within bounds that were acceptable to the Church authorities. In a town where dissent and dangerous opinions were common, Gerard no doubt saw the importance of discretion and the value of security. Inside the walls he had found scholarly disputation and strict discipline, symbolized by the monkish uniform of gray hooded gowns that the boys wore, "after the ancient usage of the Brethren," but he had also found stability.

The old world of the Catholic Church had given him security, and for all the reformist leanings, the innovative thinking, and the fascination with new skills and techniques that would mark his adult life, he never lost his instinctive sense that stability would be found in the past, in the way things had always been.

Unlike many of the Brethren's charges, however, Gerard still had no ambition for a prosperous and honorable career in the Church like his great-uncle's. The small boy remarkable for the dedication with which he closeted himself with his books became a serious and sober eighteen-year-old, with the prospect of a life dedicated to study. University life, just as much as that of the cloister, could offer support and a place to belong. The rich endowments and charitable foundations of the forty-three colleges of the University of Leuven meant that, as an impoverished but talented student, he could be excused payment of any fees there.* Although there were no formal requirements for admission, a prospective student would have to convince the doctors of his college that he was adequately prepared for the demanding course of study that the university would provide.[7] Gerard's record of study at 's Hertogenbosch, together with the patronage and recommendation of his uncle, would have been enough to do that. He was ready to take a place in the ancient university.

---

*Gisbert would have been expected to stand ready to pay his fees until he had satisfied the university authorities that he was entitled to be treated as one of the *paupeers ex castro,* the poor students of the castle.

Chapter Five

At the College of the Castle

Joining the University of Leuven was a solemn moment, a commitment like joining a monastery. On August 29, 1530, Gerard de Cremer knelt before the rector, Pierre de Corte—a man who would later prove his courage and friendship by standing up to the Inquisition on his former pupil's behalf—to take the oath of matriculation, the pupil's hands clasped between the master's in prayer and supplication. The university was a cosmopolitan place, with more than five thousand students and scholars from France, Germany, England, Scotland, and the farthest reaches of Europe—enough to create their own distinct community. The Faculty of Arts, which Gerard joined, was divided into four colleges scattered through the town. The Colleges of the Pig, the Lily, and the Hawk were all named after ancient houses in Leuven, while the College of the Castle, in the street that led up to the duke's old residence, was where Mercator received his board and lodging and most of his tuition.

When Duke John IV of Brabant had applied for papal approval to found the university early in the fifteenth Century, Leuven, some twenty-five miles southeast of Rupelmonde, was in decline. Many of the weavers whose labors had made it prosperous had left for England, frightened by the latest spasm of riots and fighting, and attracted by the lure of better profits in the growing English wool trade. Other cities had flourishing universities: Bologna, Paris, and Oxford had been attracting students for two centuries or more, and similar institutions were opening all over northern Europe. France had twenty universities in the fifteenth century, and the German-speaking countries about the same. A new university in Leuven brought not only prestige to the duke but prosperity to the town.

By the early sixteenth century, its reputation was growing. Its former rector, Nicolas Vernulaeus,[1] wrote a history of the university that described a peaceful academic town, with quiet fields and vineyards sheltered from the north winds by the hills around, and with well-swept and respectable houses—the very place, he enthused, for students seeking calm to pursue their studies. Even Erasmus had found it more congenial than the grammar school at 's Hertogenbosch. Its students, he observed, were well taught, courteous, and mature. "No-one could graduate at Leuven without knowledge, manners, and age," he declared. He had written to assure a friend: "Its agreeable and healthy climate is conducive to quiet and peaceful study; no other university can rival its intellectual life, nor the number and quality of its academic staff."[2]

The establishment of the university, by attracting scholars and businesses, had played its part in the rejuvenation of Leuven, and there was clearly much life in the town beyond the college walls. The university authorities took the possibility of youthful high spirits seriously enough to set down formal statutes banning students from bearing arms, dicing and gaming in public taverns, or even walking the streets after eight o'clock at night, and their rules were stricter still inside the college. Gerard apparently reveled in the austere, contemplative life of fasting, abstinence, and strict obedience to the *pater* of the college. The sole official record of his time at Leuven is his inscription as a "poor student" in the books of the College of the Castle, but his friends and contemporaries all spoke of a dedicated and high-minded academic, concentrating almost obsessively on his work.

In that society, at least, there should have been no shame in his poverty. But even if the somber, monkish gown, which all the university's pupils wore,[3] disguised the differences between rich and poor, there was little fraternization between them. They all ate in the same hall, but the rich took the high table, while the poor sat at the far end of the hall; the rich students lived in private rooms, while the poor shared the dormitory in the College of the Castle. Few friendships crossed such a divide, but Mer-

cator would have known the names of his rich colleagues, and one in par-
ticular would resonate for the rest of his life: Antoine Perrenot de
Granvelle, the son of Charles V's trusted chancellor, Nicholas Perrenot de
Granvelle, was starting on his rise to power.

It was customary in scholastic circles, even among poor students, to
add dignity to one's name by translating it into Latin. Gerard's schoolmaster at 's Hertogenbosch, Georgius Macropedius, had started life as
Joris van Lanckvelt. Gerrit Gerritszoon had already become known as
the humanist Desiderius Erasmus Roterodamus, and Mercator's near
contemporary Andries van Wesel would win fame as the anatomist and
humanist Andreas Vesalius. The sonorous, Latinized Mercator, or *merchant,* suited Gerard's own ambitions much better than de Cremer—
pedlar in the vulgar Flemish. In choosing his new name as he started on
his career at Leuven, he looked back to the place of his birth and the
formative years of his childhood: Gerardus Mercator Rupelmundanus
was born.

The rigid timetable of his days was punctuated, as it had been in
's Hertogenbosch, by celebrations of the Mass, and ran from dawn to
dusk, with a brief rest period in the afternoon. His course of studies in
the university's Faculty of Arts was essentially the same logic, physics,
metaphysics, mathematics, rhetoric, and moral philosophy that students
had tackled for centuries, with attention fastened as firmly on the learning of hundreds of years ago as it had been at 's Hertogenbosch. Observation, measurement, and independent thought were all dangerous
steps on the road to heresy. First among the ancient masters was Aristotle, and it was expressly forbidden even to question his teaching.

The eighteen-hundred-year-old writings of the pre-Christian Greek
philosopher were used expressly to bolster and justify the position of the
Catholic Church as guardian of thought and theology. The statutes of the
university were strict and unambiguous about how religion, philosophy,
and natural science should be approached: "You will uphold the teaching
of Aristotle, except in cases which are contrary to faith. . . . No-one will be
allowed to reject the opinion of Aristotle as heretical . . . unless it has pre-
viously been declared heretical by the Faculty of Theology."

That official position was strictly enforced by the university authorities, with the sinister power of the Inquisition always in the background. The university had done more than bring prestige and prosperity to Leuven; it had given the dukes of Brabant and their heirs—by then, the emperor Charles V—a powerful tool of religious and political repression. Though it had a degree of independence—one condition of the papal bull by which Pope Martin V had originally consented to its establishment had been that the rector should have full criminal and civil jurisdiction over its members—the university authorities nonetheless worked closely with the imperial government. There was no home within their walls for the reformist agitation so popular in 's Hertogenbosch. In 1522, Charles V had established a state-run Inquisition to work alongside the Church in quashing the reform movement, and the university authorities took an active part in its investigations. Leuven's Faculty of Theology was given the task of censoring and approving all newly printed books on behalf of Charles V, and various university officials took their places in the ponderous, awe-inspiring public processions in which the Inquisition's victims were led to punishment or public repentance. At Leuven, Mercator was studying in one of the greatest strongholds of anti-Reformation learning of the sixteenth century.

At the same time, the university boasted some of the finest teachers in Europe, who were making discoveries of their own while avoiding any direct confrontation with the authorities or the Inquisition. Erasmus had been a professor there, helping to found the Collegium Trilingue for the study of Hebrew, Latin, and Greek, and Adrian of Utrecht, one of the tutors of the young Charles V, had held the chair of philosophy, theology, and canon law before being elected pope in 1522.[4] The renowned mathematician, astronomer, and physician Gemma Frisius, who taught Mercator about the movement of the planets and helped him as he grappled with classical geometry, was no backward-looking medieval scholar.

Gemma was a sallow, thin-faced, lame, and asthmatic genius, who had taken his name from the windswept plains of Friesland where he came from, alongside the sandbanks and marshes of the Waddenzee. Like Mercator, he came from a poor family, and his parents had died during his childhood. Though only four years older than Mercator, by the time the latter arrived at Leuven, Gemma had already established a reputation across Europe as the leading mathematician and cosmographer of the Low Countries. A contemporary engraving shows him in his academic robe and bonnet, his long face impassive, with sunken cheeks and a slightly hooked nose. His eyes stare fixedly, challengingly from the frame, and his bony fingers, wrapped casually around a globe, are heavily ringed like a nobleman's—a picture of a man beyond riches, a scholar literally holding the world in the palm of his hand. While still a student and barely out of his teens, he had produced his own corrected edition of the *Cosmographia* published five years earlier by the German scholar and sometime tutor of Charles V, Petrus Apianus. The book drew on traditional ancient sources but also, through Martin Waldseemüller's world map of 1507 and the writings of other German scholars, on the transatlantic voyages of Amerigo Vespucci and the explorers of the previous forty years. The new edition had Gemma's name on the title page alongside that of its author and was widely accepted as the most authoritative account of the known geography of the world, appearing in some thirty different editions over the next eighty years.

Gemma's own writings on astronomy and cosmography, *De principiis astronomiae et cosmographiae*, were published in 1530, the same year that Mercator joined the university. He was working on the practical application of mathematics to surveying and mapmaking, while at the same time following his medical studies, which would lead eventually to his appointment to the university's medical faculty. He was a role model for the young Mercator, not just a scholar and polymath but a man who combined ancient learning with the most up-to-date research. Gemma was dedicated in particular to the practical application of his studies, the union of mathematics and geography. He had already started to produce the mathematical and scientific instruments for which he would become famous, and he was putting the finishing touches on his new technique of triangulation, the art of defining the location of a place by taking two separate sightings. His *planimetrum,* a flat wooden disk marked in degrees and fitted with a revolving pointer, could be aligned with magnetic north so that its user could take sightings of different towns across the flat Low Countries. The cathedral at Antwerp, he suggested, was an

Gemma Frisius

ideal place to start. First he would settle on a second fixed point nearby and walk the distance between it and the cathedral to check its measurement. Then, using his *planimetrum*, he would establish the angle between imaginary lines drawn from the cathedral to his observation point and from the observation point to a point of reference, such as a tower, in the distant town. He thus knew the size of one side and two angles of an imaginary triangle drawn between the cathedral, his fixed point, and the distant tower; working out the length of the other two sides, and thus the position of the distant tower, was then a matter of simple geometry. This proved the key to accurate surveying for centuries to come, and a technique which Mercator would master for his own mapmaking.

Gemma had also found time to tackle the problem of calculating longitude, which had troubled mariners for centuries, and particularly since they had started making long journeys across the Ocean Sea and to the Far East. In theory at least, working out a ship's latitude was relatively easy—instruments could measure the height of the Sun or other heavenly

Leuven, from Civitates Orbis Terrarum, *1572*

bodies above the horizon, and sets of tables would give a fairly accurate reading of latitude—but sailors had no accepted way of finding how far east or west they were. Gemma suggested in *De principiis astronomiae et cosmographiae* that it might be done with a combination of astronomical observations and the use of a reliable clock. Since the Earth was a sphere of 360 degrees that revolved once every twenty-four hours, each fifteen degrees of longitude would make one hour's difference to the time. First, Gemma advised, the navigator should take an accurate reading of the time and a sighting of the Sun when he set off. If, when he was out at sea, he then marked the time when the Sun was in the same position in the sky, the time difference measured on the clock would tell him how many degrees east or west he had traveled.* "By this art can I find the longitude

---

*One degree of longitude, or 1/360 of the total distance around the world, would result in a time difference of four minutes, or 1/360 of a day. To calculate the actual distance traveled, allowing for the fact that lines of longitude converge on the poles, a navigator would also have to know his latitude, which he could check by observations of the Sun or the stars.

of regions, although I were a thousand miles out of my attempted course and in an unknown distance," he declared.[5] There were no clocks accurate enough for such a technique—it would be more than two centuries before John Harrison's chronometer solved that problem—but the theory was impeccable. The technique was simply two hundred years ahead of the technology.

Despite the hard work of his childhood, Mercator found he lacked basic knowledge in his early days at the university. He struggled at first in Gemma's lectures on astronomy, he admitted later, because he lacked the mathematical knowledge to grasp the arguments, so he went off alone with his geometry textbooks to follow through the logic of the classical mathematicians.

He started by teaching himself elementary geometry from the books of Gemma's Friesland countryman Johannes Vögelin, which he said he easily mastered. He then tackled the first six books of Euclid, beginning with the simple, basic definitions—that a line has length but no breadth, for instance, or that a surface has only length and breadth—and gradually building up his understanding of Euclid's theoretical arguments about lines, points, circles, triangles, and the relationships between them. Mercator's method was to take a complex geometric proposition and follow it logically, stage by stage, continually referring back to earlier theorems as he went. In Book IV, for instance, he worked painstakingly through Euclid's seventeen-hundred-year-old instructions for fitting a straight line into a circle, and in Book VI, he followed through the proof that a straight line drawn through a triangle parallel to one side will cut the other two sides in equal proportions. Each proposition built upon the ones before it, so that by the time he had finished, he had mastered the technique of theoretical reasoning to the point where he could follow Gemma's lectures and understand the principles of triangulation. Mercator shrugged off this minor achievement: "In a few days, I got to the point where there was nothing in the six books that I had not diligently studied and learned," he wrote later.[6]

He worked alone but turned to Gemma for help and advice whenever he found himself puzzled by Euclid. In a mark of singular favor, he was invited for private tuition in Gemma's house as one of the *familia* of students who sat at his feet. Gemma's scholarship had won him the regard and friendship of Johann Flaxbinder, the ambassador of the king of Poland to the court of Charles V, and Flaxbinder had tried unsuccessfully to persuade him to leave the lowlands for a post as Polish court cosmographer. The books he published, which supported him during his years at Leuven, were dedicated to such figures as Charles's advisers Maximilian Transylvain and Jean Obernburger, and to Jean Khreutter, a senior councillor to the queen of Hungary. The emperor himself summoned Gemma to his court in Brussels on occasion for discussions on matters of science and geography. Gemma Frisius was Mercator's first introduction to the eminent circles on whose support his prosperity would be built.

His influence over the young student went farther. Euclid was entirely theoretical—the study of logical argument as much as lines, triangles, and circles—but Mercator's interest, like that of Gemma, was engaged from the start in its practical use. "In geometry, I only pursued those studies that were to do with measuring, the location of places, the laying out of maps, the dimensions of territories, and finding the distances and sizes of celestial bodies," he reminisced when he was sixty-nine years old in a letter to a Swiss Protestant pastor, offering advice on how a child might be taught geometry. "In mathematics, I directed my studies to cosmography alone."[7] His aim throughout was to improve his skills as a geographer, surveyor, cartographer, and astronomer.

He had other interests as well—interests that went far beyond the apparently innocent theories of geometry and took him into areas on which Aristotle and the Church had laid down unshakable rules. Ever since his boyhood in Rupelmonde, Mercator had been fascinated by the natural world, but at Leuven his interest was piqued by nature in its widest sense—not just in plants and animals but in the shape of the world and the universe. He built on his studies of Euclid to understand the movements of the stars and planets, as he described years later: "The contemplation of Nature delighted me marvellously, because she teaches us the causes of all things, the sources of all knowledge. But I delighted particularly in the study of the creation of the world, which shows us the beautiful order, the harmonious proportion, and the singular beauty which is there to be admired in all created things."[8] He saw no clash with his religious belief; to study Creation was a way to understand and appreciate its wonder, not a challenge to divine power.

The university authorities, though, were not as confident that such contemplations were free of heresy. For them, the Earth was the focus of the universe, the unequivocal center of everything, and arguments about order, proportion, and beauty were at best irrelevant and at worst a direct challenge to Holy Writ.

Aristotle had also taught that the *oikoumene,* the habitable world, was limited to the regions of Europe, Asia, and North Africa that lay between the frozen northern zone and the blistering heat of the "torrid zone." There was, he said, a symmetrical arrangement to the South, although the southern temperate zone remained uninhabited. Since the first centuries of the Christian Church, philosophers and theologians had pointed out that only descendants of the animals in Noah's Ark—safely in the northern zone—could have survived the Flood. That was a view which the church of Mercator's day supported, studiously ignoring the fact that sailors over the previous hundred years had encountered both animals and human beings around the equator and farther south.

For several hundred years, the physical reality of Aristotle had been accepted as fitting most closely with the Christian belief in an all-powerful, eternal Creator; experimentation, measurement, and empirical questioning that might throw Aristotle's conclusions into doubt were not allowed by the Church. The challenge to Aristotle was as much part of the Reformation as were the attacks on corruption in the Church. Luther's delight when he declared triumphantly, "Aristotle is going downhill, and perhaps he will go all the way down into hell,"[9] reflected Aristotle's position as one of the Catholic Church's central pillars against reform. Revolution was no less threatening to the authorities because it was in the mind; pull one brick from the towering building of medieval philosophy, faith, and theology, they believed, and the whole structure might come tumbling down.

For TWO YEARS Mercator continued quietly with his studies, avoiding any clash with the authorities, until he was awarded his *magisterii gradum*. The master's degree would have allowed him to progress from the Faculty of Arts to further studies in medicine, Church law, civil law, or theology, as Gemma had done. Instead, as he stood on the threshold of the academic career he must have dreamed of, he gave the first sign of the inner turmoil he was suffering. He remained a member of the university, subject to its rules and regulations and—crucially, as he would discover—entitled to its protection, but he abandoned his formal course of study. He left Leuven in 1532 for nearby Antwerp.

Many years later, Mercator admitted that as a young man at Leuven, he had begun to have his first doubts about the wisdom of the philosophers, and to believe that the contemplation of nature, science, and the natural world might offer a better insight into God's will. "When I understood how the world of Genesis and Moses did not agree in many ways with Aristotle and the rest of the philosophers, then I began to doubt the truth of all the philosophers, and to test it against the mysteries of nature."[10] Those words about his youthful doubts, taken from a treatise on Genesis published after his death, seem calm and judicious, but his actions at the time suggested that they hid an agonizing mental struggle.

Almost certainly, it was with these cogitations on the incompatibility of Aristotle and Genesis that the first seeds of Mercator's lifelong interest in synthesizing the various ancient and medieval accounts of history were sown. Whether his thoughts were written down for eventual publication or not, they were to develop more than thirty years later into his *Chronologia* and *Cosmographia*.

The reasons behind his decision to leave Leuven will never be known for certain, nor will the reaction of his great-uncle, who had spent so many years building his own career in the Church and keeping quiet about his reformist ideas. Mercator was not expelled—he claimed later[11] that he left "alone, and of my own volition"—and he kept open the option of returning to the university. Perhaps he had no clear idea at the time of what he would do or how he would live outside the walls of the College of the Castle. Yet in choosing Antwerp as his destination, he threw his religious belief, his academic future, even his life into jeopardy.

Chapter Six

Doubts and Dangers

THE ROAD TO ANTWERP took Mercator through the town of Mechelen, about halfway from Leuven. There is no way of knowing whether he broke his journey then and even stayed for a brief while, but once he reached Antwerp he would certainly have heard about the books, maps, and ideas that were emanating from the town. Mechelen buzzed with intellectual life. The great port city of Antwerp was unchallenged as the mercantile and commercial center of the region, and Leuven was the finest academic institution of northern Europe, but fate and the whims of mighty families had made the little town of Mechelen, under its massive thirteenth-century Cathedral of St. Rombout, a hotbed of intellectual debate and creativity. There, away from the dead hand of the university authorities, the challenging ideas of a new world found expression.

In the early years of the sixteenth century, the town had gone through a brief period of glittering prosperity, home to the court of the young Charles V's regent, Margaret of Austria. Charles himself, though born in Ghent, spent the first sixteen years of his life in Mechelen, surrounded by artists and philosophers such as the German engraver Albrecht Dürer, the humanist thinker Erasmus of Rotterdam, and Sir Thomas More, future chancellor of King Henry VIII of England. There were also spies, sending back information to their masters in the various courts of Europe about the humanist and occasionally anti-Catholic ideas that were expressed in the town. The composer and copyist Petrus Alamire* worked as a musician at the court and at various times supplied secret reports to Charles's advisers and to King Henry in England.

Even though Mechelen's glory was fading by the time Mercator traveled there in the early 1530s, the prosperity that came with such fame remained. Many businesses had been attracted to the town—among them, the burgeoning trade of printing. Mechelen was known as one of the most important centers in the Low Countries for the rapidly developing technology, and that in turn had encouraged geographers and mapmakers, giving it a widespread reputation as a place of geographic study.

Gemma Frisius and his circle were in touch with some of the town's brightest intellectual flames, among them Frans Smunck, or Franciscus Monachus. If one of them sent Mercator to meet him, it would have been done discreetly, because Franciscus was a marked man; but it seems likely that the young student paid him several visits during his months in Antwerp. Franciscus was one of a religious community known as the Minorite Friars, who believed that by practicing complete self-denial, poverty, and humility, they would lead the world back to pure Christianity. They had been outspoken in their criticism of corruption in the Church for more than two centuries, and at various times, some of their leaders had gone so far as to question the legitimacy of the papacy itself, so that members of the order had been harassed, excommunicated, even burned at the stake. Such a history meant that, at best, the Friars were regarded with suspicion by the Inquisition and the university authorities—but Franciscus had a dangerous reputation of his own as well.

A few years before, he had constructed the first globe to be seen in the Low Countries, along with a short book and a world map. The globe has been lost, but his map shows that he was one of the most advanced geographic thinkers of his day. When it was produced in 1526, the American

---

*Alamire was a shady character, believed to have come to Mechelen from Germany. He left more than eight hundred pieces of music in forty-eight choir books, most of them collected on his travels through Europe.

Franciscus Monachus's worldview

continents had gradually taken shape after Magellan's voyage around the southern tip, and Franciscus had done his best to incorporate the latest discoveries of the expeditions that had been pushing northward up its western coastline. North America floundered in a blur of guesswork, depicted as an outgrowth of Asia, and a narrow channel was shown cutting the isthmus to South America, almost foreshadowing the Panama Canal 375 years later. Petrus Apianus had shown such a channel in his world map of 1520, but he had achieved nothing like the accuracy of Franciscus Monachus's depiction of South America.

Franciscus's thoughts ran in more perilous channels as well. By the time Mercator met him he was in his midforties and was known as a critic of the Aristotelian ideas that were at the center of religious orthodoxy, a believer in the importance of observation and measurement, and a man who challenged accepted wisdom. The message of his map had been that exploration, pushing westward to the Indies, was a profitable enterprise, while in his book he had derided "the rubbish of Ptolemy," and by implication denied the truth of Aristotle's view of a five-zoned world.

The jumble of fact, rumor, report, and conjecture that surrounded the emerging Americas, let alone Franciscus's contemptuous view of the great Ptolemy, might have been meat enough for discussion between the two men, but their meetings seem to have ranged over the whole story of the Creation and the history of the world. These were more controversial studies by far than consideration of the coastline of the Americas.

For obvious reasons, Mercator never spoke about his time at Meche-len. How often he traveled there, when or even whether he saw Fran-ciscus, how long he stayed if they did meet, who else might have been with them, were all secrets he took to his grave. Despite the dangers in-volved, the two men did write to each other, though their letters have been lost. Events a decade later suggest that the religious authorities, at least, believed that their contents would have been enough to damn Mercator as a heretic.

In Antwerp, days stretched into weeks, and weeks into months, and still Mercator stayed away from the university. He seems to have been deep in study, agonizing over the conflicts between the world he saw and the world Aristotle described, between reason and the Bible, no doubt debating whether he could return to an institution that stifled original thought as Leuven did. The pleas of the doctors and professors, instructing him to return, were all ignored. It is a mark of how much he was valued as a scholar that when he did eventually go back, they swal-lowed their pride and readmitted him into the university.[1]

The practicalities of making a living from his knowledge soon took hold. Even with the support of the University of Leuven, a delight in na-ture and in the order and proportion of Creation would never put bread on his table. Philosophy, as his friend and first biographer Walter Ghim put it, "would not enable him to support a family in the years to come."[2] By contrast, geography—globes and maps, like those he had probably seen in Franciscus's cell among the Minorite Friars—was of continuing interest to wealthy sponsors. Mercator's religious anxieties, his fascina-tion with new ideas, his interest in the developing picture of the world were all genuine enough, but his later business career showed that he had a shrewd idea of where his own material interests lay—and it was not with the study of philosophy.

Mercator had been granted a license by the university to teach his own classes to young students, but private tuition was never more than a temporary way to support oneself. Through Gemma Frisius, he began to establish contacts and friendships of his own, developing his acquaintance with the young Antoine Perrenot de Granvelle, who was clearly a valuable patron for the future. Mercator needed little instruction in how to make himself agreeable to such an influential figure. "Your Grace," "Your Reverence," and "most reverend master" are among the phrases with which his correspondence with the young bishop of Arras was larded. Throughout his career, the effusive dedications of maps, globes, and books to powerful sponsors like Granvelle and his father would bear witness to Mercator's passion for developing a network of influential friends. Such contacts were invaluable to a talented and ambitious man with a career to find and no wealth on which to establish it.

Gemma, with the help of a local goldsmith, Gaspard van der Heyden, had established a workshop in Leuven several years before, to design and make scientific instruments and globes, and in the early 1530s he invited Mercator to join them. Such an invitation was immensely flattering, a mark of considerable respect from someone whose good opinion was valuable, and Mercator had no hesitation in accepting it.

Chapter Seven

Gemma's Globe

U NDER THE INFLUENCE of the painters, philosophers, and thinkers
who thronged his aunt's court in Mechelen, the awkward young
Charles V grew into a cultured and sophisticated patron of artists and
craftsmen, with his own collection of paintings and works of art. Other
leading figures in the Low Countries followed his example. Antoine de
Granvelle built a collection in the archbishop's palace in Mechelen that
eventually included at least seven paintings by Peter Brueghel, already
one of the most popular artists of his day.[1] Prosperous local merchants
and government officials bought paintings as well: The royal tax collector Niclaes Jonghelinck[2] outdid even Granvelle with a collection of sixteen or more Brueghels, and when Jean Noirot, a former minister of the
mint, was declared bankrupt in 1572, his creditors were able to auction
off dozens of paintings by leading Flemish artists. Art was a flourishing
business: The guild lists in sixteenth-century Antwerp show no fewer
than 300 artists and 124 goldsmiths living and working in a city of
around 150,000 people.

The emperor and his acolytes had, following decades of exploration,
developed a passionate interest in science and discovery. Charles was
fascinated by scientific and surveying instruments, partly for their practical use in assessing the contours of a battlefield, and partly as beautiful
artifacts in their own right. Gemma and Gaspard had been making
such instruments for several years. Gemma's *planimetrum* for surveying
the flat lowland landscape worked on very similar principles to those of
the traditional astrolabes such as Columbus had used to measure the

elevation of the Sun or the planets above the horizon, and thus calculate his latitude, and their workshop turned out both devices. Gemma also produced his own version of the astrolabe, known as the *Catholicon*, which simplified the calculations, as well as quadrants for telling the time by the Sun or the stars, various tools for mariners and surveyors, and armillary spheres, whose concentric rings around a central globe could be used to demonstrate the great circles of the heavens.

These were practical tools for navigation or study but also articles of intrinsic beauty. Manufacturing them, finely detailed and embellished as they were, was a job for highly skilled craftsmen capable both of precise engineering and delicate artistry—a challenge to goldsmiths and engravers, for the finest examples would command a high price from scholars and collectors alike.

Charles was also one of many wealthy collectors to keep a library hung with maps. The patent he granted to protect the first globe to come from the new workshop, and to prevent unauthorized copying of Gemma, Gaspard, and Mercator's work,* noted with some satisfaction that it would record for the admiration of future generations "our own kingdom which, by the grace of God, encompasses many islands and territories practically unknown to any previous century." Where the emperor and aristocracy led, the newly prosperous middle classes were eager to follow. Geography had captured the popular imagination, and the prosperity of Flanders meant there was money to be spent.

Hans Holbein's famous picture *The Ambassadors* (1533) shows Jean de Dinteville, ambassador to London from the French king Francis I, posing grandly with his colleague, the bishop of Lavour. On the desk between them lie a terrestrial and a celestial globe, one depicting the Earth, the other the stars and the planets—incontrovertible evidence of their own wealth, power, and wisdom. The globe was as much a fashion

---

*Copyright laws in the sixteenth century were concerned more with maintaining government control over what was printed and enforcing censorship than with protecting the rights of the author or artist. The rules in the Holy Roman Empire were strict but not as tightly enforced as those in France, where King Francis I established a system in 1538 by which a copy of every published work had to be deposited with the state.

Hans Holbein the Younger's The Ambassadors

statement as the ambassador's richly furred gown, demonstrating the growing control of the environment that the maritime discoveries embodied—confident symbols of the outward-looking spirit of the age.

The *idea* that the Earth was round had been widely accepted for centuries, but the full significance of it was just beginning to dawn as the trading implications of Vasco da Gama's voyage to India and Ferdinand Magellan's rounding of Cape Horn became plain. It was no longer a matter of abstract theory; vast fortunes could be and were being made by exploiting the fact that the Earth was a sphere.

Gemma and Gaspard both had some experience in the manufacture of globes. Gemma had produced one on his own in 1529 and included a sketch of it as the frontispiece to one of his textbooks of astronomy, while Gaspard had engraved the globe that Mercator's friend and mentor Franciscus Monachus had designed in Mechelen. The first globe that the three men produced together in 1535 was a delicate structure of *papieren bert*, or cardboard—a flimsy sphere just over thirty-six centimeters in diameter, barely three millimeters thick, and coated with a thin layer of plaster for strength and smoothness. Onto that was pasted a map that Gemma had created, drawing, he said, on the works of Ptolemy, Marco Polo, and the Portuguese explorer Gaspar de Corte-Real, who had traveled along the coast of Newfoundland early in the century searching for slaves.

There was more than geography to the map. Gemma knew it would need the approval of Charles's imperial court before he could offer it for sale, and he took care that Tunis, conquered by the emperor's forces only a year earlier, should be clearly marked within his domains. That was a detail, a small piece of political flattery, but across the world, Gemma was anxious to draw on the latest information. It is clear from the one surviving copy of the globe, now in Vienna's Österreichische Nationalbibliothek, that he consulted the reports of the Portuguese explorers in the East, so that the Indian peninsula, shriveled and flat on Ptolemy's maps, showed its true triangular shape, and the island of Ceylon, whose size was so exaggerated by Ptolemy, was almost the correct shape and size. The outline of Africa, which only a few decades before had been a matter of conjecture, stretching southward to join the "great undiscovered land" around the South Pole, had been fixed by years of Portuguese trading. Where once had been tracts of empty space, dozens of islands, rivers, and countries were engraved by name—the Sinus Barbaricus (Bay of Savages), off the northeast coast, or the Trogloditica Regio (Land of the Troglodytes), stretching inland. The island of "Zandibar," known by repute for centuries because of the spices that were transported by camel through Arabia to Europe, carried a regretful note—"This island not yet certainly explored"—and lay far out in the Indian Ocean, hundreds of miles from its true position.

Ferdinand Magellan's voyage had brought back more details of the islands of Southeast Asia, although that area is so damaged on the Vienna globe that much of it is obscure. To the west, Gemma accepted the amazing piece of guesswork—if that is what it was—by Martin Waldseemüller, supported by more recent Spanish vessels sailing regularly to the west coast of the Americas, and drew in a wide Pacific Ocean separating an abbreviated America from the Asian landmass. Gemma's map was a marked contrast both with the bulging Asian-American coastline of Franciscus Monachus and with Martin Behaim's America-less world.

THE NEW TECHNIQUE OF PRINTING, as much as advances in geographic knowledge, had rendered Behaim's unique, hand-painted globe of 1492 obsolete. By the early sixteenth century, most of the scores of printing houses scattered across northern Europe were producing not only typescript but also pictures and maps; the printed globe, like the book whose technology it had adapted, was sweeping across the continent. The roots of Mercator's future commercial success lay in mastering this rapidly developing medium.

Printing had established itself in Leuven within twenty years after the first books came off the presses in Germany,* but the change from woodcuts to the more delicate copperplate in the mid–sixteenth century transformed the Netherlands into Europe's unchallenged center for mapmaking and map publishing. The jewelry trade, which had developed from Antwerp's traditional commerce in gold and precious stones, had attracted the finest line engravers in the world to the city. Gaspard was only one of many goldsmiths who had adapted his traditional skills to the rapidly expanding and profitable business of printing.

Most maps printed before the mid–sixteenth century were woodcuts, but the production of large wall-maps encouraged the shift to copper. Carved wood blocks might suffer less wear in printing than the

---

*One of the new craftsmen in the town, Johan Veldener, gave the Englishman William Caxton his first lessons in handling type.

delicate metal sheets, but they were much less easily reworked—and the woodcutter could not compete with the lightly incised line of the copper engraver in picking out a coastline or a delicately lettered place-name. A woodcut surface could produce only black and white, whereas the engraver could shade or stipple a surface to show hillsides and valleys or water features; and when his burin did slip, he could tap out the error from behind, repolish the section of plate, and repair the damage. Crucially, too, a copper engraver could work faster than his rival on wood. The advantages of precision, of subtlety, and of commerce were all one way.

Under Gemma's careful eye, and with Gaspard's skillful hand to guide him, Mercator set out to immerse himself in the most dynamic technology of his age and transform himself into a copper engraver. The delicacy of the engraver demanded both the imagination of an artist and the subtlety of a skilled artisan; Mercator had to demonstrate that his hand could be as cunning as his mind was sharp. It had to be. Gemma's geography had crowded the little globe with the names of rivers, countries, towns, and islands, but also with pictures of ships with full-bellied sails, diagrams of constellations, and surprisingly unthreatening sea monsters. Reproducing them in copper was a considerable achievement by a man who had only a few months' experience in the craft of engraving, and this was acknowledged on the globe: "Gemma Frisius, doctor and mathematician, described this work from various observations made by geographers and gave it this form. Gerard Mercator of Rupelmonde engraved it with Gaspard van der Heyden, from whom the work, a product of extraordinary cost and no less effort, may be purchased."

That legend, with its unashamed self-advertisement, is the first public mention of the man who was to revolutionize not just the study of geography but the entire perception of the world. However, Mercator's share of the work was relatively minor, and Charles V's patent, which declared his pleasure in their efforts "to elucidate mathematics, revive the memory of ancient kingdoms and conditions, and present them to the people of our age," was formally granted only to Gemma and Gaspard, not to their assistant. Gemma was responsible for the cartography, and most of the detailed engraving of coastlines, rivers, and other natural features was done by Gaspard, the experienced goldsmith. Mercator, still little more than a talented apprentice, simply added the lettering; but he was learning valuable lessons from two of Europe's leading craftsmen.

Chapter Eight

Craftsman and Cartographer

MERCATOR HAD STARTED in Gemma's workshop almost as a hobby, the demanding skills of the engraver's bench a respite from the serious work in his own study. He was soon determined to become a craftsman in his own right. Antwerp and the surrounding towns were wealthy enough to provide orders for two workshops and, apparently with Gemma's unselfish encouragement, he started his own business, building upon the experience and reputation he had gained. From the start, he relied on his former teacher for help and advice, as he had done in his studies in mapmaking, surveying, and geography, and in his early ventures into geometry. He turned to him for more than instruction—when he built a forge and began manufacturing his own globes and scientific instruments, Gemma loaned him the tools—but he plainly felt that his growing reputation meant his prospects were secure enough to start building a life for himself. At twenty-four, the solitary, monastic life of a scholar was no longer enough.

On August 3, 1536, Mercator married Barbe Schellekens, the daughter of an eminently respectable Leuven widow. He had shown already, in his decision to adopt a formal, Latinized name, that appearances and social proprieties mattered to him, and, at least from Walter Ghim's description, Barbe was exactly the sort of wife that a man who was careful for his own position and his own comfort would desire. She was, said the effusive Ghim, a woman of "pure habits, submissive, and well-schooled in the care of the home, well suited to his manner of life."[1] Barbe would show later that she had an inner steel to her character, but women in the Netherlands of the sixteenth century were valued for their deference rather than their determination. The two found a home in Leuven's Parish of St. Pierre, in a street behind an Augustinian monastery, and set out on their married life—Gerard concentrating on his studies, on the development of his business, and on the nurturing of his reputation, and Barbe on the scarcely less demanding task of producing six children in as many years, while still demonstrating her unswerving dedication to her husband's comfort.

Their first son was born in August 1537, just a year and four weeks after their marriage. They called him Arnold, and with his birth, Mercator, too, embarked on a new life. His prospect as a boy and a young man had been the cloistered, celibate life of a churchman, then the similar, solitary existence of a scholar; but the speed with which he added to his family suggests that Mercator was happiest with the role of paterfamilias, and what little evidence there is gives the impression of an affectionate husband and father. Those were not common attributes. His old schoolmaster, Macropedius, reflected a clear misogynistic streak in contemporary life when he described women as being "more dangerous than fire, ocean, wild animals, or an evil spirit,"[2] and there was enthusiastic applause for his plays when they showed his female characters benefiting just as much as the children from a good thrashing. Mercator, without doubt, shared his uncompromising views on the upbringing of children—he sent his own sons off to a schoolmaster with just as stern a reputation as that of Macropedius.

Nevertheless, there are occasional hints in his surviving correspondence of a gentle and attentive father. Although few of Mercator's own letters still exist, and none of them deal with his day-to-day life at home, one from the boys' teacher and Mercator's friend and son-in-law Jan Vermeulen, written when the boys were fully grown, commented on the affection the two younger boys in particular had for their father. Bartholomew had always shown a particular warmth for his father, Vermeulen reported, and he commented too on the dutiful way that Rumold, his third son, always put Mercator's needs first. "How agreeable it is to produce children—we see God's plan in the way they lighten their parents' troubles by their devotion and effort," he wrote.[3] Even if

Mercator was a demanding father, he succeeded in winning his children's affection.

Mercator saw the opportunity to fill the huge demand for printed paper maps for travelers, wealthy individuals, and religious and civic institutions. Scores of copies could be run off from a single original, and they could not only be produced more quickly than globes, but also sold more cheaply and to more people. The main challenge was to choose a subject that would capture people's interest. Mercator would find his commercial inspiration in the most popular and controversial book of his day—the Bible.

In particular, the Church authorities feared the printed Bibles in the day-to-day language of the people that were flooding off the presses. They knew how inflammatory the Word of God could be, and the mere possession of a Bible written in Flemish rather than Latin could be enough to have a man dragged before the Inquisition. Yet despite the increasingly brutal response of Charles V, the reform movement and the new Bibles were more and more prevalent in the Netherlands. Midnight arrests, mass executions, secret hearings—nothing could stifle the demands for reform. There was widespread revulsion at the cruelty being visited on heretics, real or imagined: When guards arrived at Amsterdam just before Christmas in 1531 carrying ten severed heads to be impaled on stakes outside the town, local people refused to have anything to do with them. One of the town's burgomasters went so far as to declare bluntly that no more citizens would be delivered "to the butcher's block."

However much Mercator might have shared in this general horror at the savagery of the authorities, he was also aware that the piety of his countrymen offered an opportunity for business. In a country where people agonized over Holy Writ as the Netherlanders did, there could be only one choice for Mercator's first cartographical project: a map of the Holy Land that could be studied alongside the Bible.

In commercial terms at least, this was a safe, not an inspired, choice. More than sixty years before, Palestine had been the subject of the earliest printed regional map, included in an anonymous book titled *Rudimentum Novitiorum*, published at Lübeck in Germany; since then, generations of pilgrims and crusaders had left a legacy of itineraries, route maps, and travel books about the Holy Land. Many of them were distorted by inaccurate memories or observations and by garbled hearsay accounts, and most made no claim to precision. In 1483, the German nobleman Bernhard von Breydenbach, a deacon of Mainz Cathedral, had set off on his own pilgrimage, accompanied by a Dutch artist named Erhard Reuwich. Their intention from the start was to produce an account of their travels, and Reuwich's illustrations, based on his own observations on the journey, included a maplike panoramic view of the whole region from Damascus in the north to Alexandria in the south. Set in the center was a detailed picture of Jerusalem itself, seen from the Mount of Olives, with the holy sites marked with their biblical names.

The book, *Peregrinatio in Terram Sanctam*,[4] was an example of the popularity of the subject, still selling some fifty years later, in both Latin and German, when Mercator started work, just one of a vast number of sources on which he had to draw. Including the Bibles that had been appearing for decades with maps bound into them to illustrate different stories such as Exodus or the wanderings of St. Paul—even though many were inaccurate—the Holy Land was the most comprehensively mapped region in the world.

Reuwich's version was a panorama, and for all the detail of his observation, it lacked the accuracy of a map. By contrast, Mercator's offering of 1537, covering the region from the Nile Delta to Phoenicia, and including biblical place-names and details of the various tribes of Israel, was as precise as he could make it. Even cartographers who claimed to be exact were not to be trusted. In a letter many years later, looking back at his first venture into mapmaking, Mercator described how he referred to the work of a German geographer of the fifteenth century from the University of Ingolstadt. Jacob Zeigler[5] claimed to have plotted the longitude and latitude of hundreds of biblical sites, but Mercator found his work to be "without scale and confused."[6] Instead of simply accepting it as accurate, he tested each measurement it contained against other maps and sources—the start of a lifetime's work of synthesis, judgment, and assimilation.

Where he could not find a location to his satisfaction, he said so. Several of the camps named in Exodus as being on the route of the Israelites as they crossed into Israel are simply listed on the map as "unknown." The example of Gemma's honesty over the location of the "not yet certainly explored" island of Zanzibar was a good one to follow. Mercator's

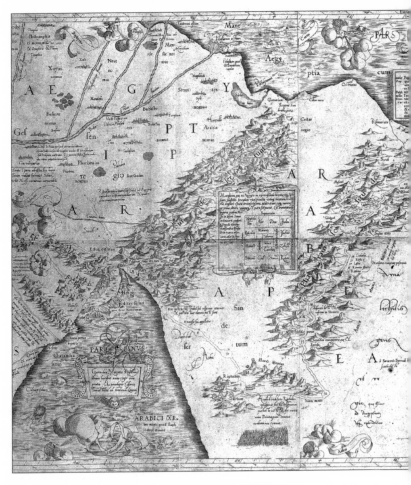

Mercator's map of the Holy Land, 1537

map—measuring some 43½ by 21½ inches when the six sheets on which it was printed were assembled—rapidly became the standard work of reference on the Holy Land. Even at that size, names on it are hard to read, and it is clearly the map of a beginner rather than a master, turned at an angle so that northwest, rather than north, is at the top. Mercator explained that his aim was to reduce the amount of useless space on the sheets, but this was not a solution of which Ptolemy would

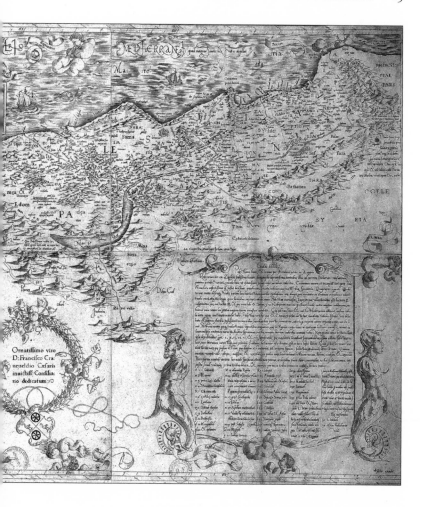

have approved. Nevertheless, there was universal astonishment at the delicacy of the drawing and engraving. Ghim declared that the map was published "to the admiration of many."[7] Mercator was barely twenty-five years old, and this was the first positive proof that he was anything more than a journeyman engraver.

Carefully measured and calculated as the locations on it were, the map was also firmly in the medieval tradition of the *mappaemundi*. The tents of the fleeing Israelites appeared close by the Red Sea, with the biblical pillar of cloud behind them. Like the Hereford mapmaker, Mercator presented the world of belief and faith as much as the physical landscape—but, 250 years on, he did so on a map that was as accurate and objective as he could make it.

For fifty years, it remained the standard map for serious students of the Bible. The Flemish Catholic Andreas Van Maes,[8] working on a commentary on the Pentateuch, the Five Books of Moses, wrote urgently to one of Mercator's friends twenty-five years after the map's publication, begging him to send a copy. "I will happily pay whatever price you ask," he said.[9] His admiration was a tribute to Mercator's scholarship, and the continuing demand for the map vindication of his choice of subject. Yet Van Maes's difficulties with the Church show there were greater risks to be considered than simple commercial failure. When his book appeared, it was immediately placed on the Church's *Index Librorum Prohibitorum,* the list of books that were heretical to read or to possess. Theological speculation, biblical exegesis, and laying out the story of the Bible on a map for common people to see were all controversial activities, encouraged by books like Van Maes's and by maps like Mercator's. Laymen who could read their holy texts in their own language wanted information about the lands in which the stories were set. Such information could only threaten the Church's jealously guarded control over knowledge; the popularity of Mercator's map simply increased the likelihood that the Inquisition would eventually take an interest in it.

Mercator's skill aside, there was then no shortage of skillful artisans. To prosper, he needed to have friends as well as talent, and to cultivate the contacts he had made at Leuven—many of them through Gemma. The Palestine map was dedicated to Frans Craneveld, another former student at the University of Leuven, a member of the Grand Council of Mechelen, and a well-known patron of the arts. He was also, significantly, a friend of Antoine de Granvelle and was intimately involved with Charles's policy of violent repression against the reformers. Craneveld had influence, and Mercator hoped he would be susceptible to flattery and use that influence on his behalf.

. . .

IN 1538, BARBE PRESENTED Mercator with another child, a daughter whom they named Emerance, after his mother. As his responsibilities at home grew, so his reputation began to spread. Even while he had been working on the map of Palestine, he had also been pushing ahead with research for another, still more ambitious project: his first map of the world.

The shape of the known world had been changing with almost every voyage. Mapping these new discoveries, setting them in context, and showing the whole world on a sheet of paper were obvious challenges for a cartographer. Another challenge was gathering information that had never been revealed before. Both trade and politics offered sound reasons why royal sponsors of explorers should want to keep their new information to themselves, and why others should want to steal it, and the mapmakers' trade often meant stitching together scraps of information that had come from spies, informers, and indiscreet seamen.

Mercator was not working alone, of course. A series of geographers across Europe toiled independently of one another, the leaked information they gathered gradually seeping through into general knowledge. Sailors, by the very nature of their job, traveled from one ship to another and from one country to another, and keeping secrets was virtually impossible. Ferdinand and Isabella, in Spain, had done their best to conceal the extent of Columbus's discoveries in the West, but within twenty years the Turkish pirate, admiral, and cartographer Piri Re'is pieced together a strikingly accurate map on camel skin—much of it now lost—showing the Atlantic and the islands of the New World. It was based, according to Re'is himself, on the recollections of an Italian seaman who had sailed on three of Columbus's voyages before being captured by the Turks in the Mediterranean.

News of Vasco da Gama's exploration to the east leaked out too. King Emmanuel declared that betraying information about Portuguese voyages would be punished by death, but his determination to keep da Gama's voyage secret was matched by efforts in Italy to find out all about it. The duke of Ferrara commissioned the diplomat Alberto Cantino to use all his influence and spare no expense in acquiring a map of da Gama's voyages, and within two years of the expedition's return to Portugal, the map was safely in his possession. Whom the diplomat bribed, bullied, or inveigled into making the duke's illicit copy will never be known, but the

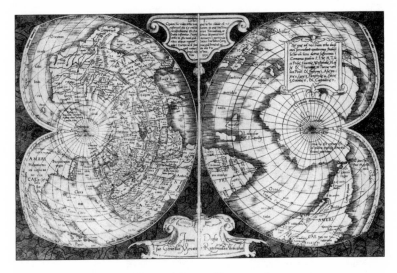

Mercator's first world map, 1538

Cantino map, showing Africa, India, and also much of the eastern coast of America with remarkable precision, now lies in the Biblioteca Estense in Modena, Italy, known to posterity not by the name of its originator or its engraver but by that of the man who sneaked it out of Portugal.

Although kings and captains failed to keep their secrets, distance, greed, ignorance, and chance could conspire more successfully to keep information from mapmakers. The Cantino map showed nothing of the interior of America, for example, or its western coast, and even when exploration started there, it was in the hands of hard-bitten soldiers, with no interest in geography or discovery unless gold was in prospect. Spanish conquistadores set out during the 1520s from their bridgehead in Mexico toward the north and south on a savage mission of conquest and destruction in which sickness and the sword between them killed some 23 million of a native population of around 25 million. Little news of their discoveries leaked out in Europe until the private papers of Bernal Diaz, one of the Spanish soldiers, were found unread in a private library in Spain more than a hundred years later. Farther south, in Peru, the forces of Francisco Pizarro were similarly laying waste to the great Inca empire with a force of less than two hundred men, and once again, they had no interest in geographic exploration. News of their exploits, too, filtered back very slowly to Europe.[10]

Mercator's map of the world, published in 1538, showed his continuing debt to Gemma—it was clearly based on the globe they had produced together three years before—but it also demonstrated how much had leaked out, and how radically the view of the world had developed from the versions of Ptolemy that were still being circulated at the end of the sixteenth century. It was a small, single-sheet map, but Vasco da Gama's voyage and the expeditions that followed it enabled Mercator to show the true peninsular shape of India, even though the southern tip was much narrower than it ought to have been. Mercator's coastline of Africa had been well charted by various Portuguese mariners, and his American continent was clearly separated from Asia by what he called the Oceanus Orientalis Indicus (Eastern Indian Ocean).

His map still showed America as a long, thin continent, but its basic shape, at least down the eastern coastline, was easily recognizable. Unlike Waldseemüller before him, Mercator clearly distinguished between North and South America, naming each one individually—his acceptance of the word *America* confirming once and for all the honor that his predecessor had mistakenly bestowed upon Amerigo Vespucci.

Mercator's world map, with its confident drawing of the east and west coastlines of South America, showed how much information had been assimilated into the accepted view of the world by 1538. But it also showed the limit of what was known. Magellan had proved in 1520 that America did not form part of some still-undiscovered great southern continent, and that there was a sea passage through the straits that now bear his name; yet Mercator, in common with other geographers of his time, still imagined the vast Terra Australis Incognita stretching up to form the southern edge of the Strait of Magellan. Ptolemy had described such a continent, and Mercator and his contemporaries saw no reason to disbelieve him. All Magellan had done, it seemed at the time, was demonstrate that the great continent was not connected to America.

In addition to incorporating the newly discovered lands into his first map of the world, Mercator was concerned with how best to project a spherical world onto a flat surface—a challenge that would absorb him all his life. The peculiar double-heart shape of the 1538 map was his first attempt to deal with the problem of projection. It was not a success. Mercator relied on a system that had been described more than twenty years before by a Nuremberg mathematician, Johann Werner,[11] a friend and patron of the artist and engraver Albrecht Dürer. Werner had produced an edition of Ptolemy in which he set out the projection, which had been designed around 1500 by another mathematician, Johannes Stabius of Austria. The two men had worked together on a sundial in Nuremberg's St. Lorenz Church—a task which, in presenting the circular movement of the Sun on a flat surface, was similar to that of reproducing the globe on a sheet of paper. The sundial had horizontal curved lines to mark the length of the shadow cast by the Sun as it changed through the day, cut by straight lines to mark the hours; the projection Stabius designed similarly had arcs centered on the North Pole for lines of latitude, cut by lines of longitude that gradually curved away to east and west from a single vertical prime meridian.

The most obvious feature of this projection was the way it presented the Northern and Southern Hemispheres separately, in a matching pair of heart-shaped frames—the so-called double-cordiform projection. It produced a very pleasing, symmetrical design and focused attention on the continent of Europe at the center of one frame, but there were serious disadvantages to it as a way of depicting the whole world. It is hard to see the relationship between Asia and the American continent, or the form of Africa and America, both of which are broken in two. The maker of any map has to choose whether to present the shape of the continents accurately or to show them the right size in proportion to each other. The adjustments necessary to reproduce the globe on a flat sheet make it mathematically impossible to do both. Mercator, following the example of Stabius and Werner, sacrificed shape. The coastlines are distorted, so that North America, for instance, can hardly be seen at all on Mercator's map.

The heart-shaped projection had been used several times before by various cartographers, but the map that it produced was essentially one to be kept in the study, rather than taken onto the high seas. It remained impossible to plot a straight course across it on a ship's chart-room table. Thus Mercator's effort was a map to be admired rather than used. The challenge of mapping the world for the navigator still remained.

Chapter Nine

The Greatest Globe
in the World

A T HOME IN LEUVEN, in the house by the Augustinian monastery, Barbe gave birth to her third child, Dorothée, in 1539, by which time Arnold was two, and Emerance a year old. Mercator's family was growing, but during the months before Dorothée's birth, he had spent weeks at a time away from home as he began an ambitious survey of much of the nearby region of Flanders. It was a fortunate choice of subject. Before it was even off the drawing board, the map was purchased by a group of leading merchants in the city of Ghent, who planned to use it as a peace offering.

Ghent, the birthplace of the emperor, had always been a rebellious, free-minded corner of the Habsburg inheritance, and when in 1538, Charles's regent, Mary of Hungary,* sent her tax collectors in to raise money to support Charles's wars against France, the hard-pressed townsmen had rebelled. They seized control of the walls, expelled the city authorities, and declared effective independence from the empire. For a few short months, a heady sense of freedom swept the city, in an open challenge to the religious as well as the civil powers. Preachers questioned the basic tenets of Catholic doctrine, while actors and min-

---

*Mary, Charles's sister, became regent on the death of his aunt, Margaret of Austria, in 1530.

strels in the streets lampooned the greed and corruption of the Church. For that short time, with Charles far away in Spain, there seemed to be nothing that the newly independent Ghent could not do.

When a message arrived late in 1539 that the emperor was on his way to visit, no one supposed, whatever his emotional ties to his native city, that he was making a sentimental journey. Charles was coming to exact retribution and reinforce the power of the empire. Some of the more headstrong of the rabble that had seized control were prepared to face him, but the levelheaded merchants of the city began to search for a way to divert his anger. They had perhaps three months in which to do so; in October 1539, Charles left Spain at the head of his army, marching to Flanders.

Ghent's brief freedom had seen the production of a woodcut map showing the city as an independent bastion of liberty, dominating the whole of Flanders. As an insult to Charles V, it could hardly have been more direct—and it gave the merchants an idea of how the city might prove its loyalty. Mercator's map could be presented to the emperor as a gesture of civic submission.

Mercator himself was enthusiastic. He had already done much of the work, and there was no better way of bringing himself to the notice of the rich and powerful than by becoming known at the imperial court. Mercator's map, even though it was never completely finished, was not only said by many contemporaries to be a better description of the topography of Flanders than anything else that had been produced; it was also an abject offering of abasement to imperial power. Ranged along top and bottom were portraits of the successive counts of Flanders, culminating in Charles himself. Flanders was part of his Burgundian inheritance, and the map's legend declared deferentially that it had always willingly bent the knee to its rulers.

Neither map nor flattery did much good for Ghent. Charles was not to be diverted from his purpose either by sentiment for his birthplace or by the sycophancy of the burghers, and his forces fell upon the town in a storm of terror, torture, and executions. Thirteen of the leading rebels were executed, great swaths of buildings were pulled to the ground, and an imposing fortress constructed on their ruins to remind the townsfolk who their master was. A long procession of burghers, guildsmen, and other citizens marched barefoot through the town, nooses around their necks, to beg on their knees for pardon from the emperor they had challenged. Yet while Ghent suffered, Mercator prospered. His map of Flanders brought him to the emperor's notice, the first work by his hand alone that had been received as a gift at the imperial court.

WHILE COMPLETING THE FLANDERS MAP, Mercator had been working on an instrument commissioned by one of his acquaintances from the university, Antoine de Granvelle, then already archdeacon of Besançon and of Cambrai, and newly appointed bishop of Arras. Exactly what he made for him is unclear; he described it as a *calvaria*, which could refer to a skull-like arrangement of three concentric rings originally designed by Gemma Frisius. Each ring was marked off in degrees to enable an astronomer to take sightings of planets and note the angle between them, but the instrument's most distinctive feature was that it was small enough to be slipped into a man's luggage.

Mercator composed a letter in 1540 to accompany the piece. It explained the difficulties he had experienced in carrying out the work and hinted delicately that he would welcome financial support. Lack of equipment, he said pointedly, meant that the *calvaria* had taken him much longer to make than he had hoped. "Since I had little equipment and I wanted to finish it, I had to seek engraving tools, which took a long time to make since as usual we had to go to other and varied shops," he wrote. "But Your Grace will count it to the good, when you see that the loss of time (if such it is) has been made good by my skill." Still in his twenties, Mercator had the outspoken confidence of a master craftsman combined with the well-modulated sycophancy of an ambitious tradesman—all of it finely judged to impress a wealthy and influential sponsor. His assurance extended far beyond mere technical competence. To Granvelle, Mercator spoke with easy familiarity about the rapidly changing state of geographic knowledge. He had taken great pains to compare the geography of the ancients with the discoveries of recent decades, he told the bishop. "Having done this diligently, I see we are still confounded by great errors.... How much we

err in the Far East, anyone who reads Marco Polo the Venetian atten-
tively will know."[1]

Many of the claims in Marco Polo's account of his travels were
mocked when his book first appeared at the end of the thirteenth century—it was known as *Il Milione* (the Million Lies)—but manuscript
copies had already been studied for more than two centuries by Mercator's time. Columbus was only one explorer to accept Polo's exaggerated
guess of how far he had traveled overland on his way to the imperial
palace of Kublai Khan in China.

Even if his account of his twenty-four-year adventure was partly
fantasy, his influence was clear in the maps that were drawn during the
fourteenth century, when the story of his travels had been widely
spread. New maps, like that on the globe produced by Gemma, Gaspard, and Mercator a few years earlier, showed a much better understanding of the size and shape of the Indian peninsula than Ptolemy
had achieved, and many of the islands of the East Indies were much
more accurately drawn, in line with Marco Polo's descriptions. But
Mercator resolved to winnow out still more truth from the errors, ex-
aggerations, and misconceptions. Along the coastline of southern Asia,
for instance, he believed after reading Marco Polo that there were four
peninsulas, not three as Ptolemy had described, and as he had shown
on his own map three years earlier. In addition, parts of Africa needed
correcting, as did Madagascar and many of the islands he had shown
before; and although he had no significant changes to make to the
coastline of America, more details had emerged to start filling out the
interior.

"In short, I am drawing all the places that others have revealed, and
fashioning a globe which will be bigger than any before, but which will
not be too big to be used," he declared confidently to Granvelle.[2]

The weakness of his world map had been its design rather than its
geography, and its lesson was that projecting the world onto a flat surface seemed to be an intractable problem of mathematics. The answer
he looked for was that of a craftsman rather than that of a mathematician. In Gemma Frisius and Gaspard van der Heyden he had had two
of the finest teachers he could have found for the techniques of globe

Mercator's 1541 globe

manufacture, and Franciscus Monachus may well have shown him his globe in Mechelen years before.

Mercator had told Granvelle in August 1540 that his work would be completed in three months from the date of his letter. It was an optimistic promise, as his predictions always tended to be: Whether because he still lacked the tools he needed, or because he simply underestimated the amount of work involved, the globe was not finished until the following year.

Barely three years after finishing his first map of the world, the information that he had at his disposal had grown so much that whole areas had to be changed. His globe had to be bigger than any made before because there was so much to put on it. His intention was clearly to make it a usable tool for navigation, indispensable not just to students but to sailors as well. He prepared instructions to enable a traveler to find his position by means of the stars, and parts of the globe were crisscrossed by loxodromes (lines showing the course that a ship would take if it followed a constant compass bearing)—an idea he took from the sailors' portolan charts of their coastal journeys. He was the first globe manufacturer to include such lines to help navigators meet the challenge they had always experienced in marking a course on the curved surface of a globe. But the way the loxodromes curved gently toward the poles was a graphic illustration of the continuing problem of projection. Lines that were straight on the map were curved on the globe.

All this, effectively a renewed, updated, and adapted version of his map of the world, was to be engraved and printed on twelve carefully shaped gores—narrow, pointed ovals of paper joined at their centers, precisely where the equator would lie on the finished globe. Each one was designed so that its length was slightly less than half the circumference of the globe and its width one-twelfth its circumference. Once the paper was wet, stretched, and pasted down, the gores would precisely cover the plaster base.[3]

At least, that was the hope. The printing was a challenge for the most sure-handed craftsman: Pasting them down would reveal not only the slightest irregularity in the surface of the globe but also any inaccuracy in the engraving. Names could be, and generally were, inscribed within single gores, but coastlines, rivers, and mountains—all the myriad fine lines that made up the map—had to match perfectly when the edges of paper were laid together. For a perfectionist like Mercator, this required the most exquisite patience. The completed gores also provided another frustrating illustration of the persistent difficulty that was troubling him. Laid out flat, the form of the map itself could hardly be seen because of the widening gaps between each delicately cut gore. Only when they were finally pasted down did the design appear as if by magic, when the lines of longitude, which had curved inexorably away from each other on his desk, wrapped themselves around the globe. To make a true, flat map, those curving lines of longitude would have to be straightened. The problem was clear, but there was no apparent solution.

The structure of the globe itself was simple, strong, and workmanlike. Gemma's cardboard construction may not have proved robust enough for Mercator's purposes, and he—or more probably a craftsman in his workshop—started by modeling a skeletal globe with flexible slats of wood, bent to shape. A cloth cover was pasted over them, and then that was spread with a thin layer of plaster. A final quarter-inch coat of mixed plaster, sawdust, and glue was then applied, accommodating any minor irregularities to produce a perfect sphere. When that coat was dried and smoothed, the precious paper gores were pasted down, colored by hand, and varnished. Copies of the actual map could be printed from the original engraving, but the painstaking work of building the globe on which to paste it had to be repeated for each new specimen. The little workshop beside his house is unlikely to have turned out more than two or three a week.

For all his skill, and for all his efforts to cover his globe with loxodromes to make it easier to follow a course, any globe was almost impossible to use for navigation at sea. The difficulties were immense. Mercator had produced the largest printed globes ever made, but they were still only just over sixteen inches in diameter—practically a toy when compared with Strabo's pronouncement more than fifteen centuries earlier that a globe should be at least ten feet in diameter, or with the world maps measuring twenty-five square feet and more that were being routinely printed. Ptolemy, while praising the accuracy of the globe as a way of reproducing the map of the world, had pointed out this problem as well. A globe, he said, was either too small to contain enough detail or too big to be of any practical use.

There were mechanical problems, too, implicit in the construction of anything as delicate as a revolving globe for everyday use. If it lost its balance, or the rod on which it was pivoted were to work loose with constant turning, the globe would be useless—a disaster for any navigator relying on it far from land. If such weaknesses were evident when the globe stood firmly on the workbench, they were likely to be still more troublesome when a small wooden vessel was tossing on the high seas. The experience Mercator had gained in Gemma's workshop, together with his own technical skill, meant he could minimize the problems. Care in fitting the rod through the plaster globe and into the wooden stand, and the most rigorous measurement of the thickness and regularity of the plaster coating, made his globes more reliable, but there were other problems that the most skillful manufacture could not rectify. Globes were bulky and awkward to handle, and due to their shape, it was often impossible to get an overview of the planned journey: The final stages of a long voyage could be revealed only by turning the globe on its axis. On a map, a navigator could at least see the whole world at a glance, whereas one side of a globe was always hidden from him.

In the end, while Mercator may have designed his globes for sailors, most of them went to stand as elegant and fashionable pieces of furniture in the homes of the wealthy, and Mercator's workshop found it hard to keep pace with demand for new globes over the next few years. Yet even as he achieved a commercial success, Mercator remained fascinated by the theoretical and practical problems his work kept throwing up. That fascination extended beyond the practicalities of cartography and the use of the globe by navigators.

WHILE SAILORS IN THE AMERICAS were discovering the limitations of the ancient conception of the world, astronomers in Europe were drawing new, staggering, and provocative conclusions about the place of that world in the heavens. Explorers and astronomers shared a growing awareness that knowledge might stretch farther than they had ever dreamed. The key to understanding the new discoveries in the skies, as well as those on Earth, was the globe.

In 1551, ten years after he started making his terrestrial globes, Mercator would produce a matching celestial globe, mounted, like the earlier one, in a carved, four-pillared polished wood stand.[4] The various constellations—forty-eight made up from the 1,022 stars listed in Ptolemy's thirteen-volume work on astronomy, the *Almagest*, and two new ones—were illustrated by finely etched human and mythological figures. He was not the first manufacturer to produce matching pairs of terrestrial and celestial globes, but as Mercator's work acquired an unprecedented popularity and fame throughout Europe, customers began to demand that their globes should come in pairs. Globe makers for the next three centuries followed this example.

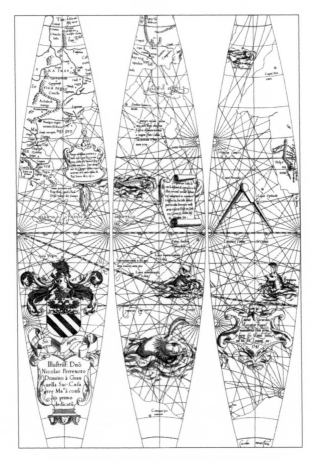

Detail of the gores from the 1541 globe

Like its predecessor, the celestial globe was the work of a dedicated artist, and he remained just as painstaking about the accuracy of his map of the stars as he had been in preparing his terrestrial globe. The telescope was unknown to the astronomers of the sixteenth century; not until 1609 did Galileo, in Italy, first hear of the new invention in northern Europe that seemed to bring heavenly bodies closer than the human eye had ever seen them. The only instruments available in Mercator's day were those such as the astrolabe and the cross-staff that could measure and track the paths of the heavenly bodies. The study of the stars had always required as much mathematics as observation.

Even more stultifying than the lack of accurate instruments was the conviction of the Catholic Church that only a universe in which the stars and planets revolved around the heavens could do justice to the magnificence of God's Creation. Aristotle had declared that the Earth was the center of the universe; so had Ptolemy. To challenge that official wisdom was to defy the Church and to invite the attentions of the Inquisition. Mercator's knowledge was based largely on Ptolemy's fourteen-hundred-year-old view of the heavens, but just as he assimilated the latest discoveries of the Portuguese and Spanish sailors into his terrestrial globe, so he studied the most recent astronomical thinking of his day as he plotted the design of his latest creation.

The ideas of Nicolaus Copernicus, a Polish-born mathematician, doctor, clergyman, and lifelong astronomer, were revolutionary enough to have been passed around by word of mouth for more than thirty years. He believed that Aristotle and the Church were wrong, and that the Sun and not the Earth was at rest in the center of the universe—a suggestion that shook traditional science and theology to its roots. Copernicus's detailed account of his theory, in the book *De Revolutionibus Orbium Coelestium* (On the revolutions of the celestial spheres), did not appear until 1543—according to written accounts, Copernicus saw a printed copy for the first time as he lay on his deathbed in Frombork, Poland—but he had been working on the ideas that it contained for some three decades.*

---

*Around 1514, Copernicus distributed a small handwritten book, *Commentariolus* (Little Commentary), to a few of his friends from his home in Frombork. It spelled out his thinking in seven axioms, the most crucial of which were that the Earth was not the center of the universe, that the apparent daily rotation of the stars was caused by the rotation of the Earth, and that the distance from the Earth to the Sun was infinitely less than the distance to the stars. It is certain that, largely as a result of the *Commentariolus,* his ideas had already spread widely by 1539, when the German mathematics professor Georg Joachim Rheticus published a summary of them in Danzig.

Once again, Mercator was determined that his work should be at least as much a precise tool for professional observers as an intriguing ornament for display; his was the first globe to be based on Copernicus's theories. In mapping the stars, as in mapping the Earth, he consciously moved away from the traditional impressionistic, subjective idea of cartography toward a new and more scientific concept.

At the same time, he was also developing an artist's fascination with the finer details of his work—an interest in the beauty of its design and the delicacy of its execution for their own sake. The artistry, the flowing lines, and the delicate textures of the mythological figures engraved on Mercator's globes were far in advance of anything that had been produced before. He wielded an engraver's burin over the copper with the delicacy of a painter touching a canvas with his brush. The muscles of Sagittarius on the globe seem to strain as he draws his bow, the bear that represents Ursa Major appears to have fur, and the feathers of Pegasus, the winged horse, are individually picked out. With his celestial globe, completed in 1551 when he was thirty-nine years old, Mercator claimed his place as the finest cartographic engraver of the age.

Every aspect of his craft fascinated him. Gemma had particularly wanted his help in producing the globe of 1535 because of the delicacy of his hand in the engraving of lettering, and Mercator had developed a keen interest in the script with which information was marked on his maps. In the original letter of 1540 to Antoine de Grenvelle about his planned globe, he had stressed his intention of making the words on it clear and uncluttered. Earlier cartographers had generally favored the thick, heavy strokes of the German alphabet, which could easily be carved out of the old woodcut blocks, even though such crude penmanship confused the design and obscured the meaning on maps whose small scale required names to fight for inclusion. The delicacy of copperplate engraving, compared to the old-fashioned woodcuts, meant that a skilled craftsman was no longer limited to the traditional letters.

On Gemma's globe, Mercator had used the italic script that had been developed during the previous century in Florence—the style of writing that Shakespeare mistakenly called the "sweet Roman hand"[5]—for its lightness and easy reading, and in his own work he was even more precise and painstaking. Roman capitals marked the different continents, empires, and oceans on Mercator's globe of 1541, and italic lettering designated kingdoms, provinces, and rivers, so that the significance of each word was immediately clear to the reader. One promontory extending north from the great southern continent was labeled *psitacorum regio* (region of parrots), while a key placed in the empty South Atlantic provided the names of some of the cities of Europe that could not be fitted onto the map itself. The italic script was concise, with an opportunity for some restrained decoration around the flourishes with which the words ended, but its main appeal for a cartographer was its clarity. Later mapmakers increasingly followed his example. It was a small improvement but a significant one: Mercator wanted his maps to be used, and every element of their design that made it easier to do so was important.

Thus, amid the hard-pressed work for his various customers and sponsors, he had set himself to produce in 1546 a punctilious little book on the use of italic script in map work. It was almost comically finicky: "There is no art so simple that its exercise doesn't demand a little study first," he wrote. "It will always be worthwhile to reduce it to a few short notes so that the student need not spend too long away from his more useful studies."[6] There would be those, he said, who would criticize him for wasting his time on something so straightforward and so unimportant—but just think how unacceptable it would be to have the Latin language in the wrong style of lettering. The Greek or German letters that were commonly used were simply inappropriate, like a king dressing in the rags of a beggar rather than in his royal purple.

No detail was too small, no instruction too basic. There were twenty-four leaves of detailed instructions on how to construct a flowing, regular script and hold a pen, "in two fingers, the index and the thumb, gently supported by the middle finger so that it is enclosed by them in a sort of triangle." Mercator offered no advice that he was not prepared to take himself; the booklet demonstrated his own skill as a calligrapher, and its woodcuts provided further examples of his talent as a carver and illustrator. Even though he was working in wood rather than his preferred copper, his lines were delicate and precise—an example to students of the standard to which they might aspire with hard work.[7] The booklet was reprinted four times and started a Netherlands vogue for similar instruction books that lasted for several years.

Mercator was shrewd enough to know that long-term prosperity lay with official favor and the patronage of the mighty—and few were mightier than the emperor himself. Hence, no doubt, the dedication of his terrestrial globe to the elder Granvelle, Nicholas. The earlier letter to the son had been a tactful way of finding out whether such a dedication would be acceptable to the father, who, he hoped, would smooth the way to the imperial court.

The world globe of 1541 sold well for decades. A quarter of a century after the first one was produced, the Spanish scholar and poet Benito Arias Montano,[8] in Antwerp as the representative of King Philip II of Spain, wrote home to Madrid that the choice in the Netherlands was between Gemma's globe of 1535 at a price of eight escudos and Mercator's of 1541 at twelve. A tribute to Mercator's reputation as well as to his globe, the Spanish thought it well worthwhile to pay the extra 50 percent. In 1568, when a pressman in his printing works might earn around one hundred florins in a year, the dealer Christopher Plantin sold Gemma's globes for eleven florins and Mercator's for twenty-four. Together they were turning Leuven into an acknowledged center for the production of globes and scientific instruments that would come to rival the famous manufacturers of Nuremberg in southern Germany.

Chapter Ten

In the Hands
of the Inquisition

ARLY IN 1542, the little workshop in St. Pierre was busier than it
had ever been. The struggle to meet the demand for Mercator's
new globe—constructing the plaster globes themselves, printing the
gores, pasting them down, mounting them on their stands, and packing
the finished articles in crates—was testing his capacity for hard work
and concentration to its limit. The household was hectic too: In 1540,
Barbe had given birth to another boy, Bartholomew, and in 1541 to Rumold, her fifth child. The following year she was pregnant with her
sixth, so there could not have been a better time for Mercator to receive
the most important order of his life so far.

Antoine de Granvelle must have been pleased with his *calvaria*, for
he had recommended Mercator's craftsmanship to the emperor himself.
Charles V was away in Spain, but from his court in Brussels came an
order for a selection of globes and mathematical instruments for the imperial collection. Mercator was required to produce terrestrial and celestial globes, a miniature quadrant for navigation and observing the
stars, an astronomical ring to show the planets in their orbits, an ingenious pocket-sized sundial, and various simpler instruments such as
compass and dividers for drawing maps and plans.

He started work straightaway, but even by the time he received the
order, the emperor was preoccupied with more pressing and dangerous
matters. His debts were mounting and his revenues falling, and his old

French enemies were moving against his possessions in the Low Countries. He looked weak, and on the banks of the River Meuse, the lesson of Ghent's crushed rebellion was beginning to fade.

The swaggering young duke of Jülich, Cleves, and Burg, William IV, had inherited the province of Guelderland and saw the opportunity for conquest and greatness. His sympathies were Lutheran, his ambitions unlimited—and Charles V's hold on the neighboring lands of Brabant and Flanders seemed temptingly insecure. The emperor's armies were once again far away in Spain, and when in the spring of 1542 William's army swept across the Meuse, it descended upon an undefended countryside. Farms and villages that stood in its way were burned, peasants and farmers put to the sword. William's aim was to reach the French armies in the west and drive a wedge through Charles's possessions in the Low Countries.

The killing was not confined to the countryside over which the soldiers trampled. In the great towns of Antwerp and Leuven, panic-stricken city authorities hurriedly seized anyone they suspected might side with the invaders. They were determined not to lose control again, as they had done in Ghent only four years before. While the townsmen were armed and sent to the city walls as an unlikely looking defense force, the soldiers rounded up anyone with Lutheran sympathies who might aid the invader.

For months, fire and bloodshed swirled this way and that across the Low Countries. The city walls held firm, but outside them Duke William's savage forces stole whatever they could move. What they could not steal, they burned or butchered. In time, Charles left Spain and made the long march to assert his authority, with nearly forty thousand Italian, Spanish, and German troops. As they approached, the myth of his weakness evaporated, and along with it, Duke William's ravaging army. The duke finished his rebellion on his knees, begging the emperor's forgiveness, just as the burghers of Ghent had done. The old lesson had been taught again.

Charles could afford to be magnanimous. William surrendered Guelderland but was allowed to keep his own lands in Germany in return for his personal commitment to Catholicism, while Charles could be well satisfied that he had imposed his power so forcefully. But it was the Inquisition that gained most from the months of violence.

It was feared as much as it was hated. In 1522, when Mercator was ten, Charles V and one of his former tutors, the new pope, Adrian VI, had brought the Inquisition to the Netherlands in a determined attempt to quash the reform movement. Pope Adrian was a lowlander himself, born in Utrecht, and like Mercator a former pupil of the Brethren of the Common Life and a teacher at the University of Leuven, but the institution he set up rode roughshod from the start over the traditional legal rights of his countrymen. Individual towns in the Netherlands had always tried criminal cases on their own authority, but the Inquisition could arrest and question anyone, even magistrates, and commit them for trial before its own courts in any town it chose. It was, Charles's successor, Philip, observed some years later, even more pitiless than its feared counterpart in Spain. Its method was terror, in particular, the terror of the stake. Purge followed purge, apparently at whim. Many died in agony, as the flames slowly blistered and burned their flesh; the lucky or repentant ones were spared the worst agonies by being strangled before the fagots were lit. Other victims were either banished or condemned to a lifetime of beggary as all their possessions were confiscated. There had been one wave of trials in the mid-1530s, when Mercator was starting to produce his globes and instruments in Leuven. Almost a decade later, another began, fueled by the political fear that Duke William and his plundering soldiers had excited.

In February of 1543, a month of biting cold, Mercator heard of the death of Gisbert, the great-uncle who had been mother and father to him, who had educated him, supported him, and believed in him. He laid aside his tools and packed his clothes into a bundle for the journey to attend Gisbert's funeral and take part in the settlement of his inheritance. Barbe would stay at home with their six children, all under eight years old. (The couple's last child, Catherine, had been born while Duke William's soldiers were rampaging over the countryside.)

Shortly after Mercator had left for Rupelmonde, Barbe was summoned by a knock on her door. She would not have recognized Pierre du Fief, although her husband would have known his name. He was the procurator general, loyal servant and theological witchfinder-in-chief to Charles's regent in the Netherlands, Mary of Hungary, and one of the most feared men in her service. In his hand was a list with Barbe's husband's name on it, using her family name to identify him: "Meester Gheert Scellekens, woenende achter den Augsteynen" (Master Gerard Schellekens, living behind the Augustinians).[1] Similar searches were going on all over Leuven: Forty-two other names appeared on the list besides Mercator's, and twenty-eight of the wanted men and women were seized in a single night.

Where was he? The question would have been short, brutal, the answers treated with contempt; the search of the house, the workshop, and the outbuildings would have started almost before Barbe had finished speaking. Arrests generally followed a pattern, a bullying tumult of soldiers swarming through the house, smashing their way inside with swords drawn, in their search for evidence against the supposed heretics. The soldiers would turn out room after room as they searched for books, documents, or letters that might help make a case against the unfortunate accused man. One of the new reformist Bibles written in Flemish rather than Latin would be enough. Women would be elbowed to one side, children savagely beaten if they dared to interfere.

When the searchers found nothing—no trembling fugitive cowering in a cupboard or under a bed—du Fief accepted Barbe's word that Mercator was gone. He had heard too many stories of convenient departures to believe her claims of a coincidental death in the family, though; if Mercator had gone to Rupelmonde, he reasoned, it was because there had been some secret tip-off about the arrest. Any attempt to flee from the Inquisition was always seen as a tacit admission of guilt, and du Fief went straight to Louis de Steelant, bailiff of the Waas region, to demand a warrant for the fugitive's arrest in Rupelmonde.

Du Fief's reputation was built partly on his brutality and partly on his thoroughness. While the doctors and scholars of the Inquisition tried to trap their victims with subtle intellectual arguments, he oversaw the process of breaking them down with physical intimidation and torture. He had headed the interrogation, trial, and execution of the English Bible scholar William Tyndale eight years before.* Tyndale, as Mercator knew well, had been hauled into the courtyard of Vilvorde Prison, strangled, and burned.

Twenty-five miles away in Rupelmonde, Mercator could not have known what danger he was in, that his fate lay in du Fief's hand. He probably stayed with his older brother Arnold, who managed the Golden Lion Inn, where the townsmen occasionally gathered for public sales; that would have been the obvious place for the soldiers to go, clutching de Steelant's warrant. The Inquisition always came in force; there was no possibility of resistance, no chance to escape, and little explanation. All he was told was that he was suspected of involvement with Lutheran heresies, that he would be investigated by the judges of the Inquisition, and that until they were ready to see him, he would be locked away in Rupelmonde Fort.

In the marketplace, and down the sloping lane that led to the river and the fort, a small crowd of locals gathered. While none wanted to attract the attention of the religious authorities, or to seem too concerned for those who had been chosen for interrogation, a low murmur of sympathy might well have arisen as the bailiff's soldiers hustled their new prisoner into view. Many of the crowd would have recognized Gerard de Cremer, the cobbler's boy. He had left Rupelmonde nearly twenty years earlier, but he had been back to visit the town since. In any case, his fame had spread. Academic, philosopher, prosperous businessman—Rupelmonde had produced few people who could claim that sort of progression. His was one of the success stories that the poor of the town might tell each other, either in hope or in envy.

From its position towering over the River Scheldt, the ancient fort at Rupelmonde brooded over the riverbank and the neighboring fields. It had already stood for more than five centuries, a blunt assertion of military might, uncompromising as a mailed fist. The arched entrance lay on

---

*Tyndale fled England as a suspected heretic in 1524, and over the next eleven years, he prepared English translations of the New Testament and the Pentateuch. These were smuggled into England, where copies were seized and burned. He was arrested in Antwerp in 1535 and condemned on a charge of heresy.

The fort de Rupelmonde

the other side of a narrow timber bridge that sloped on stilts up toward the heavy wooden gates. The towers were dark and threatening; no one could tell who was looking out from the arrow-slits that pierced the heavy stone walls. Outside the fort, the Scheldt was frozen over.

The military governor of the fortress was formally instructed that nobody was to speak to the prisoner or to give him private letters, and that any messages he received were to be handed straight to the bailiff. Until the judges were ready to hear his case, Mercator was to be kept locked up, alone.

Barbe, miles away in Leuven, had no way of knowing what might be happening to her husband, but while he languished in irons, she proved to be an altogether doughtier figure than she had ever had a chance to show. Walter Ghim, who made no mention of this terrifying episode in his hero's life, pictured her as little more than a doting mother and meek housewife, bustling around in silent awe of her eminent husband; but she did not wilt under the pressure. Rather, she set about the business of winning Mercator's freedom. She might have been browbeaten, tricked, or cajoled into telling the officers where her husband was, but once she realized what danger he was in, she rallied valiantly to his defense. Finding favorable witnesses to a suspect's character was one of the most common ways of responding to allegations by the Inquisition, and the more impeccable the religious standing of the witnesses, the more persuasive their evidence would be. Barbe went first to the local priest in Leuven, Pierre de Corte, curé of the Church of St. Peter and former rector of the university, to ask him to plead her husband's case.

Though he never wrote about his experiences in his prison cell, Mercator must have dragged his mind back again and again over the previous weeks and months. He knew nothing of Barbe's efforts on his behalf. All he could do was repeat the same questions: Whom had he seen? What visits had he made? What information could have been passed to the authorities? What did he have to hide?

De Corte did what he could. Fourteen years before, in one of the last acts before his period as rector expired, he had welcomed Mercator to Leuven in his matriculation ceremony. His later career shows that he was no friend to the reform movement—two years afterward, he was appointed as an inquisitor by Charles V and given the duty of overseeing and approving new editions of the Bible published in Leuven and Antwerp—but he responded to Barbe's pleas by writing directly to Mary of Hungary herself, Charles's sister and regent, and the ultimate authority in the Low Countries.

Even for a man with de Corte's impeccable record, it took some courage to stand up to the officers of the Inquisition in this way. "Master Gerard Mercator enjoys a good reputation. At Leuven, he leads a religious and honorable life, and is uncorrupted by heresy," he wrote.[2] It was as enthusiastic an endorsement as he could compose, but far from helping the prisoner, it simply alienated the stern regent.

Mary's personal sympathies lay with the arguments of the reformers, but the threat of Duke William's troops had put steel in her soul. She was fiercely loyal to her brother and dedicated to the extermination of heretics who might prove disloyal to him. She could be charming and feminine when she chose—the Hungarian National Museum has a flowing gown of the finest green Italian silk damask that was made for her around 1520—but she would accept no prevarication on behalf of suspected traitors. How dared de Corte intervene on such a man's behalf, she demanded in an angry reply.

De Corte had no hesitation in standing by the accused man, and he stated in a second letter that he was sure that the investigators were mistaken to suppose that Mercator had been trying to flee the authorities when he left Leuven for Rupelmonde. Mercator's work as a geographer and surveyor often necessitated long absences, and he had frequently been away working for the archbishop, for the bishop of Arras—the Granvelle name again—and even for the emperor himself, he added silkily. And as for allegations of Lutheranism, he protested: "I would have no wish to excuse it if I knew him to be corrupted by heresy—far from it, I would know how to carry out my duty to suppress evil."[3]

He then went to the university authorities to seek their help. Despite the offense that had been caused years earlier by Mercator's long absence in Antwerp, and despite the anxiety about his religious and philosophical attitudes, the scholastic community stood by him. Pierre Was, abbé of Ste. Gertrude at Leuven, was chaplain to the university, and he was persuaded to write to Mary, claiming academic privilege on Mercator's behalf. He was known for the strictness of his rule at the abbey, and he was punctilious in demanding Leuven's ancient rights. The Inquisition, he said, had no right to hold a member of the university, who could be tried only by a tribunal of the university itself. That was true enough—the rector had held the sole right of jurisdiction over members of the university ever since its foundation—but legalistic quibbles and objections that the Inquisition was overstepping its power were never likely to succeed. All the abbé's letter managed to achieve was another angry reply. Mercator had forfeited all his privileges by fleeing to Rupelmonde, said Mary of Hungary, ignoring Pierre de Corte's earlier protestations, and if Pierre Was did not take care, he might find himself the subject of a charge from the Inquisition as well.

There were more desperate pleas for Mercator's freedom, including one from the current rector of the university, François Van Som. He was a servant of the Inquisition himself, and no soft touch for heretics— Francisco de Enzinas, a Spanish reformist who saw the purge, described him as an inquisitor who was "drunk with arrogance and pride . . . full of deceits, deceptions, subtleties, blindness and cruelty . . . a devil incarnate"[4]—and yet even he was persuaded to throw his considerable influence behind Mercator.

There are no detailed records of Mercator's interrogation, but Enzinas told of a young woman, Catherine Sclerckx, questioned repeatedly about Christian doctrine by teams of philosophers and theologians, so Mercator's questioning was probably similar. Did she believe, like a good Catholic, in asking the saints in Heaven and the priesthood on Earth for their intercession with God? they asked. Was it not presumptuous, even impudent, to dare to pray to God himself, as the reformers did?

Catherine replied with a feisty speech in favor of a personal, direct relationship with God that left no room for priests or saints. If God should call to her, she asked her interrogators, should she tell him that she preferred not to reply until she had St. Peter and St. Paul at her side? This was an argument that left them with no alternative but to convict her out of hand as a Lutheran and a heretic. She was lucky to escape with her life, and a fine of four hundred florins—a working man's wage for nearly four years.

Mercator would have faced similar twisting, provocative lines of questioning, his interrogators sometimes smiling and seeming friendly, even sympathetic, as they tried to tempt him into some doctrinal indiscretion. It can have done him no harm, though, that the name of Granvelle kept cropping up in the interrogations. The chancellor, Nicholas Perrenot de Granvelle, the inquisitors told Catherine, was an intermediary with the emperor just as the Church was with God; so Mercator's close links with the family may have provided some proof of his loyalty.

Today, four and a half centuries on, what Mercator had done or said to bring du Fief and his soldiers to his door can only be guessed at. He had been circumspect while he was at Leuven, but somewhere he must have let slip an incautious word—about his views on Aristotle and the creation of the world, perhaps. In his cell, he could only guess what the investigators might know, which was precisely as they wanted it.

As THE CASES AGAINST the group of forty-three pressed slowly ahead, there was always a danger that Mercator would be incriminated by another of the suspects. After all, under the threat of the physical tortures available to the judges of the Inquisition, men and women might blurt out any name they thought their interrogators might like to hear. The inquisitors might hang their victims by their wrists from the ceiling, jerking their shoulders from their sockets by tying lead weights to their feet. They might employ the *toca*, slowly pouring more and more water down a linen strip that had been thrust into the victim's throat, or the *potro*, tightening cords around his or her naked body with the slow turn of a ratchet. Few people resisted; usually, the threat of the torture was enough.

The Inquisition was particularly interested in establishing if the suspects had met regularly, whether for worship or Bible-reading or any other heretical purpose. Early in the investigation, one of the women who had been seized, fifty-eight-year-old Antoinette van Rosmers, admitted that she had received such visits from some of the accused, but listed others with whom she said she had had no contact. Among that second group was "Meester Gheert getrouwt hebbende Scellekens dochtere" (Master Gerard, who married the daughter of Schellekens).

Mercator would never have seen that reassuring record, for one of Pierre du Fief's most effective tactics was silence. Nor would he have known that he had still more to fear from a different direction. Du Fief's men had uncovered nothing at his home, no prayers or hymns written in Flemish rather than Latin, no forbidden books or incriminating letters such as were enough to send many suspects to their deaths—but they still believed that they could find written proof of his heresy.

On May 21, du Fief sent his soldiers to Mechelen, on the assumption that whoever had denounced Mercator must have had some information about the monastery of the Minorite Friars there, the sect with which he had been in contact during his time in Antwerp more than ten years before. He was believed to have met with Franciscus Monachus, that dangerous reformist and critic of Aristotle; he had probably spoken with him and spent time in his cell—but he had certainly written him letters. The Inquisition had its spies everywhere and knew about Mercator's correspondence with Franciscus. There are no details recorded—the official record simply notes tersely that "the Friars of Mechelen have suspect letters from him"—but the bailiff was sent to read whatever evidence there might be, and to produce anything he could find that might be used against the accused man.

For the rest of the prisoners, the torture began in earnest early in June, with the screams of both men and women, according to Enzinas, echoing through the streets of Leuven. If Barbe had the stomach for it, she could have seen for herself something of the misery with which her husband was threatened. At the monastery in Leuven, close by her home, a scaffold was erected to which a sickly, aging priest named Paul de Roovere was marched for his public humiliation and examination. He was another of the forty-three suspected, like Mercator, of Lutheran heresy, and had appeared on the first list that Antoinette van Rosmers had given to the inquisitors, the list of suspects she admitted had visited her. There was still more damning evidence: The search of his home had been successful, and the Inquisition had found books and writings which they said proved his guilt.

Enzinas described the scene as the soldiers dragged him through the streets to the scaffold: "He was a small man, long-bearded and pale, haggard and almost shrivelled and wasting away with the grief and hardship he had suffered . . . a dead body, the shadow of a man rather than a man."[5]

Behind him in the slow procession marched two senior figures from the University of Leuven, taking their formal place in the awesome spectacle. There was no need for a trial; De Roovere was no Catherine Sclerckx. Under threat of execution, he crumbled, confessed his guilt, repented, and threw his books into the flames. He, at least, was saved from following them into the fire: The Inquisition spared his life because he had bowed to their authority, and sent him off to prison. For the rest of his days he was shut up alone in a tiny cell in Vilvorde Prison, between Brussels and Mechelen—the same prison where Tyndale had died—kept alive on a meager diet of bread and water. Such was the mercy of the Inquisition to those who challenged the authority of the Church.

The priest's public humiliation was a scene deliberately designed to terrify the population. Even if Barbe herself kept away, she must have heard of the gruesome spectacle. For those who defied the interrogators, there was even more suffering. Two of the accused, Jean Schats and Jean Vikart, refused to repent and were burned at the stake. To save yourself, you had to repent, but to repent, you had first to admit your guilt—and confession was not always followed by clemency. Antoinette van Rosmers—the woman whose testimony had helped to save Mercator thus far—confessed, but on June 15 she was buried alive. So was Catherine Metsys, who confessed along with her husband, the sculptor Jean Beyaerts. He was beheaded; that was as far as the mercy of the Inquisition extended. Even Paul de Roovere's sentence in Vilvorde Prison was little more than a living death, which dragged on for years.

Mercator's fate still hung in the balance at this point, four months after his arrest. Everyone involved in his case waited while, in Mechelen, the bailiff did his work. Finally, in September, the heavy wooden gates opened again, and Mercator stepped back into the light.

Du Fief had watched and waited, and had to let him go. Mercator would never know exactly what happened. Perhaps his influential contacts at the emperor's court had applied pressure behind the scenes, or perhaps the appeals of his friends at Leuven had been more successful than they appeared. Maybe the investigators had simply finished their work and concluded that he had no case to answer. The Inquisition never volunteered reasons for its decisions, and few people pressed for them.

There is, though, one fascinating, cryptic clue as to what might eventually have won Mercator's release. In the margin of the single sheet of paper that bore Mercator's name and the original damning reference to suspicious letters held by the monks of Mechelen was a brief note, with an illegible signature scribbled underneath. It read simply "*no h*," which might mean "non habent" (they do not have them).[6] The bailiff, then, failed in his search for incriminating documents. If there had been crucial letters from Mercator's correspondence, perhaps one of the monks got there first and spirited them away, or perhaps Mercator had been sufficiently cautious all those years earlier. Either way, the terse note told Pierre du Fief that, this time at least, his men had failed. They had no evidence to support their case against Mercator, and the bureaucratic little scribble authorized his release.*

The religious purge of which his arrest had been a part ground on through the rest of 1543 and much of the following year. By the time it was over, many communities of Protestants, and many groups of friends simply dedicated to the idea of reform in the Catholic Church, had been wiped out completely. Often, whole families were arrested together, questioned, tortured, and sent to the stake. Mercator had come as close as he could to the flames without being burned; he must have felt an over-whelming relief as he swore the oath of secrecy that was invariably de-manded of those prisoners lucky enough to be set free. As his oath demanded, he would never talk about his imprisonment, about anything he had been asked, or anything he had experienced. Only once, in a letter to Antoine de Granvelle written soon after his release, did he mention his imprisonment—referring to it as his "most unjust persecution."[7]

THE CRUEL TREATMENT of the Inquisition pushed many of its victims toward bitterness and greater religious extremism, and made them more determined in their beliefs, but Mercator's months in Rupelmonde Fort left a different mark. He was no revolutionary to be spurred to greater efforts, but a man who wanted to get on with his life in peace. Always cautious by nature, he became even more wary about speaking his mind on any subject that might be contentious. He remained, in theory at least, a believer in the reform of the Church, but he would never again risk at-tracting the attention of the Inquisition.

Once free, he made his study his sanctuary and locked himself away with his books and his instruments. This was a wise move—the reli-gious authorities might be less likely to trouble a hardworking scholar and a merchant of impeccable background—but it was also no doubt an

---

*Today, apart from a single tower rebuilt in the nineteenth century, there are only ditches where Rupelmonde Fort once stood. Its high stone walls and seventeen towers have crumbled away.

emotional refuge. Work was one way to get over the physical and mental effects of his incarceration, a journey back into a familiar and reassuring landscape. The study of the ancients offered contact with unchanging wisdom, while the concentration demanded by engraving and other manual tasks left no time to dwell on what he had been through. And he badly needed the money. A year spent trapped behind Leuven's city walls for fear of William's invading soldiers had crippled his business even before he had been dragged off to prison—nobody wanted to buy maps when the land itself was ablaze. Seven months in Rupelmonde Fort had brought him to the brink of ruin.

Mercator went to work finishing the globes and surveying and astronomical instruments that Charles V had ordered from him eighteen months before. They were the product of months of filing, smoothing, shaping, and measuring that had been interrupted by his spell in prison—precise, delicate, and finely crafted enough for any enthusiast's shelf. Charles received them with delight at his court in Brussels, but although he was an avid collector, he was no mere dilettante. No sooner had the long-delayed consignment arrived than the instruments were packed up in cases to accompany him on his latest military campaigns against the rebellious Protestant princes of Germany. He would use these instruments to help him study the landscapes of his campaigns, choose the ground on which to fight, and draw up battle plans that took account of the lay of the land.

In Germany, as in the Netherlands, religious and political dissent were inextricably intertwined. Protestantism was one way for the German princes to assert their independence from an emperor whose power they had always resented, while for Charles—"God's standard bearer"—the defense of Catholicism was a sacred duty. Both Nicholas de Granvelle and his son Antoine argued against war—the brutal repression of the defenseless people of the Netherlands was one thing, military campaigning against well-armed and determined armies in Germany quite another. But the emperor was immovable. He had struggled in vain for fifteen years to seek doctrinal and political compromises, and had become convinced that force of arms rather than negotiation might keep the Protestant states within the Catholic fold and enforce their loyalty to the empire.

Racked by gout and crippled by asthmatic attacks that would sometimes prevent him from speaking, he left Brussels with his troops on a long, straggling march to Ingolstadt on the Danube, deep in southern Germany. There, in the snow of a bitter German winter in 1546, he set up camp beneath the city walls, face-to-face with the Lutheran armies.

For all his physical difficulties, Charles was an inspirational leader in battle. For six days, he rode around his lines under a constant barrage of artillery fire, apparently careless both of his safety and his physical ailments, and laughing at the dire warnings of his chancellor. With him, he had the surveying instruments that Mercator had made—until a surprise raid on the farm where they were being stored overnight left the house and its outbuildings in flames and the delicate instruments reduced to ashes and a few lumps of twisted metal. The raid had little effect on the outcome of the battle; for all their superiority in artillery, the Lutheran forces were badly led and indecisive, and withdrew to leave Charles in control of much of southern Germany. At this moment of military triumph, he found time to send an urgent message to Mercator's workshop in Leuven. His precious instruments had been destroyed, and he wanted Mercator to make him some more.

Chapter Eleven

Two New Arrivals

Few skills were more important for prosperity in the six-teenth century than the ability to be on two sides at once. Simple discretion might have been enough to keep a man unnoticed and safe if he was lucky, but to thrive he needed friends, clients, and patrons wherever he could find them. The Flemish painter Anthonis Mor was known as Antonio Moro in Spain, and Sir Anthony More when Mary Tudor sat for him in England. Within a few years of finishing his portrait of Antoine de Granvelle, who tortured and executed opponents of Spanish rule in the Netherlands with such enthusiasm, he was painting Granvelle's bitter enemy William of Orange, the leader of the revolt against Spain. National boundaries, religious differences, political rivalries—all these were nothing to a man of ambition.

Whatever his secret bitterness over his treatment by the Inquisition, and whatever his reformist leanings, Mercator fulfilled his commissions for the emperor with enthusiasm. The imperial seal of approval was just the endorsement his workshop needed, and as word spread that no less a personage than the Holy Roman Emperor was one of his customers, the globes, astrolabes, and other precision instruments turned out by his team of craftsmen became more urgently sought after. If he had any private reservations about the surveying instruments he had made for Charles being used in campaigns against the Protestants, they were not strong enough to cause him any serious embarrassment.

The thriving print industry in Antwerp and Leuven, the busy docks on the river, the flourishing trading companies, and the University of

Leuven itself were all hallmarks of a busy, vibrant community that attracted determined people, whether they were scholars or businessmen. In the late 1540s, two men arrived there whose lives would become closely intertwined with Mercator's: John Dee and Christopher Plantin. They were dissimilar personalities, one an introspective and controversial scholar, the other an opportunistic businessman who battled determinedly throughout his life against a succession of setbacks and disasters. They had different talents and contrasting aspirations, and they faced the challenges of the sixteenth century in their own ways, but although their careers followed diverging paths, each of them remained a lifelong friend of Mercator's. His attitudes and achievements were illuminated by theirs; they reflected two distinct facets of his character.

In early 1547 Dee, a tall, fair-haired young Englishman with a light brown fringe of beard and an enthusiastic manner, unpacked his bags in one of Leuven's many small rooming houses, at the end of a long journey over the rough and unmade roads from Cambridge. The trip had taken him several days, and although later in his life he would become a seasoned traveler through Europe, the voyage across the Channel had been the first time he had been out of sight of land. Dee, a brilliant classical student with six years' study in Cambridge already behind him even though he was barely out of his teens, had come to the Low Countries to walk in the streets of one of Europe's most famous university towns and sit at the feet of some of the leading philosophers and scholars of Christendom.

For all its stern defense of orthodox Catholicism against the reform movement, the intellectual atmosphere at the University of Leuven was still one of inquiry, discussion, and discovery. The confidence of the town could be seen in the work that was just beginning on the new *Voirste Huys,* or town hall, one of the finest gothic buildings in the world, whose intricately carved arches and niches and six magnificent spires still dominate Leuven's central square. The university was home to some of the most highly regarded scientists and thinkers of the day, among them Mercator, Gemma Frisius, and the doctor and anatomist Andreas Vesalius, who had scandalized many traditionalists only a few years earlier by dismissing the ancient Greek physician Galen, the classical source of all medical knowledge, as little more than a fraud and a charlatan.*

Many of the lectures given by professors at the university were open to anyone to attend, and learned debate drew scholars to Leuven from across Europe. Pedro Nunes, royal cosmographer to the king of Portugal and probably the world's leading authority on the Spanish and Portuguese discoveries in the New World, was a visitor; so was the map publisher Abraham Ortelius, who started in Antwerp while still a teenager as a colorist and map seller to support his sisters, and went on to win fame and riches as publisher in 1570 of the first great modern atlas, the *Theatrum Orbis Terrarum.*

Such men, wrote Dee, would write in a single day "matter enough to require the labour of a full year for comprehension while I formerly sat at home."[1] For Dee, the fame and distinction of the thirty-year-old Gerard Mercator were something to aspire to. He was a teacher in one of the leading universities of the age, with a reputation as a scholar and thinker; and apart from his academic standing, he had already produced maps that had won acclaim across Europe. Dee admired his intellect. Unlike the Cambridge philosophers of distinction Dee had mixed with before, Mercator was able, like Gemma, to put his studies to practical use in a way the young student found refreshing and challenging. In Mercator, dividing his time between his home, his studies, and the busy life of his workshop, Dee saw a figure he might emulate, one who could dedicate himself to the pursuit of knowledge and yet thrive in the real world.

Where Mercator had been the son of a poor cobbler, John Dee's father was a successful dealer in silks and fine cloths at the court of King Henry VIII—yet their lives had followed similar paths. Mercator had sat on the

---

*Not content with such disrespect toward a figure who held the same eminence in medical studies as Ptolemy did in geography, in 1536 Vesalius had gone on to hold the first public dissection of a corpse in Leuven for nearly twenty years, and had then ridiculed the theologians for pontificating about the soul without understanding the body. There were unconfirmed stories after he died in 1564 that later in his life only the personal intervention of King Philip of Spain had saved him from the Inquisition.

John Dee

benches at 's Hertogenbosch, Dee at the little chantry school at Chelmsford in England; just as Mercator had studied through the night as a boy, Dee claimed that at Cambridge he had spent eighteen hours of every day closeted with his books. While attending the university, Dee, like Mercator, had begun to accumulate the circle of friends who would help him prosper throughout his life—men like William Cecil, later to become Queen Elizabeth's powerful treasurer, Lord Burghley.

Even so, it was at Leuven rather than at Cambridge, Dee said later, that he learned to think, that his whole philosophical system "laid down its first and deepest roots."[2] In the dusty halls and studies where the scholars met with students, he formed lifelong alliances. For three years, he said later, he and Mercator were hardly out of each other's company. "Such was the eagerness of both of us for learning and philosophising that, after we had come together, we scarcely left off the investigation of difficult and useful problems for three minutes of an hour."[3] That the twenty-year-old John Dee should show such youthful enthusiasm is only to be expected; but that Mercator, fifteen years his senior and already well established within the university hierarchy, should share in it shows not only how committed he was to intellectual inquiry but also what an impressive mind the young Dee had.

Later in his career, when he published his own maps, Dee was meticulous in deferring to both Mercator and Ortelius, "the two most celebrated geographers of this age, and both of them my singular good friends." In his famous library at Mortlake near London, where some four thousand books covering virtually every aspect of classical, medieval, and Renaissance learning were crowded onto the shelves, he would delight years later in showing occasional visitors Mercator's twin globes, which his friend had either sent to England or given to him on one of his later visits to Leuven. Dee, who saw himself as an English Mercator with his own contributions to make to the science of cartography, had carefully added his "divers reformations, both geographical and celestial." He also had a "theoric of the eighth sphere, the ninth, and the tenth, with a horizon and meridian of copper, of Gerardus Mercator his own making for me purposely."[4] The "theoric" was designed to show the movements of the different planets in their various orbits about the Earth, but since both it and the globes vanished when Dee's house was ransacked years later, there is no way of knowing exactly how it worked. Other instruments he possessed, he lamented, were "most barbarously spoiled and with hammers smit in pieces."[5] Doubtless the globes and the theoric went the same way.

Thirty years after he left Leuven, as Queen Elizabeth's court intellectual, consulted for advice on astrology, astronomy, medicine, history, and the law, Dee still wrote of and to the "honest philosopher and mathematicien Gerardus Mercator," and boasted that "sufficient Record is publisshed of our great familiarity." Dee, like Mercator, became known as one of the wisest scholars in Europe, and their lives continued to run along curiously parallel lines. During the 1550s, he was imprisoned for several months in England under the Catholic

queen Mary for his alleged involvement in "the lewd and vain practices of calculating and conjuring,"[6] and, like Mercator, he would involve himself later in his life in the practical side of geography and
cartography, advising on the planning of new voyages of discovery in
the New World and in the northern seas.

FOR ALL THEIR CLOSENESS, Dee had a passion that Mercator did not
share, to which the charges against him under Queen Mary give some
clue. Apart from his standing as a scholar, mathematician, and geographer, he developed another, more controversial, reputation as a magus, a
philosopher-magician, who had mysterious and even unsavory relations
with the spirit world. Many people believed that Dee was the model for
Ben Jonson's Faustus, "swollen with cunning of a self-conceit"[7] and
hauled off by fiends because of his pact with the devil. The old gossip and
diarist John Aubrey declared that he had been told "of John Dee conjuring at a pool in Brecknockshire, and that they found a wedge of gold;
and that they were troubled and indicted as Conjurors at the Assizes;
that a mighty storme and tempest was raysed in harvest time."[8]

The stories say more about the malice of those who told them and the
gullibility of those who listened than about Dee, but there was reason for
them. Dee was irresistibly drawn toward necromancy and magic. In his
later life, he spent several years in earnest communion with angels, with
the help of a crystal ball and a mysterious scryer, or medium. For all his
protestations that he was innocent of witchcraft, he certainly believed
that he, or at least his scryer, had the mystical power to summon spirits.

Such activities, like astrology and alchemy, sometimes teetered on
the brink of heresy and were often the stock-in-trade of the charlatan,
but they remained an obsession in sixteenth-century Europe. The
boundary between science and superstition was hard to define. Stories
of trickery, spirit-raising, and magic gathered around the lives of men
like Dee, although he always protested that there was nothing blasphe-
mous or heretical in his dealings with the unseen, that his work was another way of interpreting a divine plan of Creation.

Mercator, like Dee, was fascinated throughout his life by the natural
world, by what he could see and interpret, and by its place in God's awe-

inspiring plan, but he believed that astrology misrepresented the mystery of Creation. His approach of constant measurement, checking, and interpretation fitted into the scientific revolution that would dominate the seventeenth century rather than the tradition of mysticism that lingered on from the Middle Ages. Many of Dee's interests, by contrast, over the next few decades would come to seem shady, disreputable, and even fraudulent. Even so, this difference in philosophical approach did not stand in the way of a lasting understanding between the two men: Mercator never criticized Dee's interest in the occult, and for the rest of his life he remained a regular correspondent and a close friend.

THE OTHER NEW ARRIVAL in Antwerp, Christopher Plantin, was a business partner rather than a close friend,[9] but he faced the same great dilemma as Mercator as the 1540s drew to an end: how to live and prosper under the increasingly savage religious persecutions of Charles V and the Catholic Church. Plantin was a reformist by conviction, and a devotee of several heretical Anabaptist sects, but he was also a master of the art of supporting two sides at once, and he stayed in Antwerp to make his fortune.

When he arrived with his wife from the French town of St. Avertin, near the city of Tours, the prospects for a peaceful life in Antwerp could hardly have been worse for a printer and would-be publisher. In the early 1520s, Charles had issued the first of a series of edicts, or *plakkaten,* threatening "loss of life and property" for a range of religious crimes, and in the second half of the 1540s, they were renewed no fewer than six times, with copies posted in public places as a terrible warning. All signs suggested that purges like the one that had swept up Mercator would get worse—and for anyone concerned with the printing of books, as Plantin was, the bloody campaign against heresy was close to home.

In 1546, the Leuven theologians issued a preliminary list of forbidden books, and four years later, Charles's notorious Edict of Blood decreed that the possession, selling, or copying of any heretical work would be punished by death. Supporting the decree was Antoine de Granvelle, whose influence continued to grow: In 1550, on the death of his father, he slipped effortlessly into his place as keeper of the emperor's great seal.

Christopher Plantin

Plantin had arrived with his wife a couple of years earlier, in 1548.[10] Two years younger than Mercator, as a young child he showed a remarkable aptitude for Latin and astounded his teachers by his appetite for scientific books. In Antwerp he set up a bookbindery, and then, in 1550, he was listed as a *boeckprinter* in the register of the city's Guild of St. Luke. At first, he survived on the money from a small haberdashery business run by his wife, but within five years he had established his own printing works, and by 1563 he had five presses turning out books in one of the most profitable enterprises in Europe.

Like Mercator, he spent his life building up a thriving family business; Plantin's personal motto, *labore et constantia* (by hard work and tenacity), could have applied just as well to Mercator, whose maps he supplied to clients in the Low Countries, Germany, France, and England. His records show that apart from selling Mercator's maps and globes, he provided him in return with some twenty-two thousand sheets of the best-quality paper over a five-year period. Theirs was a mutually profitable partnership—though they, too, had different priorities.

Plantin's success was built on trimming, switching loyalties, and watching for the sudden changes in power that could lead either to prison or to profit. He began by printing clandestine broadsheets with secret funding from the reformers, avoiding arrest in 1561 only by being away in France on a lucky business trip when the soldiers came for him. Unlike Mercator, he had traveled far enough to be out of their reach, and he stayed in France for nearly two years. All his goods were confiscated and sold, but when he came back in 1562, he set about cultivating rich merchants and political contacts, among them Antoine de Granvelle. Plantin abandoned his old reformist friends and attached himself unashamedly to people in power. Within a few years, he had a dozen printing presses turning out not inflammatory reformist pamphlets but prayer books, Bibles, and other religious tracts with such success that he was named arch-typographer to the king of Spain. Plantin had not just shifted loyalties; he had immersed himself in the profitable trappings of Catholicism.

His company's records show that between 1571 and 1576 he shipped 18,370 breviaries, 16,735 missals, 9,120 Books of Hours, and 3,200 hymnals to Madrid. A business that had started on the fringes of the law became the trusted collaborator of the Spanish monarchy and the Catholic Church. The portrait by Peter Paul Rubens in Antwerp's Plantin-Moretus Museum shows him as a successful businessman, clutching a book and the golden compasses that he had adopted as the symbol of his company. He is a thin-faced figure, with the sidelong, calculating glance of a man who has taken risks and until then emerged triumphant.

When Spanish soldiers mutinied and rampaged through Antwerp, burning, raping, and ransacking buildings, Plantin paid out a fortune in bribes to save his new business premises in the Friday Market, the Vrijdagmarkt. "Nine times did I have to pay ransom to save my property from destruction; it would have been cheaper to have abandoned it," he declared ruefully.[11]

For more than fifty years, the shifting rivalries between Catholics and reformers, between Spaniards and nationalists, meant for Plantin a lifetime of delicate maneuvering and frantic tacking against the changing winds. His nature was to adapt, not abandon; Mercator could never have done the same.

As the 1540s drew to an end, neither man had any immediate reason for fear, but Mercator's whole career shows that, whereas Plantin seemed to revel in courting danger and avoiding arrest, he sought peace and security to pursue his studies and bring up his family. Life in Leuven would have been uncertain and threatening, even though he was too cautious to allow himself to be trapped with forbidden books or to consort with suspected heretics. The contact with Franciscus Monachus and the "suspect letters" had been a young man's careless slip that would not be repeated. Though the Inquisition had cleared him, though he had kept the oath of secrecy that had been the price of his freedom, and had powerful friends and contacts, the times were ever more threatening. Plantin stayed, and bent with each fresh wind; Mercator left.

In 1551 William, duke of Jülich, Cleves, and Berg—the same Duke William whose soldiers had ravaged Flanders not ten years before—invited Mercator to take the chair of cosmography in a new university he was planning to open in the German town of Duisburg. Time and the humiliation of his defeat by Charles had tamed the blustering young adventurer whose army had swarmed across the border; the old lesson of Ghent had been learned afresh. He was a tolerant and enlightened ruler, who had been performing his own religious and political balancing act for years. For himself, he maintained the nominal Catholicism that Charles had demanded, but the reformed Church that had been established in his dukedom since his father's time remained unaffected. In the three duchies that lay astride the lower Rhine, Lutheranism and Calvinism were both flourishing. Compared to the constant vulnerability of existence in the Low Countries, his realm was a haven of religious freedom.

The new role that Mercator was offered was appealing as well. The *Oxford English Dictionary* notes the first use of the word *cosmography* in 1519—a new name in Mercator's day for an ancient discipline, the study of the Earth and the universe and their relation to each other. The cosmographer could take virtually the whole field of natural science for his own, looking back to the ancients and forward to the new discoveries that were being made both on Earth and in the heavens. There was, or there seemed to be, no conflict between the quest for knowledge and Mercator's deep religious sense. Cosmography was the homage of the intellect to God's Creation, a study which, in its breadth and depth, was made for a man who declared himself to be so fascinated by "the most beautiful order, the most harmonious proportion, and that singular beauty which is admirable in all created things."[12]

From Duke William's point of view, the presence in Duisburg of the leading geographer of his generation would reflect greatly to his own credit and bring prestige and renown to the university he planned; Mercator had the prospect of a new life in which he could devote himself to the intellectual challenge of his studies and enjoy the standing to which his learning entitled him. There was no reason why involvement with Duke William's new university should threaten his growing prosperity; the duke's backing and sponsorship would be assured, and Mercator's study and workshop could support each other. Although Leuven had become Europe's center for the production of globes and scientific instruments, Mercator's reputation already spread far beyond the town. He traveled to the trade fairs around the Low Countries, France, and Northern Germany, and had built up such a range of patrons and customers that he could work just as profitably from Duisburg as from Leuven.

Mercator said little about his decision to leave his old university town, other than to observe, years later, in a flattering message to Duke William, that Jülich was where his life had truly begun. Rupelmonde in Flanders was his birthplace, but in the dedication written in the first volume of his Atlas in 1585, he told the duke, "I was conceived under your protection, in the territory of Jülich, by parents from Jülich."

But there was clearly more to his decision than a sentimental retracing of Hubert de Cremer's footsteps of nearly four decades before. There were clear practical reasons to go to Duisburg. Life in his old university town had been limiting. He had enjoyed the profits that instrument making brought him, but he had achieved no standing in the town, no position of social eminence. He could never be sure, but he must have wondered whether he was living all the time in the shadow of his past. Seven years had passed since he had crossed the wooden footbridge out of Rupelmonde Fort, but perhaps the taint of suspected heresy still hung about him. Under Duke William's protection, he could make a new start far away from the memory of the Inquisition.

His children had grown considerably by this time. Arnold, the eldest boy, born about a year after his marriage, was thirteen years old; in another couple of years, he would be the same age Mercator had been when he left for 's Hertogenbosch. The girls, Emerance, Dorothée, and Catherine, would stay with their mother, as was the custom, and Rumold and Bartholomew, at nine and ten years old respectively, could be taught at home for a while longer, but he would soon have to be thinking about their education.

For all that, it was not a straightforward decision. Uprooting himself, his family, and his business took some courage, but if he lacked Plantin's moral and political suppleness, he never had difficulty in showing a degree of adaptability. Mercator accepted Duke William's offer in 1551 and began the preparations to leave with his family for a new life in Duisburg. His was a well-planned and dignified departure, with all the precious engravings for his maps, all his books and documents, painstakingly packed up and prepared for the journey. In a very real sense, he was going home.

Chapter Twelve

A New Life

TWELVE YEARS BEFORE Mercator's arrival at Duisburg, in the
duchy of Cleves, Duke William's sister Anne had set off on her ill-
fated mission to England to become King Henry VIII's fourth wife—a
short-lived and unhappy adventure. The six-month queen had realized
quickly that her best policy was to avoid confronting the powerful
monarch, bow to his will, and reach the best deal she could, and as a
result she lived on in comfortable seclusion in England, with the confusing title of King's Sister and a generous pension of five hundred
pounds a year. This was the same lesson that her brother had eventually learned from Charles V. His reward for accepting the power of
the emperor after his adventure in Flanders was a quiet life for him
and his dukedom.

Duisburg was a snug, backward-looking town of the old German
Empire, clinging to the right bank of the Rhine where it was joined by
the Ruhr, and filled with ancient buildings, fading memories of its
former glories, and barely three thousand inhabitants—more than in
Rupelmonde but less than a quarter the population of 's Hertogenbosch. It offered none of the cosmopolitan life of Leuven, nor of the
hectic commerce of Antwerp. A bird's-eye view drawn later by Mercator's friend and fellow lowlander Johannes Corputius showed its
compactness and neatness, with a network of narrow streets huddled
around the great Salvatorkirche (Church of the Savior) and the central market, all protected by a defensive wall and a moat channeled
from the river. Yet it gave no idea of the overwhelming scale of the

Rhine,* on which Duisburg relied for its very existence. Like Rupelmonde, the town stood at the confluence of two rivers, but the Rhine, fed from the Swiss Alps some four hundred miles upstream, was vaster than anything Mercator had seen before.

The origins of the name of the Rhine are lost in its pre-Roman, Celtic history,† and it has always been one of Europe's great natural boundaries. To the conquering Romans, the river and the dense woods through which it ran had been as much a frontier of the known world as the mythical sea of Oceanus was to the Greeks. The Roman chronicler Tacitus, writing at the end of the first century AD, saw the Hyrcanian Forest as marking the very edge of civilization. In Mercator's day, by contrast, Corputius showed the trees tidily dotting the riverbank outside the city walls, where they were carefully tended and felled for timber. Then, as now, the Rhine was an important trading route south into the heart of Europe, with barges carrying furs, rye, and wheat from Russia, grain and salted fish from the Baltic, and wool and linen cloth from as far away as Ireland. Back downstream came cargoes of delicate glassware from Venice, and silks and spices that had passed through the Italian cities from Arabia and the Ottoman possessions in the Balkans. There was an abundance of fish in the river as well, and the floods that followed the spring thaw would leave a deposit of rich, fertile black silt for the local farmers. The forests supplied not just timber for building but also partridge and quail for Duisburg's marketplace. Thanks largely to the Rhine, Duisburg was not, at least when Mercator arrived, a town that knew privation.

Duke William's sharp reminder of the realities of power had been learned in the Low Countries, not Cleves, and Duisburg had been untouched by war. Behind its walls stood tiled houses, many of them with gardens and orchards, and all the institutions of a peaceful town: a Latin school, a corn mill, and a market. The trees outside, undamaged

---

*Even today, with the massive cranes and docks of the biggest inland harbor in the world, the black waters of the Rhine dominate the town.

†Two suggestions are that it derives from *der Rinnende* (the flowing) or from *Rein* (the clear).

THE NETHERLANDS, FLANDERS, LORRAINE, AND GERMANY
CIRCA 1570

North Sea

DENMARK

Rantzau

Lubeck
Hamburg

ENGLAND

FRISIA

Bremen

Elbe R.

THE NETHERLANDS

Amsterdam
Leyden

Ems R.

Weser R.

HOLLAND · Utrecht

ZEELAND

GUELDERLAND

s'Hertogenbosch

Bruges · Rupelmonde · Antwerp

CLEVES · BURG

GERMANY

Ghent

BRABANT

Duisburg

Ruhr R.

Mechelen

Sichem

Neuss · Dusseldorf

Meuse R.

Scheldt R.

Brussels

Leuven · Gangelt

Cologne

FLANDERS

Maastricht

JULICH

WESTERWALD

Gembloux

Namur

Somme R.

EIFEL MTNS.

Rhine R.

Frankfurt

THÜRINGERWALD

Main R.

Aisne R.

Reims

Mosel R.

HUNSRÜCK

Paris

Marne R.

Meuse R.

Verdun

Metz

Nuremberg

Seine R.

Toul

LORRAINE

Rhine R.

Necker R.

FRANCE

Strasbourg

SCHWARZWALD

Ingolstadt

Danube R.

BAVARIA

SCHWÄBISCH

Rhone R.

FRANCHE-
COMTÉ

Basel

JURA MTNS.

ALPS

0   Miles   50   100

0   Kilometers   100

© 2004 Jeffrey L. Ward

by rampaging armies for generations, were a mark of 140 years of quiet prosperity. Duisburg was dominated, literally and figuratively, by the spire of the towering Salvatorkirche; by the mid–sixteenth century, for all the tensions between different Protestant factions, Lutheranism was the accepted and settled religion. A welcoming calm greeted scholars and philosophers, and much that was familiar to a lowlander as well: Flourishing trade with the cloth manufacturers of Ghent and Bruges meant that the sounds of Flemish echoed in the marketplace as merchants haggled and shouted over their bales of cloth.

Not only traders traveled to Duisburg from the Low Countries. Soon after Mercator arrived, a well-known humanist and teacher from Ghent, Johannes Otho, set up a school for twenty-five "youngsters of good birth" in the town. He had left Ghent in a hurry with his wife and children, after a summons to appear before the Inquisition—one more heretic who had slipped away to the safety of Duke William's tolerant rule. The magistrates in Duisburg, well used to new arrivals with such problems behind them, wrote a formal note to Ghent, assuring the authorities there that Otho was a respectable Catholic, but it did no good. All the possessions he had left behind were seized, and his house in the town's Talboonstraet was sold off. His future depended on the school he had established in Duisburg, and Mercator's children were among his first pupils, working through the Latin grammar he had published in Flemish and poring over his learned translations of Plutarch.

Mercator's home in the Oberstrasse, a short distance to the northeast of the church, was destroyed by Allied bombing in World War II.[1] A model in the local museum, constructed from old photographs, suggests it was built around a central courtyard, with an office and a workshop facing the living quarters. A high stone wall with a thick wooden gate topped by an iron grille ran along the street frontage; even in peaceable Duisburg, a prosperous merchant and a man with a family—"an honest citizen of modest fortune," as Mercator described himself[2]—needed to protect himself against thieves and vagabonds. It was an old and spacious two-story house of stone, ideal for a man whose business and family life were closely intertwined. There was space for his growing collection of printed books and manuscripts on history, philosophy, and theology—his "most amply furnished library," according to Walter Ghim.[3] Rolls of maps, sent from correspondents in Italy, Germany, England, France, and the Low Countries, lined the walls.

In marked contrast to the rambling rabbit-warren of rooms and alcoves in Antwerp's Vrijdagmarkt, where Christopher Plantin ran his printing works, the workshop in the Oberstrasse was small and compact. Where Plantin was an industrialist, Mercator remained a scholar and craftsman to the day he died. There, with the help of his sons as they grew older, and with a small team of artisans, he produced the globes and scientific instruments for which he was renowned.

A perfectionist, Mercator liked to be closely involved at every stage of a job, but it was almost universal practice for the routine tasks to be carried out by apprentices. The new art of copperplate printing, for instance, involved a production line of ancillary tasks both before and after the delicate work of inscribing the lines of the map onto the metal plate. First, an assistant would spread a wafer-thin layer of wax over the heated surface of the plate to provide a suitable medium onto which the map could be copied in reverse for engraving. The copying, too, could be carried out with training and practice by one of the team, delicately tracing the lines of the original map onto the hardened wax. Mercator, though, remained the master craftsman: His hand was on the graver which moved across the wax surface to carve through into the copper beneath, and Mercator, too, cut out the place-names in the flowing italic script in which he took such pride. This was the traditional skill of the jewelers and craftsman-engravers on which Antwerp's early dominance of the printing industry had been based, the skill that Mercator had learned in Gemma's workshop.

Once the carving was complete, the copper plate had to be covered with ink, with an assistant squeezing the sticky black fluid into the incised lines before wiping away the excess, and cleaning and burnishing the face. Then the plate would be positioned in a wood frame over a sheet of paper that had been dampened so that it would squeeze into the depressions on the plate, and finally screwed firmly down in a press modeled on the ma-

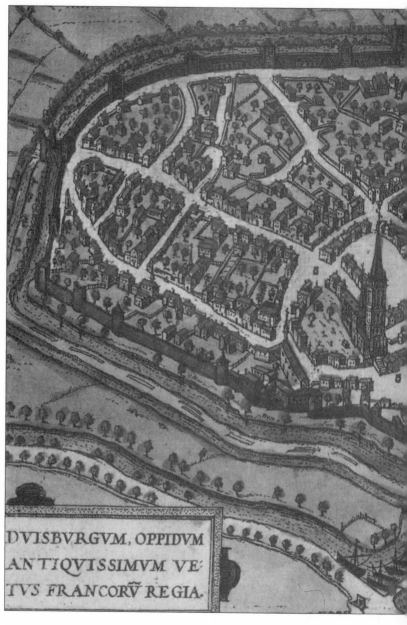

DVISBVRGVM, OPPIDVM ANTIQVISSIMVM VE: TVS FRANCORṼ REGIA.

Duisburg, from Civitates Orbis Terrarum, *1572. Mercator's house was near the foot of Oberstrasse, which ran between the main square and its gate in the town wall.*

chines that had squeezed olives and grapes for centuries. With the whole process of cleaning, inking, and polishing being repeated before each new impression was taken, there was plenty to occupy his team of craftsmen. For them, as for Mercator, the workday would have been long, starting as early as 5 AM in the summer, and lasting until the light began to fail at dusk. Wages in printing houses and workshops were small, and there were fines for unsatisfactory workmanship.

SUCH A STRICT REGIME would have won the approval of Walter Ghim, one of Duisburg's leading townsmen and civic dignitaries, who was to become Mercator's close friend and first biographer. Ghim lived close by and offered gushing descriptions of his friend in the life story he wrote shortly after Mercator died. "In time of good fortune, he behaved with moderation; in adversity, with great patience," said Ghim. He was calm of temperament and sedate and serious in his bearing—a model citizen. "During the 42 years that he resided here in Duisburg with his family he never exchanged a harsh word with any of his fellow citizens. . . . He paid the magistrates the honour and respect that was due to them. Wherever he lived, he always got on well with his neighbours; he crossed nobody's path; had proper regard to the interests of others; and did not put himself over anybody else."[4]

Respect for the magistracy would have been a quality particularly dear to Ghim's heart—he was mayor of Duisburg no fewer than twelve times and obviously relished his position—but there is not a word of criticism, of controversy, anywhere in his account. He never mentioned Rupelmonde Fort and the Inquisition, nor hinted at any religious doubt or difficulty; Mercator's life, according to Ghim, was a serene tableau of intellectual rigor and bourgeois virtue. "From the time when Gerard Mercator came to live here, I saw a lot of him, but I never found him idle or unoccupied. He was always heavily engaged in reading one of the historians or other serious authors, of whom he had a fine stock in his library, or in writing or engraving, or was absorbed in profound meditation. Although he ate and drank very little, he kept an excellent table, well furnished with the necessaries of civilised living. He took the greatest care of his health. . . . He always did his best to help those who

were poor and less fortunate than he, and throughout his life, he cultivated and cherished hospitality."[5]

Virtually nothing is known today of Ghim except for his twelve
terms of office as mayor and his relationship with Mercator, and he
survives only in the reflected light of his friend's renown. By his own
account, he was a frequent visitor, and his conversations were detailed
enough for his biography to remain one of the most important sources
of information about Mercator's life. Even its omissions, like the story
of the Inquisition, are significant: They show what Mercator wanted
to cut out of his life and forget. Ghim did not write about them because Mercator no doubt did not talk about them. Ghim clearly
revered his friend's learning and scholarship—and he, in return, represented the stability and social position that Mercator had lacked as a
young man.

Mercator had authority: not that of simple physical size—Walter
Ghim says he was a small man, well-formed and good-looking—but
the confidence of a man at ease with himself. These early years in
Duisburg were probably the happiest, most contented period of Mercator's life, even though the project for which he had originally come
to Duisburg foundered in financial and political problems. Duke
William had been premature in planning a university without having
received formal approval from the pope, and twelve more years passed
before the official license was granted. By that time, the scheme had
lost its impetus, and the university would not ultimately open for another ninety years.*

Even without the university, Mercator had plenty to occupy his time.
He manufactured mathematical and astronomical instruments, but the
terrestrial globe that he had originally designed ten years before, coupled with its new celestial counterpart, was still the most important
product of his workshop. He was gradually building up production;

---

*By the time Pope Pius VI did grant his license in 1576, Duke William was already crip-
pled by ill health, and his enthusiasm for the project was gone. Mercator's only direct
connection with it came more than three centuries later in 1972, when it was renamed
the Gerhard-Mercator-Universität.

apart from consignments he regularly sent to Christopher Plantin in Antwerp,* globes were sold at the annual fairs in various German and French cities, and also shipped off to individual buyers across northern Europe. In addition, Mercator had ambitious plans for the expansion of his house in the Oberstrasse, with porticos, halls, courts, dining rooms, gardens, and orchards.[6] He spent long evenings in his library, discussing the finer points of science or theology with Ghim and other townsmen, and wrote detailed exchanges by letter with scholars all over Europe and beyond.

One of Mercator's most regular correspondents was a friend from Leuven, Jan Vermeulen, well known by the Latinized name Molanus, who was a humanist and a historian. As a young man, he had staggered his examiners at the university by reciting an entire book of Aristotelian philosophy by heart, without a pause or a stumble; but he had another, more controversial, reputation as a passionate champion of religious reform. He had been forced to flee the Low Countries during Granvelle's religious purges and established himself in the Protestant town of Bremen in north Germany, where he ran a school for orphans. Ten years younger than Mercator, over the years he became not only his friend, confidant, and correspondent but also the teacher of his sons and eventually his son-in-law.

The two men wrote to each other regularly for at least two decades.[7] Most of their private letters are lost, but those that remain show something of the similarities and differences in their characters. Their religious devotion was clear—"Remember you are a citizen of heaven, and must live by heavenly laws," Vermeulen exhorted his friend in one letter.[8] "The will of the Father should be stronger in us than the injuries of all the wicked." On another occasion, writing in reply to a letter from Mercator, he told him ardently, "Your letter burns with your eagerness to celebrate the divine goodness."[9] Only a single letter survives from Mercator's side of the correspondence, but he fell as naturally as his

---

*Plantin's accounts, quoted in Colin Clair's *Christopher Plantin* (London: Cassell, 1960), show that a few years after Mercator's arrival in Duisburg, between 1558 and 1589, he supplied Plantin with a total of 1,150 maps and globes

friend into formal Christian expressions such as "Greetings in Christ" or "Brother in Christ." Another surviving letter, written to a Protestant pastor in Zurich later in his life, shows how comfortable Mercator felt in the company of reformers whose friendship in Leuven would have been enough to have him convicted by the Inquisition. With the solemn devotion of his friend Vermeulen, Mercator wrote: "I thank God that He bound me in friendship with such good men of great piety. What can be more sweet in life than to enjoy the company of those whom we know to be superior members of the body of Christ?"[10]

Mercator was calm and measured in contrast to the fervent religiosity of his friend. Vermeulen seethed with anger against a society that he believed rejected the teaching of the Bible—"The sons of men are liars and more fickle than vanity," he told Mercator[11]—and he had no hesitation in confronting the politics of religion head-on. "The tyranny of the Pope is like the devastation of the Turk," he declared angrily[12]—a remark that gives some clue to the shared attitudes of the two friends. Vermeulen had the reputation of an outspoken critic of the Church, and as a result he spent much of his life on the run. Such high-principled recklessness was not for Mercator, who, in any case, lacked the angry dogmatism that characterized much religious discussion. However much he may have privately sympathized with Vermeulen's position, his public instincts were those of a conformist, a man who was unwilling to involve himself in controversy.

One letter in particular, written to Vermeulen in July of 1576, reveals his scholarly quibbling over the minutiae of his faith as well as his refusal to be drawn into the narrow bigotry of the time. It shows how open-minded he could be, even in the overheated atmosphere of the Reformation. In it, he discussed the doctrine of transubstantiation—the question of whether the bread and wine of the Communion literally become the body and blood of Christ. It was one of the most bitterly disputed issues between Catholics and Protestants, traditionalists and reformers, but Mercator's was a voice of easygoing pragmatism. He had the measured calm of Erasmus. It was nothing more than a fight about words, he said; picking over the detail of the argument would produce only useless quarrels.

"This is a bigger mystery than can be understood, and is not part of the necessary articles of faith. . . . Therefore if anyone thinks this or that, provided it is piously, he is not thinking heretically, and I am not convinced that he should be condemned, nor do I think he should be excommunicated," he wrote.[13] Elsewhere in Europe, people went to the stake over their beliefs in the "this or that" of religious dogma. The nub of the case made out by the Inquisition against the unfortunate priest Paul de Roovere all those years ago, at the time of Mercator's arrest, was that he had questioned the literal presence of the body of Christ in the Communion. Where de Roovere had crumpled in the face of threats, bullying, and constant questioning, Mercator's was the voice of calm tolerance and common sense. His final thought, though, was of discretion. "Don't communicate this to anyone, lest my enemies learn of it, and it be criticised," he cautioned, anxiously.[14] Such tolerance on either side of an argument over religious practice was rare, and even in Duisburg, he sensed, the slightest whiff of doctrinal scandal could be dangerous.

Over time, Mercator's skills were called upon in Duisburg as a surveyor, as an arbitrator in property disputes, and even as a representative of the town on formal occasions and delegations. He was a regular guest at official banquets and other civic occasions of a community that set great store by public service and public events. He began to be known, for all his sobriety, as an entertaining and expansive guest who could be relied on to enliven a late-night table. The town records for 1561 show Mercator presented with "a fine salmon of 35 pounds," presumably as a reward for his services in some semiofficial capacity; in the same year, he was awarded eleven and a half quarts of wine from the city's cellars, with which to welcome a visit from his married daughter Emerance.

IN 1552, HAVING DILIGENTLY fulfilled the order to replace the scientific instruments lost at Ingolstadt, and having moved to Duisburg, Mercator started work on a new imperial commission, a task of such importance and such delicate craftsmanship that Charles V would only entrust it to him. The emperor wanted a pair of globes for his collection—not the usual large instruments, which, placed in a wooden stand, would dominate the library, but a pair of tiny concentric models, terrestrial and celestial, one fitting snugly inside the other.[15]

Walter Ghim almost certainly watched his friend at work on these globes, and later, he described them in admiration. "One [was] of purest blown crystal, and one of wood. On the former, the planets and the more important constellations were engraved with a diamond and inlaid with shining gold; the latter, which was no bigger than the little ball with which boys play in a circle, depicted the world in so far as its small size permitted, in exact detail."[16] Judging from Ghim's description of their size, the world presented on the smaller globe can have been little more than a sketch—certainly not detailed enough for serious study. With their shining gold inlay, they sound more like a rich man's toys than instruments of scientific precision.

Mercator carried the finished globes personally to the emperor in Brussels, so that he could gain the maximum personal advantage from the order. Because Charles was on the move for much of his life, in military campaigns or journeying between the different parts of his empire, he spent little time at his court in Brussels. In normal times that city was a glittering, luxurious place, its mood very different from the restrained atmosphere of Duisburg. The emperor gave lavish banquets and surrounded himself with fine paintings, famous choirs, and magnificent Flemish tapestries. This, though, was a somber occasion: Charles, broken in health and in spirit, was preparing his abdication.

The victories that followed the battle at Ingolstadt in 1546 had proved to be the high point of his military campaigns. In 1552, France declared war on Charles and occupied the ancient cities of Metz, Toul, and Verdun, on the French borders of the empire, and at the same time, the Protestant German princes formed a fresh alliance against him, spurring him back into military action. First, he was forced to flee humiliatingly from Innsbruck by the soldiers of the Protestant prince Maurice of Saxony, who declared derisively that he wanted "to seek an interview with the emperor." Then he gathered his army around the imposing fortifications of Metz, meaning to recapture it by siege from the French. He camped outside the walls with some one hundred thousand men in the middle of a cold November, but this time there was none of the jovial encouragement of his men's morale that had marked his conduct at Ingolstadt six years earlier. His Spanish and Italian troops, huddled miserably in open trenches in the freezing weather, died by the thousands of cold and disease, and on New Year's Day of 1553, he withdrew in confusion. Some thirty thousand of his men had lost their lives, and with them perished not only Charles's hopes of regaining the city of Metz but also any chance of imposing his will on the German princes.

Charles was still only in his early fifties, but he was worn, bent, white-haired, and prematurely aging. The gout that had troubled him for years had left him a virtual cripple, unable to grip with his hands and struggling to mount his horse. In this painful state, with one leg resting on cushions on his saddletree to ease the pain, the mightiest ruler of the world made his halting way across the frozen countryside back toward Brussels. A journey that usually lasted just over a week took him thirty-six days, and he arrived in Brussels early in February 1553. His main interest lay in making arrangements for his retirement to the remote Spanish monastery of San Jeronimo de Yuste in Estremadura. He had been planning this retirement for several years, and with his life there in mind, he had ordered the twin globes from Mercator. The Flemish-born emperor, rejected as a foreigner by the Spanish, the Germans, and the lowlanders as well, would return to Spain, where he spent his remaining years surrounded by his collection of scientific instruments, clocks, watches, maps, and globes.

Upon receipt of the globes, the weary emperor formally installed Mercator with the grandiloquent title of *Imperatoris domesticus* (member of the imperial household), an honor that is proudly listed on his memorial in Duisburg's Salvatorkirche. This final gesture of appreciation came, ironically, just as events were about to make clear how wise Mercator had been to leave Leuven.

Two years later, in the great hall of the castle of Brussels, Charles formally handed over rule of the Netherlands to his son, Philip, and within a few months added his possessions in Spain to the inheritance. When, in 1556, Charles's brother Ferdinand was named as the new Holy Roman Emperor to rule over the German and Austrian possessions, his withdrawal from power was complete—but his legacy to the Netherlands was a terrible one.

Over the coming years, Mercator would hear of the torments of his native land with horror. Between them, Philip and the egregious Granvelle, who slipped smoothly from one master to the next, would turn the country of broad horizons that Mercator remembered from his boyhood into a smoking wasteland.

Chapter Thirteen

Our Europe

CROWDS OF REFUGEES had been leaving Leuven, religious reform-ers and their families fleeing Granvelle's latest purges. Mercator's outspoken friend Jan Vermeulen had left a couple of years earlier, head-ing in abject poverty for Bremen, some 220 miles to the northeast, where his religious views would be more acceptable.[1]

The contrast with Mercator's position was marked. His business was flourishing, and he was enjoying the prosperity it brought him. The small globes he made for Charles V are lost, but other productions of his workshop demonstrate both his obsession with accuracy and the extent of his reputation. A magnificent pair of his globes, prepared as a gift for the Ottoman sultan Murad III, was auctioned in Europe in 1991 for over $1.8 million.* The globes, made in gilt metal and bearing the sultan's of-ficial *tughra* (imperial cipher), were less than twelve inches in diameter, standing in finely carved and precisely matching wooden stands—big-ger, perhaps, than the ones he made for the emperor, but still too small for a serious scholar to use. The terrestrial globe, though, includes all the details of Mercator's own world map, while the celestial one is carefully based on the star map of Nicolaus Copernicus. His reputation rested not

---

*The globes were never delivered to Murad, who had a reputation for indulging his love of beautiful things. One order from his palace in Istanbul was for one hundred thousand tulip bulbs, while others were for clocks and other instruments to add to his magnificent collection. It is not known why he never received Mercator's globes, which remained in the possession of the same family in Germany for some four hundred years.

just on the beauty of his work but on its accuracy as well. For Mercator the perfectionist, scientific instruments had to be finely designed and articles of beauty, while the slightest conversation piece had to be as accurate as his skill and learning could make it. Commercial success and social standing came at a price, however. For more than twelve years, Mercator had produced no new maps.

Before he left Leuven, he had engraved the plates for the first three or four sheets of a great map of Europe that he intended to be the definitive record of the continent. Carefully wrapped in cloth, they had been transported to his workshop in the Oberstrasse, where, soon after arriving in Duisburg, he resumed work on the biggest scheme he had undertaken so far.

He had described his plans to Antoine de Granvelle as early as 1540, with his usual overconfidence about the speed with which he could complete the work: "My next job is to put in order our Europe, and the most part is done, except Spain, but since it is a huge work, it will take much time, at least one year in the fabrication."[2] In fact, the first edition of the map appeared fourteen years after that letter, so clearly "the most part" must have been an optimistic exaggeration. It was planned in fifteen separate sheets, which would eventually be pasted together in three rows of five sheets each, to form a map some 65 inches wide and 52¾ inches high, covering an area that stretched from Iceland in the north to western Morocco and the Nile Delta in the south, and from the Atlantic coastline and the British Isles in the west to the upper Volga and the Syrian desert in the east.

From the start, there had been little doubt that it would sell. Martin Waldseemüller had produced the first map of the whole continent as a woodcut in 1511, and it was still selling well, though much of it had been rendered out-of-date by a great surge in regional mapmaking across the continent. As Mercator set himself to complete his own work, he had four more decades of research by geographers, scholars, and printers on which to draw. Even the work that he had described to Granvelle as finished in 1540 was revised and improved over the years as Mercator gathered new information from other mapmakers, from ancient sources, and from mariners. Where Mercator's map required fifteen sheets to include all the names and other information he had gathered, Waldseemüller's had been completed on just four.

Apart from the many maps of the various regions of Europe, there had been several attempts at a map of the whole continent in the years following Waldseemüller. In 1535, the German cartographer Heinrich Zell had published an eight-sheet woodcut map of Europe with a descriptive commentary, and nine years later, the young French nobleman Nicolas de Nicolay d'Arfeville, court geographer to King Charles IX, produced a map on four sheets that showed Europe and the north African coastline. Both mapmakers were primarily interested in regional cartography—Nicolay later made the first marine chart of the coast of Scotland—and their maps of Europe were highly derivative of Waldseemüller's work. Neither of them attempted the detail with which Mercator filled his map.

The new interest in making local and regional maps had been inspired by the techniques of triangulation and surveying that Mercator's friend and teacher Gemma Frisius had introduced in the early 1530s. Mercator's map of Flanders in 1540 was part of the explosion of cartography across the continent. In Mechelen, Jacob van Deventer produced a series in which he surveyed, measured, and mapped the lowland provinces of Brabant, Holland, Zeeland, and Frisia in intricate detail, while in Paris a mathematics professor, Oronce Finé, had surveyed and mapped the whole of France. The Paris booksellers encouraged a brisk trade in other regional maps by craftsmen such as Jean Jolivet, Jean Chaumeau, and Gabriel Symeone.

The breadth of knowledge of the mapmakers all over Europe was astonishing. They were not only polymaths, but scholars who had the same quality that John Dee had noted in Leuven—the ability to turn their learning to practical effect. One of them, a professor of Hebrew and an amateur mathematician from the Rhineland named Sebastian Münster, had established himself at Basel University in Switzerland as the leading German geographer of his day with an edition of Ptolemy's *Geographia*, supplemented with original maps of European regions. He had worked in the printing industry and published his own works on Hebrew, cosmography, geography, and applied mathematics.

Münster died in 1552, a victim of one of the outbreaks of plague that periodically swept through European cities, but he had maintained a widespread network of correspondents and had appealed to scholars, princes, and burgomasters for descriptions and sketch maps to be incorporated into a detailed study of the region. Much of that legacy of research, surveying, and measurement, incorporated into the 649-page *Cosmographia* that Münster published in 1544, almost certainly found its way to Mercator's desk.

Among the maps on which Münster drew was an anonymous woodcut, produced as early as 1499 to guide pilgrims heading through central Europe on the way to Rome for the papal Holy Year celebrations of 1500—*Das ist der Rom Weg*, as its title explained. Its printer, according to a note below the map, was the Nuremberg illuminator Georg Glockendon—the same artist who painted Martin Behaim's globe—but the map itself is usually ascribed to a craftsman in the same town named Erhard Etzlaub. He was an instrument maker and engraver, like Mercator, and he also produced two compasses with sundials that have maps of Europe, the Mediterranean, and North Africa engraved on them. What is most immediately striking about these apparently crude and simple maps, engraved in 1511 and 1513, is the way they are drawn with south at the top. But for all the roughness of their lines, they were constructed to a revolutionary and deceptively simple design. Etzlaub's lines of latitude were drawn progressively farther apart the farther north they moved.

There is nothing to suggest that Mercator ever saw Etzlaub's maps, let alone modeled his famous projection on them—they were one-of-a-kind metal artifacts, not printed maps, copies of which might have been sent to him—but the interest in regional cartography across Europe did present him with a flood of new information that had to be assimilated into his map of the continent. The development of printing meant that he could pore over many of the maps at his own desk; others were described to him in letters from scholars across the continent. Judging from his letter to Antoine de Granvelle in 1540, he had been studying such maps and reports on and off for more than ten years, first in Leuven and then in Duisburg, his problem as much one of evaluating information as of gathering it.

Often, the new maps were unsatisfactory: Other mapmakers, he grumbled, were less conscientious than he was and ignorantly reproduced the false along with the true. "This is obvious in the maps which have come to us from Italy," he wrote testily to his friend Abraham Ortelius some years later. "The later works are more corrupt than the earlier ones even though they are made by the same author. If one follows this thread, then all of geography must be entangled and obscured in inextricable error."[3] Even accurate descriptions could be corrupted by careless copyists and engravers.

Mercator's own map of Europe finally appeared in 1554. He had kept Antoine de Granvelle informed about its progress from the start, and he dedicated the finished map to him, in return for an honorarium that, says Ghim, amply demonstrated "the magnanimity and exceptional generosity of this magnificent personage."[4] The Baltic area and the far north of Scandinavia were still uncertainly sketched in, but due to the work that had been done by regional mapmakers like Finé, Münster, and their collaborators and correspondents, towns and cities were marked much more accurately, as were the great rivers such as the Rhine, the Danube, the Loire, and the Volga. The entire map was surrounded by a two-inch decorative border of human figures, animals, and mythical beasts, maintaining the medieval tradition of using the map to exemplify the variety of God's Creation.

The printed sheets would leave Mercator's workshop in bundles of fifteen, ready to be pasted together to hang on the wall. Some dealers, like Ortelius, who branched out into selling maps soon after starting work as a colorist and illuminator, would color them by hand for their customers; some would paste them together and sell them as a completed, rolled-up map. However it was offered for sale, the map of Europe was a huge success and continued selling briskly for years. In 1566, for example, Christopher Plantin's records show more than four hundred copies sold from his Antwerp bookshop—nearly half the sales in a single year that Waldseemüller's map had achieved over four decades. Its immediate effect was to reinforce Mercator's position as the unchallenged leader among the geographers and mapmakers of his generation. It was his most important creation so far: From the multiplicity of information on which he had drawn, he had produced a map that showed almost every part of the continent with greater accuracy than had ever been achieved before. For example, Ptolemy had given the length of the Mediterranean Sea as sixty-two degrees, an estimate that Mercator had reduced to fifty-eight degrees on his globe of 1541. On the new map, shifting Cape Finisterre and the adjacent Spanish coast eastward, he reduced it farther to fifty-three degrees—longer than the forty-one degrees shown on modern maps but a considerable improvement.

Still, he was not satisfied. In the legend to the map, he appealed directly to those who bought it to supply him with yet more information, more sketches of particular areas, more mathematical coordinates and estimates of distances between places. He was planning a new world map, he said, and such information would make it more complete and more accurate—but he would also use it in revising and updating the second edition of his map of Europe.

While traveling to the Frankfurt fair in autumn of 1554 to sell his new map, he renewed his acquaintance with Abraham Ortelius, the young map colorist-turned-dealer from Antwerp. Ortelius, fifteen years younger than Mercator, had an even keener eye for a bargain or a business opportunity than he did, as he would show when he produced the world's first atlas some years later. He traveled to fairs in England, France, and Italy to buy and sell maps, and avidly developed friendships with geographers and cartographers who might be useful to him.[5] After their meeting in Frankfurt, he became a close friend and lifelong correspondent of Mercator's.

The work of revision kept the map of Europe on Mercator's desk for nearly twenty years. It seems to have sparked an explosion of the intellectual work that remained closest to his heart, as if the move to Duisburg and the rush of regard and acclamation that greeted the map had released a new flood of energy in his middle age.

In mapping the continent, he was trying to produce a still image of a moving target. The surveying work of the regional cartographers gave him a firm foundation on which to build a map of the settled lands of old Europe, but in the less inhabited areas, the known coastline was changing almost as rapidly as it was in the Americas and the Far East.

While Spanish and Portuguese expeditions were pushing their discoveries farther west and east, the English were dominating the northern seas. Mercator was not satisfied with the maps that were available of the Far North, and he was delighted to advise in the planning of new expeditions in search of a northeastern passage to the Orient.

His old friend and pupil John Dee was instrumental in involving him in this northern campaign, deftly exploiting his ties with Europe's most honored cartographer in his efforts to persuade Queen Elizabeth to back the expeditions from the 1550s onward.* He showed Mercator's maps and quoted his name and reputation to lend powerful support to his arguments. Such involvement, even at a distance, in the arguments of the English court, with its seething religious and political dissent, its spies and informers, would later draw Mercator into danger; but then, he was well satisfied with the new information that filtered back to him from the English expeditions. By the time the second edition of his map was published in 1572, he was able to correct the errors on the northern coastlines that had troubled him before. He redrew the northern extremities of the Scandinavian peninsula and the adjoining White Sea, together with a new legend acknowledging his debt to "the most famous navigation by the Englishmen of the north-east sea." Moscow was moved to a new and more accurate latitude on the fifty-sixth parallel, and the rivers and mountains to the north of the Black Sea were extensively redrawn. In all, six of the fifteen original plates were beaten out, repolished, and newly engraved.

THE LATER HISTORY of Mercator's European map is a somber example of the fragility of large printed maps. It was believed for centuries that all the hundreds of copies of the 1554 edition that were printed,

---

*The first expedition, which left in 1553, aiming to reach Cathay and the Indies by sailing around the north of Russia, ended in disaster, with two of its three ships icebound and stranded off the coast of Lapland. Their crews, more than seventy men, died from scurvy and exposure, while men from a third ship, the *Edward Bonaventure,* had to struggle overland to seek help at the court of the Russian tsar Ivan the Terrible in Moscow. A second attempt to find a northeast passage in 1556 also ended in failure but established a profitable trading route to Russia through the White Sea.

many of them colored, varnished, and hung in noble houses, church buildings, and other public places, had been either lost or destroyed. The map survived only in references by other contemporary geographers and in the writings of Walter Ghim, who said that it "attracted more praise from scholars everywhere than any similar geographical work which has ever been brought out."[6] Then, toward the end of the nineteenth century, a student in Breslau municipal library, then in Germany and now in Poland, found a torn and crumpled document filed away in the archives: A single copy of Mercator's great work had survived.[7]

That precious map vanished, probably forever, in the confusion of 1945, another victim of World War II. It had been meticulously reproduced, but experts assumed that there would never be more than a modern copy of Mercator's map to be seen—until 1967, when a Dutch schoolmaster was thumbing through collections of prints in a Brussels shop, looking for views of old Amsterdam. Among the assorted boxes of photographs and tattered cardboard and paper sheets was a book of some fifty maps, about 16½ inches tall and 11½ inches wide, torn and frayed around the edges, which had apparently been rebound, recolored, and occasionally "improved" by an eighteenth-century Cistercian monk, who had written his name on the first page.

Today, the book is one of the most treasured possessions of London's British Library.* Handwriting experts confirmed that the pen strokes and flourishes were identical with the style of Mercator's own handbook on italic writing. Further detailed study showed that two of the maps, showing Tyrol and Lombardy, had been drawn and annotated by Mercator himself—the only manuscript maps by him that are known to have survived—and that the rest of the book had been produced by cutting sections from several prints of his wall map of Europe. Mercator's lost work, or almost all of it, had been rediscovered for a second time.

One theory is that the book was compiled for the use of Duke William's gifted eldest son, Karl Friedrich, who set out on a tour of Italy in the 1570s, shortly before his death from smallpox at the age of eight-

*The library invested $1.2 million in buying the book at auction from a private collection in 1997.

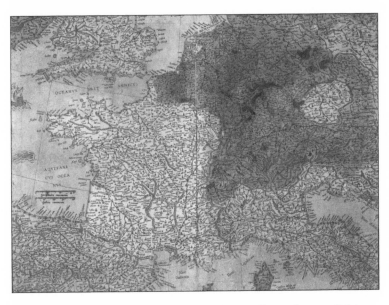

A section from Mercator's 1554 map of Europe, featuring France, Germany, Belgium, and the Netherlands, as well as parts of England, Spain, and Italy

een. In view of Mercator's dismissive criticisms of the work of Italian cartographers, it is significant that the two manuscript maps of Tyrol and Lombardy, drawn by Mercator himself, cover some of the areas of northern Italy where the boy was to travel. Making up the patchwork atlas would have been a relatively quick and easy way of maintaining contact with the ducal court—Mercator was always alive to such commercial opportunities—which might also be a source of geographic information. Duke William's chief magistrate, the strongly Catholic Werner von Gymnich, was traveling with Karl Friedrich, and Mercator wrote to him later asking for information about the journey to be incorporated into his later maps.

The original printed map of Europe was cut into sections and bound to form the book, so it is impossible to see the full sweep of the design as

Mercator intended.* Two soft, curling sheets of gray cardboard are all that are left of the original covers, with one remaining scrap of leather still clinging precariously to them; paper strips hold the boards together in place of a spine. Inside, some of the pages are patched and mended, and the ancient pasting that holds others together in a delicate jigsaw of paper fragments is starting to come away. Carefully propped on a lectern now, it has none of the grandeur of a finely balanced globe; there is no feeling of wonder as there might be in touching the delicate brass machinery of an astronomical instrument, no sense of sheer imposing size as there would be with a wall map. It is impossible even to be sure that it was Mercator himself, rather than some assistant in the workshop, who cut and pasted the original map to make the book. And yet it is hard not to be awed by the thought that Mercator's own hand once drew the two manuscript maps of Lombardy and Tyrol that are among its pages, and that the "lost" map of Europe has survived.

*In the library now, the book is carefully preserved inside a sturdy modern slipcase and is jealously guarded—a note in capitals inside the case warns that it "must not be issued without the permission of the reading room supervisor, and then it should only be issued under very close supervision"—but for all the attentions of its eighteenth-century restorer, and for all the care of the library authorities today, it seems somehow an incomplete memorial to the great cartographer.

A Mysterious Commission

I N BREMEN, Jan Vermeulen's school was struggling. By the summer of 1559, there were only twenty pupils at the desks, and the death of his wife meant that he had to cope with all the tasks of running the school alone. Mercator saw an opportunity to bring his old friend to Duisburg to join him.

That same year, a group of leading citizens had set out proposals for a new preparatory school—in theory at least, a first step toward setting up the ill-starred university, and a source of students for it once it opened. Mercator was called on to draw up the curriculum and study-plans, and to offer lectures in mathematics to the most talented pupils. There was no need for papal approval for such a venture, and on Wednesdays and Saturdays at 9 AM, Gerard Mercator the cosmographer, the internationally known cartographer, and the civic dignitary became once more Mercator the pedagogue, with students sitting around him in Duisburg's old market hall as he returned to the teaching life he had last tried at Leuven twenty years before. Among his pupils was Johannes Corputius, who would later use the mathematical skills Mercator taught him in constructing his famous bird's-eye panorama of Duisburg.

Judging from his attitude toward his sons' education, he would have been a hard master, as ready as the teachers of his own youth had been to resort to beating his pupils to impress his lessons upon them. In his teaching, as in his studies, he was painstaking, thorough, and intense— qualities that may have been less appealing to the boys than they were to their parents. He demanded much from his young charges, as is shown by his response to an invitation toward the end of his life to take over the education of a young boy from Zurich. Writing to the boy's father,[1] the Protestant pastor Wolfgang Haller, he recommended a program of lessons based on his own methodical studies of Euclid, working painstakingly through to the detailed study of the classical geographers.

Vermeulen was the ideal choice as rector, and soon after the school opened, Mercator used his influence to persuade his friend to join him in Duisburg. He was, as Vermeulen put it in a letter, "honouring an old friend with a position of standing,"[2] but he was also recruiting a teacher whose high standards matched his own. Vermeulen's reputation—not least with Mercator's own two younger sons, who had spent time in the school at Bremen—was that of a harsh disciplinarian whose lessons were punctuated with strict physical discipline. His indignant reply to a letter from Bartholomew complaining about his time as a pupil inadvertently gives a vivid picture of life in one of Vermeulen's classes.

"What are those 'blows of students' which you mention? What 'whippings'? What 'sticks'? What 'harsh slavery' does your mind imagine?" he demands.[3] Bartholomew's original letter is lost, but the message of Vermeulen's denials is clear enough—although grumbles about strict discipline did nothing to damage his standing in Mercator's eyes. Vermeulen recognized that the main interest of the city authorities was that he should be "intent on his teaching, and not troublesome in matters of religion."[4] They had clearly heard of his outspoken rigor in the cause of Church reform, but Mercator's recommendation was enough to ease their anxieties. A little later, he showed his regard for the widowed Vermeulen in the most convincing way possible: A few months after the schoolmaster's arrival in Duisburg, the town's municipal accounts recorded a gift of sixteen quarts of wine to celebrate his wedding to Mercator's daughter Emerance.

Mercator's involvement with the school lasted only three years, and in 1562, he handed over his duties to Bartholomew. His cartographic studies were taking up more of his time: The revisions of the map of Europe were a constant anxiety, and the success of the map had brought more commissions. Mercator was already known across Europe and in particular, thanks largely to the efforts of John Dee, in the court of

Queen Elizabeth of England. He had never crossed the English Channel, but Dee, who had provided maps and advice on navigational techniques for expeditions to the Far North since the first attempt in 1553, quoted his name and his opinions frequently in pressing the case for northern exploration. The new map of Europe and Dee's recommendations reinforced his fame among sailors, explorers, philosophers, and mapmakers in England. Together, they were at least partly responsible for the arrival on his desk in the early 1560s of a mysterious new map that threatened to draw him into the fringes of the Tudors' world of secrecy and intrigue.

Even in the security of his home in the Oberstrasse, Mercator was almost obsessively cautious in his dealings with authorities and always anxious not to make enemies. Just as he never spoke about his fearful time in Rupelmonde Fort, so he never mentioned this map and its clandestine connection with English politics. There are no names, and no firm dates;[5] it is only possible to piece the story together by deduction and guesswork from scraps of evidence, hints, and account books.

The traveler who arrived at Mercator's workshop in Duisburg was expected, for he carried a precious package with him that would not have been allowed out of its owner's hands unless the project and its price had been agreed in advance. Like John Dee, who had made the trip from Cambridge to Leuven about fifteen years before, he had traveled for several days over rough and unmade roads on the grueling journey from England, but the name of the town he started from, the route he took from the Channel to the Rhine, who he was, and who had sent him will never be known.

This was a straightforward commission, although one of a type that Mercator had never accepted before. The traveler brought with him a map, already researched, drawn, and finished, from which he wanted a copper printing plate prepared. There was no doubting the need for a new map of the British Isles and, on the face of it, nothing more natural than that Europe's leading cartographer and engraver should be asked to produce it. However, researching it, designing it, comparing one record with another, obtaining measurements and coordinates as he had done so successfully in the map of Europe, were not part of the commission. Mercator was simply to engrave a plate of a map drawn by somebody else.

That sort of work was common enough for most of his contemporaries, but Mercator always prided himself on his skill as an original cartographer as well as an engraver. This was, in any case, different from the usual printing commissions. From a cartographical point of view, it was exciting enough—a highly detailed map of Britain of a quality that had never been seen before, and a piece of work that a dedicated mapmaker like Mercator would appreciate—but politically, it brought with it the smell of the execution fires. If such a map had fallen into the wrong hands in England, it would have been enough to send its author, its owner, even the man who carried it, to the gibbet.

The early years of Queen Elizabeth's reign were tense and apprehensive. In 1561, the new queen had been on her throne for barely three years. She had inherited the crown from her half sister, Mary, replacing the latter's fervent Catholicism with a strongly nationalistic Protestantism, and ending the hopes of the Spanish that Mary's marriage to King Philip of Spain might win England back to the true faith without a fight. Tudor England was agog with talk of Catholic plots and Romish priests slipping secretly from country house to country house.

To the north, the government of the young Mary, Queen of Scots, had called in French troops in an attempt to stave off a Protestant uprising, and looking south, years of tension with France had exploded into open warfare, with English soldiers fighting on behalf of Protestant rebels in Normandy. Catholic France and Spain were unpredictable enemies; England was on tenterhooks, waiting to be invaded.

If these were not normal times, this was not a normal map either. Most of the work in preparing it was evidently done during the early years of Queen Mary's Catholic regime, and it showed a country that was apparently loyal to the Catholic Church. New bishoprics, which had been established by Henry VIII in defiance of the pope, and which Catholics at the start of Mary's reign had hoped might be abolished, were not shown on the map at all. Many Catholic monastic establishments were marked; so too were the areas controlled by Scottish and Irish Catholic clans. At best, the image of Britain that it presented would not have found favor in

Queen Elizabeth's court; at worst, it was a map designed for an invading army.

When Queen Elizabeth had come to the throne in 1558, she inherited a debt-ridden country, and her "navy" consisted of just twenty-two usable vessels. The continuing sense of military tension in England as much as a simple lack of skilled engravers had prevented the printing of new maps. For more than fifty years, successive governments since Henry VIII in 1509 had been aware of the use invaders could make of reliable maps of the country, and had been determined to take control of any cartographical work that went on. Detailed maps would show a potential invader not just possible landing grounds and routes across the country but also the exact places where they might find Catholic allies. The great flowering of new cartography in the mid–sixteenth century never reached England. It had been one of the best-mapped countries in Europe in the Middle Ages, but there had been no maps published there since the introduction of printing, and no globes constructed.[6]

Mercator never revealed the name of the man who had asked him to engrave the map—he had been supplied with the drawing by "an English friend," he said—or that of its original creator. There are some clues: One convincing suggestion* is that the map might have been the work of a Scottish priest, John Elder, who had close connections with leaders of the French Catholics, particularly the cardinal of Lorraine, uncle of Mary, Queen of Scots. Elder was also a confidant of the close-knit and subversive circle of exiled English Catholics—although he himself was no longer in exile. He had returned to England late in 1561, first promising Elizabeth's secretary of state, Sir William Cecil, that he could be of service and then secretly offering his loyalty to the Scottish queen.

Elder was a spy, a double agent—"as dangerous for the matters of England," said Sir Nicholas Throckmorton, Elizabeth's trusted ambassador in France, as anyone he knew[7]—and a man with a network of alliances among English, French, and Spanish Catholics. Cecil

*Made by Peter Barber, map librarian at the British Library, in *The Mercator Atlas of Europe,* ed. M. Watelet (Pleasant Hill, Oregon: Walking Tree Press, 1998), and in conversation with the author.

himself was warned by one of his many informants that Elder had "the wit to play the spy when he list"[8]—surely a masterpiece of understatement. He was, at the very least, under the close eye of the authorities, and a risky man with whom to have dealings. It is possible that Mercator himself never knew who had compiled the map—even more likely that he did not want to know—but if he did, such a tangle of secret loyalties and deceptions would have been a powerful reason to keep quiet.

Despite Mercator's lifelong silence about the project, Christopher Plantin's order-book in Antwerp tells an interesting story. Over the next twelve years, he sold ninety copies of the map of the British Isles—forty of them in Paris, and more to Spanish officials and their friends on the European mainland. Several went to the Jesuit Douai College, which was closely associated with the Catholic seminary that smuggled priests into England.

The map itself would have tempted Mercator to become involved, despite its lack of a grid of latitude and longitude and its occasionally distorted coastline. It gave him names, locations, and other details about the British Isles that he would later incorporate into his own work, and that he could not have found elsewhere. At about 35½ inches by 50½ inches, it was the largest and most detailed printed map of the country to have been produced, and it had some 2,500 names marked on it. Nevertheless, Mercator took pains, in the legend he wrote and printed on it, to deny any responsibility for its content: "A certain friend offered me this depiction of the British Isles. I present it to you just as it was brought to me."

Duisburg was a long way from England, but if the map had seriously worried Sir William Cecil and Elizabeth's agents, they could certainly have reached Mercator to do him harm there. Years earlier, he had faced imprisonment and possible execution by the Catholic authorities as a dangerous reformist; by accepting the unorthodox commission, he found himself involved in Catholic intrigues against a Protestant ruler. He had shown before, in the alacrity with which he supplied surveying instruments to Charles V, that his own religious and political feelings would not stand in the way of commercial profit, and with the English map he demonstrated that geographic information, the indispensable raw material of his mapmaking, could also tempt him into dangerous areas.

DEE'S ENTHUSIASTIC PROMOTION of Mercator's name at court was part of a determined effort to encourage exploration in the Far North. This effort to find a new passage to the Orient, either to the northwest or the northeast, was the focus of English attempts to gain a share of the profits to be made from exploration and discovery for most of the sixteenth century. It was the result of years of frustrated ambition dating back almost to Columbus's first voyage of 1492.

A year after Columbus's first landfall, the Spanish cleric Rodrigo Borgia sought to bring order to the changing map of the world. But where Mercator, decades later, strove to do so through years of dedicated scholarship, Borgia acted with a single stroke of his pen. It was an act of monumental arrogance, even for a man who had bribed and maneuvered his way through the Catholic Church with a silky determination that had brought him honors and unimaginable wealth. His ecclesiastical career, like that of Antoine de Granvelle in the Low Countries, had also brought him a new name—but whereas Granvelle had to be content with a cardinal's hat, Rodrigo had won the ultimate prize and became God's vicar on Earth, Pope Alexander VI.

He had been proclaimed pope in August 1492, while Columbus's ships were still battling through the Atlantic, and within months of his election he drew a line around the globe to share it between Europe's great maritime powers, Spain and Portugal. The world he divided was barely understood—it still seemed likely that Columbus had reached Asia rather than discovered a new continent—but Pope Alexander's line circled it with brash confidence. It ran due north and south a hundred leagues to the west of the Cape Verde Islands,[9] giving all the newly discovered lands to the east of the line to Portugal and those to the west to his native Spain. However, instead of settling a dispute, the division of the globe started years of skirmishing and bitterness.

Pope Alexander appeared to have merely formalized an arrangement that already existed in practice. Columbus's voyage had established the interest of his Spanish sponsors in routes to the west, and Portugal's well-defended control of the seas that led to the Spice Islands in the East appeared unchallengeable. At least that was the theory. But as there was no reliable way to fix a line of longitude, there were constant quarrels between the two nations about where the line on the map actually fell across the globe.

By the time Charles V inherited the Spanish throne in 1517, there was growing dissent, too, from the nations who had missed out in the pope's arbitrary division of the spoils of exploration. Francis I of France, who had been Charles's rival for the imperial crown and whose constant wars against him brought both leaders to the brink of bankruptcy, declared sarcastically, "I should very much like to see the passage in Adam's will that divides the New World between my brothers Charles V and the King of Portugal."[10] In England, the serpentine Sir William Cecil was uncharacteristically blunt when he later told the Spanish ambassador to London, "The Pope has no right to parcel out the world, and give and take lands to whomsoever he pleases."[11] Elizabeth's privateers made the point more forcibly by unofficially plundering Spain's ships and settlements in the Americas, and even made their own voyages through the Portuguese East. But for all the skirmishing and bad-tempered diplomacy about trade, the fact remained that the Spanish and Portuguese had got there first.

For the English, the only way was north. If they wanted a share in the apparently limitless wealth to be gained through trade with Cathay, they had to find their own way there. The English diplomat Robert Thorne, who was living in Seville and had already invested in Spanish expeditions to the Americas, wrote to Henry VIII as early as 1527, summing up the general sense of frustration. To east and west, there seemed to be simply nothing left to find. "There is one way to discover, which is to the North. For out of Spain they have discovered all the Indies and seas occidental, and out of Portugal all the Indies and seas oriental," he told the king.[12]

Where that "one way" north to the Indies would be discovered, whether to west or east, was bitterly disputed by merchants, scholars, and sailors, but the incentive was clear. A new route to the Indies would revolutionize the trade routes of Europe as surely as Vasco da Gama's voyage to India had done. If English seamen could reach the East by sailing around the north of either America or Russia—a much shorter route than the Spanish and Portuguese took to the south—they might challenge their trading rivals on their own terms.

That determination faltered as the Muscovy Trading Company, set up to mount fresh expeditions, turned its attention to building profitable trading links with Ivan the Terrible in northern Russia, from where ships brought back furs, ropes, fish, and timber for Elizabeth's growing fleet. During the 1560s, there were bitter theoretical arguments at the court over whether the northeastern or the northwestern route offered the best chance of success, but no more expeditions.

Mercator's world map of 1538, still the most authoritative view of the world available, showed chains of mountains blocking any sea route around northern Russia to the Mare glaciale and the so-called Eastern Indian Ocean, while to the northwest, he marked a passage[13] running temptingly through to the uncharted western coast of the Americas and thence to the Indies. There were old stories of Indians blown onto the coast of Europe, presumably driven from Cathay through a northwest sea passage.

The early expeditions of 1553 and 1556 had concentrated on finding the northeast passage despite Mercator's map. There were stories to support that possibility too, eagerly seized on by its proponents: The horn of a unicorn, an animal well known to thrive in Cathay, had been found on the shores of the Barents Sea north of Russia. How else could it have got there, other than by floating down the clear waters of a northeastern passage? And where the horn of a unicorn could go, a well-equipped merchant ship could surely follow.*

For Mercator, the expeditions were the first of a series of disappoint-

---

*Today, with no unicorns found in Cathay or anywhere else, it seems more likely that the fabulous "horn" would have been the spiral tusk of a narwhal—impressive, perhaps, but no sign of a seaway through the East—but that piece of evidence carried great weight for a while among the acriminous exchanges in the English court.

ments that were to blight the final decades of his life. They started in excitement and optimism. The geography of the Far North was one of the most frustrating uncertainties of the age, and around the North Pole itself, there was an infuriating mixture of myth, rumor, and ancient stories; a passage to either the northwest or the northeast would have settled once and for all one of the remaining mysteries of geography. Mercator died still believing that one would eventually be found. But for all the amendments the reports of the explorers enabled him to make to the detailed depiction of northern Scandinavia and Russia on his map of Europe, the big questions about the form of the North Pole and the coastlines of northern Russia and America still remained unanswered.

Those first explorers also focused attention on the problem Mercator had already faced in his first world map: the contrast between the curve of the Earth and the flatness of the map. The simplistic projection of the maps they used meant they were virtually useless. Each line of latitude was a circle divided into 360 degrees of longitude, but the closer it was to the Pole, the smaller was its circumference, so that each degree represented a shorter distance to be sailed. The sailors knew that, since lines of longitude converge on the poles, the value of each degree of longitude would change the farther north they went, but they had no way of calculating exactly how great that change would be—and traditional maps ignored it completely.

It was almost impossible for a navigator either to calculate his position precisely or to map the complex network of islands, inlets, and peninsulas through which the expeditions had to thread their way. When the stranded ships of the first major expedition to the Northeast in 1553 were found by Russian fishermen a year later, the written log of the dead captain was recovered. One entry described how they sighted a deserted coastline and fixed its location: "This land lyeth from Seynam east and by north 160 leagues, being in latitude 72 degrees." But for all the navigator's attempts to leave some record of his achievement, the details were too inaccurate for later travelers to be sure exactly where the observations had been taken.

Over all the expeditions loomed the unanswerable problem of projection. For all their bravery, the mariners lacked the means to navigate their vessels with any certainty or to record the discoveries they made. Neither courage nor seamanship could solve the problem—but mathematics might.

Chapter Fifteen

In the Forests of Lorraine

IN THE EARLY 1550S, as the English were starting to extend their influence into the far northern seas, King Henry II of France suddenly pushed his power to the east, seizing the bishoprics of Metz, Toul, and Verdun from the duke of Lorraine. This was the invasion that prompted Charles V to lay siege to Metz, and which led to his debacle before the city walls, his retreat to Brussels, and his abdication—but at the same time, it showed Duke Charles of Lorraine that he was faced on both sides by overwhelming power.

His dukedom was a magnificent and gilded trap. The lands that he assumed on the death of his father in 1544 were sandwiched between the borders of the kingdom of France to the west and the Holy Roman Empire to the east, putting him in the position that any leader dreads—caught in the middle, between two powerful enemies. He was the son-in-law of King Henry and related on his mother's side to the emperor Charles V,[1] but with the two great powers sporadically at war throughout his reign, there was no security in family connections. His lands were part of the "Spanish road," the crucial supply line through which Charles could move troops from his Italian possessions to Germany and the Low Countries—a route of march that caused perennial consternation among the French as large bodies of well-armed and disciplined soldiers marched along their borders. Only through astute diplomacy backed by military strength could Lorraine hope to maintain its independence of either side, and Duke Charles's policy was to talk peace and prepare for war.

The dukes of Lorraine had always had sharp teeth in the face of attack—it was at the walls of their ancient capital of Nancy that Charles the Bold, one of the ambitious dukes of Burgundy, had fallen in 1477—but Duke Charles's response in the years following the French attack in 1552 was particularly imaginative and determined. Antonio de Bergamo, one of the finest Italian specialists in military design, was brought in to rebuild Nancy as an impregnable stronghold; the mines and salt pits that produced the duke's revenues were reorganized to make them more profitable; a single system of weights and measures was introduced to encourage trade; and strict new laws were enforced against the vagabonds, footpads, and unemployed mercenary soldiers who infested the roads. And Duke Charles commissioned a map of his lands.

Such a new map would be of immense military value in organizing the defenses of the dukedom, and it would be important in encouraging efficient administration—but it would also be a powerful statement of the independence of Lorraine. The Italians were known throughout Europe as the finest military architects, and in Antonio de Bergamo Charles had commissioned the most famous of them. In the same way, he looked for an expert to make a complete and original survey of his dukedom, using Gemma's methods of triangulation.

The request was made formally early in 1564 through Duke William, at whose court Mercator was official cosmographer, but by the time it reached Mercator himself, it was more an order than an invitation. Duke Charles had asked for him by name, Duke William had agreed to the request, and the project was so wide-ranging and of such importance that it required Mercator's personal attention. He had already carried out numerous small-scale surveys for private commissions in Duisburg and had surveyed much of Flanders for his map of 1539, and he attacked this fresh challenge with the vigor and physical determination of a man in his twenties. It tested his mastery of every aspect of his craft, from surveying to designing and drawing. The project became one of the longest and most taxing of Mercator's career, and it almost killed him.

Mercator's sons, Arnold, Bartholomew, and Rumold, were all in their twenties, helping him in his workshop and developing their own skills.

Bartholomew, at twenty-four, had already taken over many of his teaching duties at Duke William's preparatory school and with his father's patient instruction had become proficient with Gemma's *planimetrum*. Mercator therefore brought him to Lorraine, and they spent long months in the field, crisscrossing the dukedom with their imaginary triangles. It was an extremely challenging task: Lorraine stretched for more than 250 miles southward toward the towering barrier of the Vosges Mountains, with little-used tracks that suddenly plunged into dark valleys, and endless hillsides of barely penetrable forest. Gemma had developed his method of surveying by casting imaginary triangles for miles across the long, flat horizons of Flanders; in Lorraine, Mercator and Bartholomew had to work piecemeal, moving slowly from hill to hill and from village to village.

There were some existing documents on which Mercator could draw—Martin Waldseemüller, who came from the town of St. Dié, in Lorraine's southern Rhineland, where there had been a flourishing tradition of local cartography, had presented Duke Charles's grandfather with a map of his lands some fifty years before—but Mercator and his son carried out the most detailed survey of the dukedom that had ever been made. Mercator's practical skill as a surveyor is one of the traits that marked him out from other cartographers who were working at the same time, and he took his own measurements whenever he could, a grueling and physically demanding operation.

Exactly what happened to Mercator in Lorraine is uncertain. From the sketchy account Walter Ghim gave, it appears to have been another crisis about which Mercator himself wanted to say very little later in his life. "The journey through Lorraine gravely imperilled his life, and so weakened him that he came very near to a serious breakdown and mental derangement as a result of his terrifying experiences," Ghim wrote.[2] His frustratingly coy account is the only record. Some later writers have put forward a theory that Mercator may have been attacked by one of the many armed gangs of robbers that infested the forests of Lorraine, but this does not seem to be borne out by Ghim's words. Ghim said he was weakened by the journey—a phrase that suggests exhaustion rather than any robbery. The most likely explanation of Mercator's collapse is that he simply succumbed to the physical and mental pressure of a cripplingly onerous task.

Whatever the cause of Mercator's illness, it forced him to return to Duisburg and take to his bed for several months, and the duke's commission had to wait. Although Ghim says that from his first arrival in Duisburg his friend always "took the greatest care of his health,"[3] after the crisis of Lorraine Mercator started to mention bouts of illness in his own letters.

Of the map itself, nothing remains, apart from copies published many years later in Mercator's atlas, but he was evidently proud of his work and anxious to gain the maximum credit for it. Working from the observations he had completed, and from other readings taken by Bartholomew after he had returned home, he prepared "an exact pen-drawing."[4] Just as he had taken care whenever he could to present his commissions to Emperor Charles V in person at his court in Brussels, so, still weak from his illness, he set out for Duke Charles's palace in Nancy and delivered the map in October 1564.

Charles was duly grateful, though he never published Mercator's map. Lorraine, no less than Tudor England, was in constant danger of attack from outside, and the same considerations of security that made mapmaking such a sensitive operation for England's Queen Elizabeth were doubly applicable to a ruler in the delicate position of Duke Charles. Few items were more valuable to an invader than a detailed map; the information on this map could have affected the very survival of the dukedom. Such knowledge was a rare commodity in the sixteenth century, and the map stayed locked in the duke's library, where he could consult it, but where it would be safe from any potential enemies.

DESPITE THE HEALTH CRISIS precipitated by his trip to Lorraine, Mercator continued to travel far afield, marketing his globes and instruments. He remained a regular visitor to the trade fairs in the various German cities, where he met scholars and merchants who would sell his instruments, and especially to the book fair in Frankfurt.

The annual Frankfurt fair dates back at least to the twelfth century. For hundreds of years, apart from silks, wines, jewels, fine carvings, and other luxury items, there had been manuscripts for sale from monks who had traveled across Europe with their wares. From the moment the clanging bell at the fairground announced the start of trading, merchants were free to move about and trade as they wished. The city was also one of the main centers of the new printing trade in Germany, and by the end of the fifteenth century, so many booksellers were coming that an area close to the River Main became known as the Buchgasse, or Book Alley. By Mercator's time, it was firmly established as a separate book fair and provided fertile ground for finding new customers for his maps and globes—part of a network of trade that stretched across the continent and beyond.

Travel, though, was both wearying and dangerous. It was often difficult to tell the difference between gangs of bandits and the groups of unpaid and undisciplined soldiers and mercenaries who wandered the countryside. As a result, one of Christopher Plantin's agents, who had been seized by robbers as he traveled from Brussels to Namur, had a clause written into his contract requiring the bookseller to cover half the cost of any ransom demand. Merchants gathered in groups for protection, often with armed guards provided by the civic authorities for at least part of the way, but the risks and the hardships remained.

Mercator would have traveled either by horse-drawn wagon, with books, maps, globes, and other goods for the fair packed into barrels, or on board one of the creaking barges that plied regularly up the Rhine to Cologne and on to Frankfurt. At times, the fighting between the Spanish and Italian troops of King Philip and the rebels of the Low Countries made travel across country almost impossible. For example, in 1585, with Antwerp besieged by the Spanish, Plantin traveled with Ortelius from Amsterdam to Hamburg by sea, on to Frankfurt by stagecoach, and then back downriver to Cologne. It was a round-trip of about a thousand miles, either over unmade roads or on the bare boards of a Rhine barge, encumbered with barrels and boxes of merchandise, and under the constant threat of robbery.

There are no such detailed accounts of Mercator's traveling, but one small reference not only demonstrates how far he journeyed but also suggests that his expeditions were not all business and sober study. In 1560,

Europe's leading cartographer was in the town of Poitiers, in western France—"a town of priests and monks," one later traveler[5] said dismissively. However, it also had a flourishing printing industry, it boasted a university that had been established a century and a half before to rival the one in Paris, and it hosted the annual Fair of St. Luke—three good commercial reasons for Mercator to have made the six-hundred-mile journey. In addition, about half a mile outside the town stood the famous Pierre Levée, the Raised Stone, an ancient monument that was casually referred to as a Druids' stone or a Celtic antiquity. Today, the town has engulfed it, but the huge flat stone on five massive legs of rock—the word *dolmen* comes from the Breton for "stone table"—was there long before Poitiers, the Druids, or the Celts. Modern estimates suggest that the "tabletop," some twenty-two feet long by sixteen feet across, was maneuvered into position on its six-foot legs of rock more than three thousand years before Mercator's day, making it more or less contemporary with Stonehenge in England. Its original religious or ceremonial purpose is a mystery, but by the sixteenth century it had become not only the center of St. Luke's fair but also a rendezvous for townsmen and scholars from the university.

Around the time of Mercator's visit, a local writer described how people, "when they have nothing else to do, pass the time by climbing up onto the stone and banqueting there with large quantities of bottles, hams, and pastries, and inscribing their names in the capstone with a knife."[6] Mercator was traveling with three friends and professional colleagues, the cartographer Abraham Ortelius, the engraver Frans Hogenberg, who would later produce most of the maps in Ortelius's atlas, and his friend Filips Galle, another map engraver and publisher. Apparently, they left their inscriptions on the rock like hundreds of others, before and since. Hogenberg later collaborated with the book designer Georges Braun to produce a best-selling compendium of panoramas and sketches of European towns, the *Theatrum Urbium*—and in that book, on a sketch of the rock, appear the four names, with the date beside them, though no trace of the inscriptions survives today.[7] For all Walter Ghim's remarks about his hospitality and good humor, the picture of Mercator that emerges from his letters, from official documents, and from other descriptions is one of almost unleavened seriousness; the Pierre Levée incident presents a fleeting glimpse of a different, more relaxed character.

FOLLOWING HIS INTENSIVE WORK on the maps of Europe and Britain, and his surveying project in the forests of Lorraine, Mercator began to turn his attention to the skies, watching and predicting the movements and eclipses of stars and planets like many of his contemporaries. The first telescopes would not be devised for a good half century, but astronomy had a long history as a pastime for scholars, philosophers, and especially geographers.

The early geographers had developed their theories about the form and structure of the Earth from observations and measurements of the stars. The imaginary triangles with which Mercator surveyed the Earth could be constructed in the heavens as well. His earlier studies in Leuven had been based mainly on his readings of Ptolemy's words and his understanding of the new researches of Copernicus and other modern astronomers, but in the 1560s he began his own careful, systematic watching of the skies.

Perhaps Mercator built his own observatory in the house in the Oberstrasse, for his notebooks record an eclipse of the Sun in April 1564 and one of the Moon in October two years later. There was a religious motive in his work, as there was in his studies of cosmography, a feeling that gaining understanding of the workings of the universe was one way of paying homage to the great mystery of Creation, but plotting the movement of the planets was a challenge, an intellectual game as well as an act of religious piety. "How I delighted in making early predictions of the eclipses of the sun and the moon," he reminisced as an old man.[8]

In the sixteenth century there was little distinction between astronomy, the study of the stars and the planets, and astrology, the study of their supposed influence on life on Earth. Some of the most famous names of the century were involved in astrological predictions and interpretations. Copernicus himself learned mathematics and astronomy in preparation for the use of astrological charts in his medical career, and in England John Dee was a devoted adherent of astrology. He created several detailed birth charts, including one that plotted the positions of the planets at the time of his own birth. The charges of witchcraft and conjuring that led to his imprisonment under the Catholic queen Mary were based on allegations that he had drawn up similar horoscopes for the queen, her husband, Philip of Spain, and her sister, the future Elizabeth I.

Even the popes had relied on the interpreters of the stars for generations, and astrology remained for many people a respectable and trusted science. Yet to Mercator, astrology and the occult were nonsense and blasphemy. "They misunderstand the entire celestial system," he wrote of astrologers. "The purpose for which the lights of the sky are created is much greater than mere astrological prediction—it is to reveal to mankind the almighty power, the majesty, and the divinity of their Creator, not to be at the service of the vanity of the astrologers."[9]

Mercator rarely expressed his feelings so forcefully; even so, this was still not a modern response. Mercator asked the medieval question "Why?" rather than the modern scientific question "How?" and answered it with a conventional reliance on the might and majesty of God. He remained, to that extent at least, consistent with his age: In the sixteenth century, the word *science* carried none of its modern implications of dispassionate, empirical objectivity. On the other hand, his dismissal of astrology as superstition and vanity was the attitude of an individual thinker; in an age before science, Mercator's instincts were those of a scientist, not a magician.

Chapter Sixteen

Tragedy

E ARLY IN MAY 1563, just as he was about to start on what would be the busiest period of his life, a sinister incident had occurred that would cast a shadow over Mercator for years to come. In his garden one morning, he found an unsigned letter, apparently thrown over the wall from the Oberstrasse, that threatened to shatter the comfortable respectability he had established for himself in the town. Exactly what it accused him of is now as uncertain as the name of his secret tormentor. The only surviving account is simply that it said he was "addicted to the most shameful practices,"[1] had published libels and satires about various important personages in the duchy, and had committed other, unspecified crimes.

He might have shrugged off a single note to himself as the work of some jealous enemy, but he found to his horror that a series of similar messages had gone to leading figures in Duisburg and elsewhere in the duchy. The precise charges are unlikely to have had any justification; for all Walter Ghim's enthusiasm about his friend's geniality, Mercator's surviving writings—letters and poems as well as his books and prefaces—are devoid of any sense of humor, let alone satire. In any case, it seems barely credible that a man so single-minded in his pursuit of the good opinion of the wealthy and influential should have put his position at risk by spreading gossip about them. He habitually larded his correspondence with such phrases as: "I will be eager to be worthy of the benefits granted to my work by your Roman Majesty"; "I congratulate myself that I have been considered worthy of [your] friendship"; and "I wished to gratify your Illustrious Majesty by first sharing this work with you and showing my eagerness to honour you." These are the words of a man whose fault, if he had one, was sycophancy, not disrespect.

However, the passion with which he responded to the letters showed how seriously he took this unexpected attack. He immediately visited Duke William to plead his innocence of the allegations and to press for an investigation into them. They would have been brought to the ducal court in any case, but Mercator judged it better to confront them and declare his loyalty in person, rather than allow them to go unchallenged.

In many other cities, Mercator might have faced sudden arrest, imprisonment, even execution after such an anonymous letter to the authorities. The secret denunciation, so popular with the Inquisition, had long been a favorite tool of both envious individuals and repressive governments. In Venice, for example, it had been formalized as a tool of state security, with confidential public letterboxes shaped like lions' mouths set into the walls of the streets for informants to drop in their unsigned accusations. Duisburg was not Venice, but at the very least a scandal could have turned Mercator's well-connected sponsors and clients away from his business, or worse, threatened his security.

The inquiry he begged for was held, and found no substance in any of the various allegations made against him, but Mercator's response did not end with the sensible step of clearing his name in official circles. He remained a welcome guest at the court and the trusted servant of the duke and his highest officials, yet even this reassurance could not ease his anxieties. The incident would prey on his mind for years; for all the self-assurance he had shown before, the letter writer had touched a vulnerable spot deep in his soul.

The secret malice behind the letters, rather than the allegations themselves, was what ate at him. Years before, in the dark months in Rupelmonde Fort, he had wondered bleakly for days on end whether he had a secret enemy and who it might be. This new campaign of malevolence was a cruel reminder of how fragile everything he had achieved might still prove to be.

For more than twelve years, fresh letters would appear sporadically, without warning, either sent to Mercator himself or passed to his friends or to leading figures at the court. None was signed, but each one contained the same allegations of shameful behavior and disloyalty to the duke. Even though there was relative harmony between Catholics and Protestants in Duisburg, the "shameful practices" that Mercator denied so vehemently obviously referred to religious or doctrinal matters. There was just enough truth in such suggestions to hurt; Mercator's tolerant attitude left him with a foot in each camp, vulnerable to attack from both sides. In letters to his friends, he gave his anonymous slanderer a name, calling him Flavius Dorpius—Flavius being the name of the Roman emperor Domitian, who "wallowed in noble blood,"[2] and Dorpius that of a professor of divinity at Leuven who had accused the humanist Erasmus of being insufficiently critical of Lutheranism.[3] In putting their names together, Mercator created a personality for his mysterious enemy that combined savage malice with religious bigotry.

The scandal itself extended no farther than Duisburg and the court in neighboring Düsseldorf, but six years after the first letter, Mercator was still printing impassioned denials in the prefaces to his books that would be bought and read across Europe. He was the victim of a calumny, of a campaign of secret plotting, he declared. "How could anyone suppose me capable of writing such libels and pamphlets—me, devoting myself as I do solely to the beautiful studies of geography, cosmography, and history? . . . Nothing in the world gives me greater pleasure, and other occupations, even when they are necessary, are a burden to me," he protested.[4]

He wrote poems—now lost—attacking "Flavius Dorpius" and returned again and again in his private letters to the theme of his injured probity. The obsession blighted Mercator's life. Vermeulen was astonished that "the hatred of one wretched man" could have such an effect and begged him not to take the matter further. "I ask you and beg and plead with you by our old friendship to stop torturing yourself, and cast aside as far as you can those unhappy thoughts about Flavius Dorpius," he wrote in 1575. "It is a hallucination that you will receive help or protection from the advisors in the Court. . . . Whatever way you handle Flavius Dorpius, you will stain your name for posterity, and be smeared by the association."[5]

Yet Mercator would not be calmed. He was convinced that there was something more sinister to this mysterious enmity than jealous spite or religious prejudice: "I feel that those who don't know the nature of my conversations and studies are often led to suspicions of evil," he said.[6] He lived in an age that burned heretics and witches with the same grisly enthusiasm, and although he was no dabbler in spells or summoner of spirits, many of his fellow scholars had been suspected of sorcery. John Dee, his house and library ransacked by the mob, had seen the passions such stories could arouse. Mercator's scholastic work and his delight in "the contemplation of nature . . . the causes of all things, the sources of all knowledge" seem blameless enough today, but experimenters and thinkers threatened the treasured myths and idols of the past; "suspicions of evil" could confuse natural science with necromancy, love of knowledge with love of the Devil.

In the mid-1570s, the anonymous letters ceased as abruptly as they had started. There are suggestions in Vermeulen's letters to Mercator that the man they suspected was behind them was leaving Cleves for Holland—where, Vermeulen added darkly, Mercator's friends would see to it that "Flavius Dorpius" would find "someone who both can and will bridle his insolence."[7] Whatever happened, he vanished from Mercator's life and was mentioned no more. The damage that had been done—and Mercator's old age was plagued by increasingly frequent periods of black depression—had been caused not by his malicious accusations but by Mercator's own obsessive response.

BY THE TIME the letters stopped coming, Mercator had suffered more personal tragedies—heart-wrenching reminders of individual mortality. The world that he had drawn on his maps was changing shape with almost every new voyage, but the world in which he lived in Europe could be horrifyingly like that of the Middle Ages.

Throughout his life, Mercator doted on his family. He had delighted in his children when they were small and ran errands around the workshop in Leuven, and had planned their upbringing meticulously; just as his great-uncle, Gisbert, had given him his grounding in Latin, grammar, and the basics of schooling, so he had looked after the education of his sons and daughters. They remained a close and affectionate family, even though by 1567 the six children were all in their twenties, well embarked on their own adult lives. All his three girls were respectably married, Dorothée to a merchant in Antwerp and Catherine, like Emerance, to a schoolmaster. His sons were following in their father's footsteps, carving out their own roles in the family business. They had their own children, too, running through the workshop as their parents once had. The future, it must have seemed to Mercator, was assured well into the next generation and beyond. The family's prosperity, though, rested ultimately on trade, and trade had always brought more than profits, spices, and fine silks to Europe.

Two centuries before Mercator's time, a flotilla of Italian merchant ships returning from the Black Sea had docked in Sicily with their crews raving with fever. The dying sailors were mottled with red and black spots, and they screamed with pain from the blisters and swellings around their armpits—symptoms that would become agonizingly familiar over the following months. There was no cure. This was the beginning of the most devastating epidemic ever to hit the Continent, either before or since. Within a few days, the mysterious disease had spread to the nearby city of Messina and the surrounding countryside: Bubonic plague, which in just five years was to claim more than 25 million lives across the Continent—a third of the population—had arrived in Europe.

Outbreaks continued for three hundred years, wiping out whole towns and villages. No one knew either cause or cure. Even in Mercator's day, bands of religious zealots still wandered from town to town flogging themselves to atone for the sins they believed must be responsible, while the less devout clutched nosegays before their faces, in the vain belief that the infection might be carried on the rank smells of the town. Others, still more desperate, tried to keep it at bay by breathing in the fumes from the festering contents of chamber pots. Prosperity was little protection; the plague killed rich and poor without distinction. During Mercator's own lifetime, one bout that struck the University of

Leuven all but wiped out the professors of the Faculty of Medicine, who struggled heroically to care for their sick colleagues.*

The plague's course was well-known. It began with shivering and feeling cold; then came nausea and vomiting, deep sleep, and a high fever, sometimes followed by paroxysms, convulsions, and madness. There might be blisters and tumors or dark red spots on the skin. The pain could send victims into delirium, while such treatment as there was—lancing and cleaning the swellings, without any anesthetic—was as agonizing as it was fruitless. Some patients were dosed with laxatives, others made to vomit, and there were treacles and potions boiled up from exotic ingredients such as snakeskin. Yet almost everyone who showed the symptoms died. Each new outbreak, each new infection, was greeted with abject terror among the communities where it struck, making people brutal as well as fearful: Sufferers were often driven away from frightened communities, to die uncomforted and alone.

The overwhelming modern view is that the disease was a combination of bubonic and pneumonic plague, but the rats, which we now know carried the infected fleas that spread it, went unnoticed and unsuspected. The fleas, *Xenopsylla chepsis*, were riddled with the plague bacteria, which left them voraciously hungry. Every time they bit, they would vomit infected blood from their stomachs into the wound, a hideously efficient way to spread the disease. The busy docks of a trading port like Bremen in north Germany were an ideal breeding ground.[8]

Spring, when the fleas began to breed again after the cold of winter, was the worst time, and twenty-five or thirty people were dying each day in Bremen when, in mid-April of 1567, Mercator's eldest daughter, Emerance, and her young son arrived there to rejoin her husband. Disillusioned by the failure of the university project in Duisburg, Jan Vermeulen had left there four years before to reopen his school in Bremen. The staunchly Protestant town had sheltered him when he originally fled religious persecution in Leuven years before, and he hoped it might offer him a fresh start in life again.

---

*This outbreak lasted from August 1578 to May 1579.

Emerance was returning from a few weeks with her father in Duisburg, where she had taken several of Vermeulen's pupils to escape the
latest cases of plague. Like her grandmother arriving in Rupelmonde
many years before, she was heavily pregnant as she returned to Bremen.

The letter that arrived at Duisburg from Mercator's son-in-law in
May 1567 should have brought good news. Instead, it left him shattered
and heartbroken. Only a few days after their arrival, Mercator's grandchild Jan—named after his father—was struck down by sickness. "For
four days, while we looked on, the plague tormented my little son, the
half of my soul, and on the fifth day, it took him," Vermeulen lamented.
"He died in our arms. No fear of danger or death could drag me or
my wife from the needs of the child. He had scarcely died when I
dragged my wife away into another house, having changed clothing.
We arranged a funeral."[9]

All the clothes in the house were burned in case they carried the
plague, and the grief-stricken parents fled to another lodging to try to
escape the contagion. There, they found more misery: The plague had
spread panic among the population, and they were forced out onto the
streets again by the threats of a neighbor wielding a knife, who was ter-
rified that they might have brought the disease with them. Vermeulen,
at his wits' end, found shelter for himself elsewhere and hurried his
wife away with some friends to the nearby town of Emden, which still
seemed to be plague-free.

At first, Emerance's friends told themselves that her shivering fit
might have been brought on by her pregnancy, by the journey, or by her
experiences in Bremen, but first the plague struck one of her friends—
sick on the seventh of May, dead on the eighth, and buried on the
ninth—and a day later she was getting sick herself. The account Vermeulen sent his father-in-law and friend is heartrending in its bleakness:
"A church woman sat with her; a doctor was there, and a surgeon. . . . On
May 10 at 8.00 she delivered a male child, who lived only a few moments.
The midwife was there with some ladies." Her "brothers and sisters"
were with her too, and a Protestant minister, but they were too familiar
with the course of the plague to have any real hope of her recovery,
though they watched by her bed for three days. "At evening, she asked

that Arnold [Mercator's oldest son] be summoned, since her time of death was at hand. Having talked about the faith and after some prayers, struggling a little with the pains of death, she slept in the Lord."[10]

Emerance was only twenty-nine when she died. Mercator was distraught, and along with his grief he had a fear that it is almost impossible for a modern mind to comprehend. The Italian writer Giovanni Boccaccio said the victims of the plague often "ate lunch with their friends and dinner with their ancestors in paradise";[11] they could be dead within a few hours, with all their sins upon them, and with no time for the confession or repentance that might save their immortal souls.

Mercator wrote an anguished letter to his son-in-law, begging for hope that her soul would have been saved. The letter is lost, but the reply, written two months after her death, survives. "I am in no doubt about your daughter's salvation," Vermeulen reassured him. "As long as I live, it will always be a pleasure to remember with what piety and entirety of faith Emerance, Mercator's daughter, lived with me. . . . She had learned to pray with tears, which are, they say, the blood of the soul."[12] Mercator may have stood at the doorway of the modern age, but at a time of crisis, he plunged back into the personal mental hell of the Middle Ages. Science and scholarship were powerless before the awesome and incomprehensible power of God.

The plague in Bremen vanished as suddenly as it had struck. "The plague which raged seems to be buried in the same tomb as my heart," wrote Vermeulen just two months after Emerance's death. "No traces of it appear. Everything will be a burden with my wife gone, but what can I do?" Mercator, friend as well as father-in-law, had clearly attempted to encourage Vermeulen, even as he grieved for his daughter, as Vermeulen's reply, in the same letter, indicates. "I really wonder how at this time you can say that I should seek a remedy for my loneliness. . . . Loneliness is a trouble, especially when abroad, to a man like me who has neither friend here nor relative, nor anyone to close his dying eyes. But, since life is so short, and I see my grey hairs, I think of nothing less than trying my chances again."[13]

As some consolation, he sent his father-in-law the last letters Emerance had written during the few short days between the death of her son and her own sickness, but even that mournful comfort was snatched away. Perhaps the messenger he chose was nervous that the package might be infected with the plague; perhaps it was simply mislaid on the journey. Whatever the reason, the letters, at the time surely the most precious possessions either Vermeulen or Mercator could have had, were lost, and the bereaved father never saw them.

THERE WAS STILL ONE MORE crushing blow to come. Mercator had watched with pride as his sons grew, taking their places in his workshop, each inheriting different skills. Arnold, the eldest, named for Mercator's brother, the innkeeper of Rupelmonde, was the practical artisan, the man to whom the burghers of Duisburg turned when they needed someone to repair the town clock, as well as a skilled manufacturer of scientific instruments. His work was compared with that of his father, and he was also becoming known as a meticulous surveyor in his own right. His youngest brother, Rumold, was an engraver, who had already worked alongside his father on the map of Europe, and who was being groomed to take over the commercial side of the family business. He worked with booksellers in Antwerp and London, learning the trade that had made his father's fortune.

In mapping Lorraine, Bartholomew, the middle son, had worked more closely and more consistently with his father than either of the others, promising from an early age to match Mercator's scholarship. After his schooling with Vermeulen, Mercator had sent him away to the Protestant college in Heidelberg to immerse himself in philosophy, Greek, and Hebrew, and he had returned to take over his father's teaching duties in the school at Duisburg. Yet it was in the field of geography that he was making his mark. He had already published his first book by the time he was twenty-three, a learned work describing the manufacture and use of terrestrial and celestial globes, based on Mercator's teaching and on the experience he had gleaned in the Duisburg workshop. He also had his father's unerring eye for a useful connection: He had dedicated the book, published in Cologne, to Mercator's own patron at the court of Duke William, the duke's chancellor, Henri Barsius Oliferius.

A few months after the tragedy of Emerance came news of the death of Bartholomew, just twenty-eight years old, who had so tried Vermeulen's schoolmasterly patience as a boy. Exactly what killed Bartholomew is unknown. It was probably another outbreak of the plague, though there were plenty of other diseases and infections in sixteenth-century Germany to carry off a young man in the prime of life.

For his father, still grieving the deaths of his daughter and grandson, it was another wholly unexpected disaster. After the struggles in Lorraine, Mercator had faced the possibility of his own death; with the loss of two of his children and a grandchild, mortality was all around him.

Chapter Seventeen

The Sum of
Human Knowledge

D ETERMINED THAT TRAGEDY should not be allowed to triumph, Mercator spent much of a decade, starting in the mid-1560s, shut away in his room, focused on his researches and his books, his only complaint that business affairs and other worries interrupted his work. The day-to-day running of his business, the surveying tasks, and the management of his financial affairs in the town were delegated more and more to Arnold and Rumold.

He had been working sporadically for years on what would become a 450-page manuscript on the subject of chronology, endeavoring to establish the dates of historical and biblical events by making calculations on the basis of lunar and solar eclipses mentioned in ancient records.[1] Mercator's original seeds of doubt in Leuven over the compatibility of Aristotle and Genesis had led him through the years to ponder ways of synthesizing the various accounts of history, and during the 1560s he turned to these desultory researches more seriously. He brought together Bible stories from the Old and New Testaments, the dates included in Ptolemy's great astronomical work, the *Almagest,* and the writings of various diarists and historians from medieval times up to his own day. He was aiming to produce a study of the Creation of the world, blending the Old Testament account with the historical knowledge he had gleaned from his studies of ancient texts, and showing how all history led inexorably to the religious upheavals through which he had lived. He

recorded the chaos across the Low Countries, where in Antwerp, 's Hertogenbosch, and the towns of Mercator's youth, Calvinists, Anabaptists,
and reformers were even then smashing religious statues, ripping down
pictures, and burning churches. He chronicled the eclipses of 1564 and
1566, which he had observed for himself in Duisburg. The stately movements of the planets in the heavens and the violent eruptions on Earth
each in their own way figured the inexorable passing of time, which, he
declared at the end of the book, would lead within a few short years to
the long-predicted Apocalypse and the return of Christ to his kingdom
on Earth. The world, he said, was 5,544 years old, and the whole of history fell neatly into three stages, as ordained by God. The first had led up
to the birth of the prophet Abraham, the second to the coming of Christ,
and the third would complete the work of Creation with the approaching end of time.

Astronomers were describing the regular movements of the stars,
and the shape of the world was being discovered and set out for study,
so logically time itself should have a pattern, a beginning, a middle, and
an end, which could be revealed and admired in all its awe-inspiring
symmetry. The message of the *Chronologia* was that humanity, like individual humans, had a birth, a life, and a death—a beguiling, if somber
train of thought that had added poignancy for Mercator as he mourned
the deaths of Emerance, Jan, and Bartholomew.

When the time came, he could hardly bear to send the *Chronologia* to
be published. Ghim declared later that only under the greatest of pressure from his friends and the printer would he let the manuscript out of
his hands. When the book appeared in 1569, it was a personal triumph—
his favorite, the one he preferred "to all the other brain-children which
he had sired in his life."[2] In the preface, he declared proudly, "I have succeeded in discovering a variety of things which, if I go more deeply into
them and put the finishing touches to them, will be found worthy of immortality."

Not only Mercator's resolute perfectionism made him unwilling to
release his manuscript. While he was raking over the writings of his
youth, bringing them up-to-date with new researches, and compiling the
detailed list of dates that would appear in the book, he had conceived the

idea of a great new work that would bind together his life's studies. Preparing the *Chronologia* opened his eyes to the possibility of preparing an even wider-ranging study of the growth of human understanding. The original idea of an all-embracing history of the world had grown into the vision of an encyclopedic *Cosmographia*, in which he would present the synthesis of existing knowledge of geography, history, and the creation of the world. This, he believed, was his life's great purpose, which would secure his enduring fame.

The task he set himself was both awe-inspiring and essentially medieval. For centuries, monks and scholars had toiled to fit their knowledge of the world and the entire body of learning contained in ancient literature into a single Christian framework. Ptolemy's *Geographia* was the universal source for the cosmographers of Mercator's day, but there were attempts even before the rediscovery of his work in the fifteenth century. In the seventh century, for example, St. Isidore of Spain had produced his twenty-volume *Etymologiae,** also known as the *Origines,* which claimed to trace the whole history of human development. Only one of the twenty volumes was devoted to the origins of words; the rest dealt with a vast range of subjects, including languages, peoples, kingdoms, medicine, law, rhetoric, and the history of war. In the twelfth century, a monk from the French cathedral town of Tours named Bernardus Silvestris wrote his *Cosmographia*, which attempted to fuse Christian, pre-Christian, and pagan stories into a long poetic account of the Creation.†

The aim of the cosmographers was to justify the medieval conception of a world under the overarching control of God, in much the same way as the Hereford *mappamundi*. The Christian emphasis on Aristo-

---

*The *Etymologiae* were written sometime around AD 620, toward the end of Isidore's life, and throughout the Middle Ages were considered the most important storehouse of classical learning. They were originally circulated in manuscript copies but were printed ten times between 1470 and 1529.

†Bernardus also included Arabic astrology in his mystical and allegorical description of the way that primal matter was fused with the spirit of nature and divine wisdom to create humanity. His poem circulated throughout the Middle Ages and can still be read in translation. (*The Cosmographia of Bernardus Silvestris,* trans. Winthrop Wetherbee [New York: Columbia University Press, 1990].)

tle's geocentric view of the universe was the product of a similar attitude of mind: an attempt to reason out a system that would explain the whole of Creation.

The doubts that grew out of Mercator's efforts to reconcile Aristotle and Genesis, pre-Christian and Christian accounts of the Creation, had been at the root of the youthful rebellion that had taken him out of Leuven and onto the road to Antwerp, Mechelen, and Franciscus Monachus. More than three decades later, he confronted those doubts directly, drawing together all his learning about geography, history, astronomy, and the creation of the world, all for the glory of God. He aimed, he said, "to celebrate the work of God, to make the infinite wisdom and the eternal goodness burst out afresh. . . . That is the end to which I will direct all my efforts, all my reading, all my thoughts."[3]

In this, as in so much else, he followed the examples not just of Ptolemy and the medieval cosmographers but of his old friend and teacher Gemma Frisius, who had first made his name forty years before with his reworking of the *Cosmographia* of Petrus Apianus. Apianus, too, had sought to produce a universal digest of knowledge, which included a map of the world as it was known in the 1520s. His *Cosmographia* had also included ingenious working paper instruments, enabling the user to find the positions of the Sun, the Moon, and the planets at various times—in its way, the first pop-up book.[4]

The details of Mercator's plan developed over the years, but it was wide-ranging and ambitious from the start. Mercator immersed himself in the writings of the past; as his maps sought to reconcile classical wisdom with modern discoveries, so he intended that his *Cosmographia* would bring together the undoubted truths of Christianity with historical records and pagan authors in one great synthesis of learning. His aim, above all, was to reconcile faith in the teaching of the Bible with the growing knowledge of the physical world that seemed to call it into question. The *Chronologia* was to be the first of five books. In the second, he would present his view of the universe and astronomy, basing it on the celestial globe he had produced in 1551; the third and fourth would deal with astrology and the creation of the elements; and the fifth would describe the geography of the world as Mercator knew it to be, alongside the most accurate rendition yet attempted of Ptolemy's *Geographia*. In his dreams at least, Mercator was putting himself beside the great Alexandrian.

It was an impossible project. He was already in his fifties—a considerable age in the sixteenth century—and he tortured himself for the rest of his life with the growing realization that he would never achieve his grand design. His second volume remained unfinished, the third and fourth were never even started, and the final book was also incomplete when he died. But while working on the *Cosmographia*, Mercator made the discovery that would win him the immortality of which he dreamed.

THE STUDY OF GEOGRAPHY, which had taken up so much of his life, had traditionally been based on measurement and calculation, and, perhaps responding to the random, unpredictable nature of the tragedies that had struck him, he turned to the rational certainties of mathematics and the discipline of abstract thought. Central to the final part of the *Cosmographia*, the description of the current state of geographic knowledge, was to be a new map of the world. His map of 1538 would not do: The long, straggling shape of North America, which had represented the sum of knowledge three decades earlier, would have been laughable by the 1560s. In the Far East, there was more detail to be drawn in along the southern coast of Asia, and the English voyages to the northern seas had yielded detailed knowledge of the coastline of Scandinavia and northern Russia. More than this, the map of 1538 was useless for navigation. The double-cordiform projection that left America clinging helplessly to the edge of the design made it impossible to see how one part of the world related to another. Africa and South America were split between the two halves of the old map so that it was impossible to see their shape. Mercator needed to find a new way of reducing a three-dimensional image, the globe, to the two dimensions of a flat map—solving the problem of projection.

Artists and geometricians had been struggling with a similar prob-

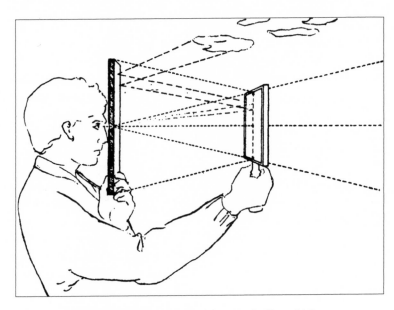

Diagram showing Brunelleschi's converging lines of sight

lem for centuries. About 150 years before, the sculptor, architect, and engineer Filippo Brunelleschi, one of the most influential figures of the early Italian Renaissance, had calculated a mathematical way of producing the illusion of depth in a painting. Parallel lines in his picture of Florence's Piazza Duomo[5] all met at a single vanishing point, and the size of an object was proportionate to its supposed distance from the observer.

This was the first modern example of a theory of linear perspective—"the rein and rudder of painting," according to Leonardo da Vinci a few years later[6]—and it is not too much to say that this one discovery was responsible for much of the unprecedented artistic flowering of the Renaissance over the next hundred years. Brunelleschi produced no written record of the experiments by which he established the principle of converging lines of sight—his contemporary Leon Battista Alberti some twenty years later explained the geometric principles behind it*—but his technique was essentially mathematical.

Brunelleschi demonstrated that perspective was a trick, an optical illusion. He was a showman by nature as well as an artist: He invited guests to look at the Duomo in Florence's Piazza through a small hole drilled in the back of a painting on a wooden panel. According to his biographer, Antonio di Tuccio Manetti, Brunelleschi "had made a hole in the panel . . . which was as small as a lentil on the painting side . . . and on the back it opened pyramidally, like a woman's straw hat, to the size of a ducat or a little more."[7] What the guest was actually seeing was not the Duomo but a small mirror reflecting Brunelleschi's painting of it; by removing and replacing the mirror so that his guest was alternately seeing the building and the painting, the artist could demonstrate the precision with which he had re-created the scene.

Brunelleschi's perspective was a theory built on rediscovered knowledge. Classical philosophers had written about it centuries before. In the first century BC, for example, the Roman architect and military engineer Marcus Vitruvius Pollio had described perspective as "a method of sketching a front with the sides withdrawing into the background, the lines all meeting in the centre of a circle."[8] Nobody before Brunelleschi, though, had developed the theory as a practical method of creating an apparently three-dimensional image on a flat surface, and other artists were quick to take advantage of his discovery.[9] The simple lead-backed mirror, a discovery of the thirteenth century, and another means of achieving the same effect, was a standard piece of equipment in an artist's studio, producing real-life examples of perspective to which the artist could refer.

---

*Alberti's book, *On Painting,* first appeared in 1435. It described how an artist should frame his picture within a rectangle and then choose a single focal point within it, from which lines should be drawn to various points along the baseline of the rectangle, forming a series of triangles. The changing distances between these lines as they converged on the focal point would then show precisely how dimensions should be adjusted in the painting to give the illusion of depth. The book is available in a modern translation, with introduction and notes, by John R. Spencer (New Haven: Yale University Press, 1970).

Brunelleschi and the artists who followed him had a relatively simple objective: to give depth and emphasis to the scene they were painting, from the particular viewpoint they had selected. Cartographers could use similar principles—Ptolemy had done so in constructing his map projections*—but the challenge they faced was much more sophisticated. A map is a diagram, not a picture; there is no one viewpoint from which the entire globe can be seen, so perspective alone cannot solve the problem of transferring its curved surface onto a flat sheet of paper. That had been recognized for more than fifteen hundred years as a problem without a solution.

Some three-dimensional geometric forms, such as a cylinder or a cone, are capable of being laid out flat without distortion—"developable," in the mathematicians' jargon; others, such as the sphere, are not. While a mathematician can produce formulas to prove this, a layman can simply try to lay the peel of an orange flat on a table. If the spherical Earth is flattened out into two dimensions, like the orange peel on the table, it will always be distorted in some way, whether in the size or shape of the land, the distances between points, or the direction from one place to another. This means that a map projection, a system designed to lay the globe out flat, can never be perfect; all the designer can do is minimize some elements of the distortion at the expense of others.

For Ptolemy and the philosophers of classical times, this was a mathematical oddity as much as a practical problem of geography or cartography. The known world covered only a portion of the globe, and the knowledge of coastlines, the routes of rivers, and the relative positions of towns and physical features was so hazy and inexact that the distortions of projection were insignificant. In any case, there were no recorded journeys long enough to make projection a serious difficulty for sailors and navigators. Ignorance as much as mathematical law had limited the traditional worldview.

---

*He had written explicitly about geometric optics in his book *Optica,* which reappeared in the West in 1154, after being translated from an Arabic version.

Even so, repeated attempts had been made to find the most accurate means of producing a flat map. Ptolemy, having set out his own proposals in his *Geographia*, had effectively thrown up his hands in despair and recommended a globe as the only truly accurate way of studying the world. The globe, though, had disadvantages of its own, as he freely admitted: It could not be made large enough to show sufficient detail, it was awkward to handle, and one half of it would always be obscured from view. He described two different projections in detail, building on the efforts of other Greek philosophers hundreds of years before him, who had set out systems of parallels and meridians—the grid of latitude and longitude lines—to provide a basic framework for constructing a map.[10]

The commonest such systems produced a network, or graticule, which was either square or rectangular. All parallels—the east-to-west lines of latitude—were straight and horizontal, regularly spaced according to the changes in latitude; the meridians, or north-to-south longitude lines, were similarly straight, equidistant, and parallel, crossing the lines of latitude at right angles. For the purposes of the map, each line of latitude on the globe was considered to be the same length. The projection was as straightforward to understand as it was to create, simply representing the globe as a cylinder rather than a sphere, and then unrolling it. Such a projection was ideal for maps of smaller areas, on which the inaccuracies as one moves north and south would be unnoticed.[11]

Although it may be easy to create, a straightforward cylindrical projection simply ignores the way that lines of longitude—the meridians—converge on the two poles. By straightening these curved and converging lines, the projection forces them apart. In addition, while every line of longitude is of equal length, running right around the world, lines of latitude are parallel circles, with only the longest one—the equator—running around the full circumference of the Earth. The rest get shorter the closer they approach to the poles—which means that each degree of longitude, being $\frac{1}{360}$ of the length of a given line of latitude, will similarly represent a progressively shorter distance on the face of the Earth. A degree of latitude on the globe always represents the same distance, but the value of a degree of longitude becomes smaller as it gets farther from the equator. Those changes on the globe could not be properly reflected by a cartographer: Distances, areas, and—most important of all to navigators—directions were hopelessly distorted over much of the map. The laws of mathematics continually frustrated efforts to produce an accurate representation of the world.

Ptolemy's efforts, which survived only as mathematical descriptions rather than completed maps, were ambitious, being based on the idea of viewing the world not as a cylinder to be unrolled but as a cone. His parallels of latitude were concentric arcs rather than straight lines, and his longitudinal meridians either straight, evenly spaced radii, broken by an angle at the equator, or—in his more complicated version—a series of evenly spaced arcs. The curvature of these lines gradually reduced toward a single, straight prime meridian, producing a map shaped like a cloak spread out on the ground, gradually increasing in width from north to south.

This second projection, which Ptolemy said he preferred—"for me both here and everywhere, the better and more difficult scheme is preferable to the one which is poorer and easier"[12]—had the advantage of keeping different areas of the map more precisely in proportion to each other. Most cartographers who produced versions of his maps in the fifteenth and sixteenth centuries, however, were less conscientious and used the simpler version.

There were other proposals over the centuries. Globular projections, for instance, showed an entire hemisphere in a circular form and were used in the Islamic world for astronomical maps, and by medieval scholars such as the English philosopher Roger Bacon in the thirteenth century. Bacon, an English friar who studied at Paris and Oxford, quoted ancient Hebrew sources to support his view that it was possible to reach Asia by sailing west, and produced a circular map to demonstrate this. The map had parallel, straight lines of latitude crossing a single, straight, vertical central meridian at a right angle, with the curves of the other meridians gradually increasing on each side to form the outline of the globe. The world map of Franciscus Monachus, which inspired Mercator in his youth, was designed on a similar globular projection.

By Mercator's day, this mathematical theorizing had become important. The world was changing and growing, and the old guidelines for depicting it were increasingly inadequate. To the south of Europe, Africa and South America were known to stretch into areas that would be hopelessly distorted by any simple projections, while to the west, a great new continent had been discovered. Ptolemy had designed his projections to fit the world as he knew it, and cartographers had to find a way to incorporate the new knowledge that had been gained.

Some of their maps simply extended the arcs of Ptolemy's meridians, while others, such as Waldseemüller's world map, gave a much sharper break in the line of the meridians at the equator. At the start of the sixteenth century, Johannes Stabius and Johann Werner were working together in Nuremberg on the church sundial that would eventually lead them to their own heart-shaped or cordiform world map. The result of their work, the basis of Mercator's first world map in 1538, had been to increase the curve of the meridians in Ptolemy's second projection.

One factor common to all these attempts was that they were virtually useless for navigation, because the straight course along a single compass bearing, which was simplest for a sailor to follow, was effectively unplottable on the map. Portuguese ships returning from Brazil found themselves as much as seventy leagues off course as they approached the Azores, and King João II's cosmographer royal, the mathematician Pedro Nunes, who had visited Leuven while Mercator was there, had recognized the problem and made his own contribution. He had calculated the curve across the map that might represent such a straight course across the sea; but although such a course might be shown on a map by a theoretical straight line along a compass bearing between the point of departure and the destination, actually following such a bearing on the sea would send a ship increasingly off course as the curvature of the Earth distorted its direction. Nunes, in effect, had defined the problem; a practical answer to it was yet to be found.

A straight line on any existing map could not be translated into a single compass setting on the sea. Navigators were faced with the unenviable choice of either plotting their course on a globe, with all the consequent inconvenience and inaccuracy, or making constant adjustments to their calculations as they proceeded. In practice, since lines of latitude could be figured out relatively easily from the height in the sky of the Sun or the planets, they had generally minimized the problem by setting a course well to either east or west of the destination they were aiming at and then sailing along the line of latitude until they found it—a hit-or-miss technique that could add days to a long voyage, without inspiring much confidence in its outcome. What had been a theoretical challenge for cartographers was a matter of immediate practical concern. Not only were ships sailing greater distances than they had ever done before, but they were venturing farther north and south, where the problems of projection were intensified.

The task Mercator had set himself was to produce a map that sailors could use, on which a straight line was also a straight line on the sea. He spelled it out in Latin in an explanatory panel on the world map he eventually produced in 1569: The projection, he said, "spreads the surface of the globe out flat so that places are in the correct position relative to each other, both as regards direction and distance, and with the correct latitudes and longitudes." His intent was not just to update the existing picture of the world but to produce a new type of map, with a new purpose, useful to scholars and sailors alike, representing the true shape of the continents with a minimum of distortion—not just a new version but a new vision of the world.

Chapter Eighteen

The World Hung on the Wall:
The Projection

W ALTER GHIM LIKED TO CLAIM after Mercator's death that he
had been in the mapmaker's studio when work started on the
great map of 1569. He watched, perhaps, but Mercator worked alone.
"In this vast undertaking, he had no help or assistance, but engraved
the whole of the map himself with the exception of the margin," Ghim
declared.[1]

Exactly when Mercator hit on the idea of a map that would be as useful to sailors as it was to scholars is impossible to say. Twenty-three years
before, he had written to Antoine de Granvelle about the failings of
navigational charts: "When the courses of ships are correctly measured,
the latitudes shown are often greater than they truly are, or sometimes
smaller. When the latitudes shown are correct, then the distances are inaccurate." In that letter, Mercator was concentrating on the question of
compass deviation that had so troubled Columbus, rather than on the
specific mathematical challenge of projection. In any case, he had more
pressing concerns on his mind: In 1546, he was still rebuilding his business and his life after the trauma of Rupelmonde Fort. Even so, in the
same letter, he had set down his plan for the future. "There is much else
to be said about the correction of voyages and marine charts. . . . If I am
ever relieved of my heavier obligations, I have decided to pursue and
solve this matter properly."[2]

All his life, with his habitual passion for accuracy, Mercator had been squirreling away maps and reports from the expeditions that had extended the boundaries of the known world during the previous eighty years. He was in touch with other mapmakers and geographers across Europe and beyond—for example, he regularly exchanged letters with a Portuguese scholar-monk named Philip Sassetus who lived in Goa, on the Indian coast—and John Dee was only one of many foreign scholars who came to see him, as eager to meet the great man as he was to pump them for information. Mercator described later how he had prepared the ground, comparing Spanish and Portuguese charts with each other, and then studying other printed and handwritten accounts from past centuries, patiently reconciling Spanish with Portuguese, past with present. "It is from an equitable conciliation of all these documents that the dimensions and situations of the land are given here as exactly as possible," he wrote in the legend to the map.

The maps of the Spanish and Portuguese explorers and of the English expeditions to the North—or at least descriptions or summaries of them—were the pure gold that cartographers like Mercator sought, but there was also valuable information to be gleaned from the portolan charts drawn up by professional seamen to make their own regular journeys more reliable. The *navigatorias chartas* to which Mercator had referred in his letter to Granvelle were almost certainly such handdrawn seamen's sketch maps. The two trades, chart maker and cartographer, had grown up separately, but what the seamen's charts, or cards, lacked in sophistication, they made up for in hard-won and up-to-date experience. It is impossible to say how many such charts[3] reached his desk, but these were what he was hoping for in return for the help he had given John Dee in planning the English voyages to the Far North; Mercator's son Rumold, who was working for a bookseller in London, also did his best to find what pieces of information he could.[4] The sketches, distances, and descriptions contained in such maps and in the written directions that often accompanied them were "equitably conciliated" along with Mercator's other information.

Ever since he had produced his first globe in 1541, he had been tackling the problem of projection in reverse—preparing flat maps that had to be shaped and pasted to fit a spherical globe. He had seen how the wet, pasted map could stretch if not handled properly, pulling all the lines out of shape. Calculating the curve of the individual gores and cutting them precisely was as much a problem of manual dexterity as of intellect, but such work had left him constantly aware of the limitations of Ptolemy's theories of projection. By considering the Earth as a cone to be unrolled, Ptolemy had forced the lines of longitude out of true, making them converge some distance above the pole. That led to significant distortions of direction on maps drawn according to his prescription; but then, straightening the lines of longitude so that, as parallel lines, they never converged at all would necessarily stretch the lines of latitude and lead to still more inaccuracy. But what if the distances between those lines of latitude were to be altered in the same proportion—if the map were to stretch not randomly, as had occurred when he pressed the wet gores against the plaster coating of his globe, but proportionately, in every direction at once? Then the distances between places, the sizes of islands and continents, would be exaggerated, but their positions relative to each other would remain true.

Mercator went back beyond Ptolemy to the older and simpler cylindrical projections. First he straightened the meridians of the globe, so that, instead of meeting at the North and South Poles, they continued as parallel lines on his map, just like those of the original rectangular graticules of the ancient Greeks. Doing that necessarily stretched east-west distances on his map as it got closer to the poles, and also distorted the directions in the same proportion—lines of latitude, which grow progressively shorter on the globe, were shown as equal in length.[5] The resulting exaggeration of distances as the map approaches the poles is a feature of any cylindrical projection. However, maintaining the true direction was Mercator's priority, and so he next extended the gap between his lines of latitude in the same proportion as he had earlier moved apart the meridians. On the map, that results in lines of latitude appearing farther apart the closer they get to the two poles—and as a result, the distances Mercator showed were grossly distorted in the polar regions. Islands such as Greenland and Spitzbergen were—and are—shown much larger on a Mercator map than in real life.

Mercator had intended that his map of the world be used at sea, not just in the study. And the title of the map leaves no doubt about this: *Nova et aucta orbis terrae description ad usum navigantium emendate et accomodata* (a new and improved description of the lands of the world, amended and intended for the use of navigators).

Thus, though the distances may have been expanded, the *directions* on his map precisely reflected the course a navigator would need to steer on the sea. For sailors and navigators, the relative size of the lands they sailed to would be a matter of little importance compared with the ability to follow a straight course across the map. As a practical matter, the fact that Europe appeared bigger on the map than the mysterious and unexplored lands in the tropics was a positive advantage to a cartographer who had much more information to include about the lands close to home compared to what he knew about the equatorial region. Mercator's was a Eurocentric map for a Eurocentric age.

Today, with the advantage of hindsight, his innovation—like many other great discoveries—strikes us as beguilingly straightforward. In essence, he was simply lengthening the lines of latitude and of longitude in equal proportions; any one of the cartographers who had wrestled with creating a world map in the centuries since Ptolemy might have done the same. Ironically, it was in part Ptolemy's own achievement in setting out his suggested projections that had prevented them: In a world where few long journeys were made to the Far North or South, there had for centuries been little incentive to produce a map like Mercator's. Ptolemy's projections were good enough for the world he knew, and, with minor adjustments such as those of Waldseemüller, they were acceptable for much of the sixteenth century. The English explorations of the northern seas had exposed their true limitations, and Mercator's map was drawn at a time when the need for a new projection was becoming clear.

The new projection had its own limitations. It could not, for example, show the shortest distances for long voyages. That could be demonstrated by stretching a piece of string around the globe between the point of departure and the destination, and would have appeared as a long curve on Mercator's map. Actually following such a course—the so-called great circle route—involves so many changes of compass bearing that it would have been practically impossible for sailors with the skills and instruments of the sixteenth century. Mercator's map, then, offered an alternative that was both reliable and simple.

Previous projections were simply not adequate to map the world that the explorers had revealed. Mercator summed up the problems with traditional maps that navigators on expeditions to the North had noted: "It is inevitable that the shape of the lands is enormously distorted, and that for this reason not only longitudes and latitudes, but also directions and distances are far from correct. Great mistakes result."[6] On his map, the problem of distances remained, but those of longitude, latitude, and—crucially—direction had been solved.

Like Brunelleschi working out the technique of perspective drawing a century and a half before, Mercator left no notes or clues to the process by which he arrived at his great discovery. For all Walter Ghim's boasting that he watched him at work on his map, the real preparation of the new projection was done in private. Whether it was calculated from mathematical first principles or worked out by trial and error is not known. Although an accomplished mathematician like Mercator must have had some idea of the theoretical basis of what he was doing, he most likely drew the projection with geometric instruments such as dividers and protractor—mechanically, rather than theoretically.

ONLY THREE COPIES REMAIN today of the map that emerged from Mercator's lengthy process of gossiping, checking, comparing, and designing. One, colored and bound into an atlas by a later hand, is in Holland, at Rotterdam's Maritime Museum. Another is in the university library in Basel, Switzerland. The third is kept at the back of an office storeroom in Paris's Bibliothèque Nationale, hanging in a rack with other maps, almost like washing on a line. Here, Mercator's work can be viewed as he intended. The eighteen individual sheets have been carefully pasted together to make a large map (52¾ inches wide by 83½ inches long). Reproductions in books, though, are no substitute for the delicacy and scale of the real thing.

At first sight, the map is oddly unimpressive. The Hereford *mappamundi*, with its deep ochre coloring and the strange, idiosyncratic world

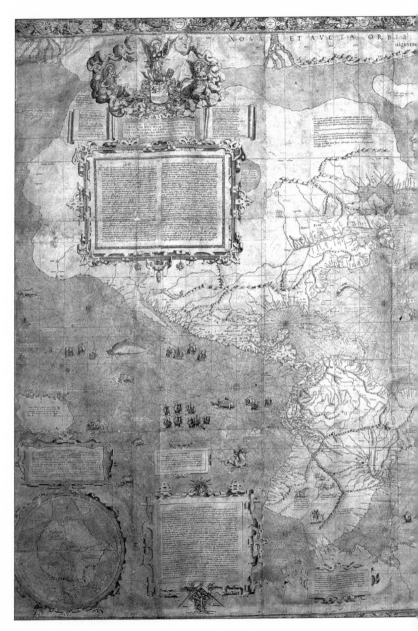

Mercator's 1569 world map, later called "Mercator's Projection"

it portrays, gives an immediate sense of great age. Mercator's map of 1569 may mark a turning point in people's appreciation of the world around them, but at a glance it seems little more than a simple black-and-white line drawing, with notes, sketches, and brief essays all jostling for attention. Only when one climbs the stepladder to study it more closely are the map's intricacy and detail revealed. The Amazon River snakes through the interior of a strangely bulbous South America, and delicately drawn dense forests cover much of Russia. The former Aztec capital of "Tenuchtitlan" is marked in Central America, as are, farther south, the Incas' ancient city of Cuzco and also Lima, the thirty-five-year-old settlement of their Spanish conquerors. Much of the rest of the world is dotted with towns and settlements; some of them, like Exeter, York, Paris, or "Duysborg" itself, are well-known, but others, filling the center of Africa and the deserts of Arabia, never existed. For all Mercator's careful researches, this map, like the Hereford one, was in part a compendium of what people believed.

The sketches of biblical stories, which were such an important feature of the maps of the Middle Ages, are gone, but Mercator could not restrain himself from adding a few drawings depicting other, more modern, tales and fables: In South America cannibals are cutting up and cooking an unfortunate victim, and a strange kangaroolike animal is suckling its young; in the middle of Africa the mythical Prester John sits serenely at the center of his empire.[7]

LIKE THE HEREFORD *mappamundi*—like all maps—Mercator's world map is a self-portrait as well as a depiction of the world, reflecting the age in which it was conceived. For all its creator's personal religious devotion, Christianity no longer held an unchallengeable, overarching role in European society. On most maps, Jerusalem had lost its medieval place of honour at the center of the world a century or more earlier; on Mercator's, it can barely be found at all, the tiny letters *Irlm* squeezed in among the other biblical names. The Holy City had been reduced to an abbreviated afterthought.

Instead of the reliance on God and the Church that the medieval mapmakers exhibited, Mercator's map depicts a world that is confident in itself. The towns that fill Europe, Africa, and Asia, whether real or imagined, suggest a landscape that has been tamed. The scattering of names in the areas of Spanish influence in the New World and elsewhere, as well as the empty spaces—vast areas of America and Russia without a town in them—speak of a conviction that European culture will eventually spread there too. Even the huge sea monsters with which Mercator decorated the Atlantic and the Pacific don't seem to pose a threat to the ships plowing the treacherous seas. This, the map seems to say, is the age of trade, which will carry all before it.

In the Eastern Hemisphere, Mercator had thirty years of exploration on which to draw since his last map of the world, and the coastlines, particularly in Southeast Asia, are much more recognizable today than those he had drawn in 1538. To the west, America was no longer the mysterious and intriguing land it had been. Repeated voyages across the Atlantic and around Cape Horn had revealed much of its coastline. While many geographers were still arguing about whether the new continent was simply an extension of the Asian landmass, Mercator had no doubt. "Those who say that New India continues with Asia are mistaken," he declared,[8] confidently drawing in the west coast of America and the whole Pacific Ocean.

In his depiction of America, Mercator provided more details than ever before. Although the squat, bulging outline he drew of the southern half of the continent may appear grotesquely distorted, the western coastline of North America was much more accurately drawn on his map than it had been earlier. Seven years before, the Spanish cartographer Diego Gutierrez[9] had produced a wall map of America that showed nothing of the northern half of the continent beyond the eastern seaboard. Mercator, by contrast, depicted a long sweep of western coastline, including the peninsula of Baja California, which Waldseemüller and other cartographers had shown as an island, and also attempted to show mountains and rivers in the hinterlands of both North and South America.

Anyone looking at Mercator's map for the first time would have been struck by the size of the new continent. America seemed to have swallowed up a quarter of the world. On earlier maps, including his own, it had looked small and unimportant, but on the map of 1569, it had swelled to fill almost half of the Northern Hemisphere. New information from the voyages to the Americas had led Mercator practically to double the width of the northern part of the continent from 80 degrees on his first world map to around 155 degrees on this one.[10] This revision reflected Mercator's realization of the huge scale of the discoveries that were being made in the Western Hemisphere; it was also a shrewd way to recognize Spain's King Philip, whose domains in the New World were shown stretching impressively across more than 40 percent of the globe, a graphic representation of power.

But there was more than new information and political circumspection to explain the huge increase in size of North America. Because of Mercator's projection, which progressively increased the linear value of each degree of latitude and longitude as the map extended north and south, the sixtieth parallel, which ran across the widest part of what is now Canada, was twice as long on the new map as it should have been. He believed that the continent extended nearly twice as far around the globe as he had thought before. In addition, as a result of the projection, each degree of its breadth stretched twice as far as it had on his earlier map. Mercator's projection had turned America into a monster.

The same thing had happened to an even greater extent at the bottom and top of the map. Ptolemy's influence remained: Like Waldseemüller some sixty years before him, Mercator had followed the Greek master in drawing the great southern continent that reached almost to the tip of South America—"the Southern Lands, not yet discovered at all," as one early map put it, with appealing ingenuousness. Mercator had drawn this mythical continent on his earlier world map, separated from South America by the narrow Strait of Magellan, with Tierra del Fuego a headland rather than an island, and he had no reason to change his mind. The long, sweeping, and entirely imaginary coastline almost reached the southern coast of Africa and the East Indies. The sheer extent of this land was striking: It ran from one side of the map to the other. It would have to exist, Mercator reasoned, in order to balance Africa, Asia, and Europe, and maintain the equilibrium of the globe.[11]

In the North, a similar belt of land extended above North America and Russia. For all the efforts of the English explorers, the North Pole remained in practice, like its southern counterpart, unseen and unsee-able, but with this new projection, both poles were also unmappable. At the points where lines of longitude converge on the globe—the two poles—degrees of latitude and longitude alike were stretched to infinity.

This was only of theoretical interest, as no explorers of the sixteenth century were going to reach either pole, but in the North, Mercator tried to meet the difficulty by including a small inset, drawn from a different viewpoint from that of the rest of the map. From directly above the pole, he showed a group of four islands, separated by rivers running into the "indrawing sea" that covered the pole itself. At its center, at the point where the waters were sucked into the depths of the Earth, stood Mercator's mythical *rupes nigra*, the black rock that he believed was the source of the Earth's magnetic field.[12] In the legends to the map, he added stories of strange pygmy tribesmen, myths of ships drawn toward lodestone mountains, and horrified accounts of irresistible storms and currents in the Far North. With no firm information from sailors to draw on, Mercator had to rely on tradition and superstition, which had coalesced to produce a grotesque tale that could have been told by Herodotus more than a millennium earlier.

Other gaps and glaring errors remained. Much of the unknown hin-terland of North America was conveniently hidden behind a rectangular block containing the legend to the map; the vexed question of whether a northwestern passage to Asia existed was avoided with the aid of a care-fully placed and heavily decorated dedicatory panel, although Mercator was more confident in showing a simple eastern route along the northern coastline of Russia. The search had been going on unsuccessfully for six-teen years when the map appeared, but he had no doubt that some future expedition would find its way past the frozen islands and ice-bound seas into the warm waters that lay beyond. Many of the rivers of the Americas, like those of Africa and much of Asia, were drawn from imagination or from ancient tales, as they had to be.[13] Exploring coastlines was one thing, but several centuries would pass before expeditions reached and surveyed the hinterland of the new continent.

For all his insight and innovation, Mercator still protested his loyalty to traditional authorities. On the legend to the map, he maintained that the

Portuguese explorations in the East had provided no improvement on Ptolemy's classical descriptions, and yet a glance at Ptolemy's depiction of the coastlines of India, Ceylon, and the whole of southern Asia shows how inferior was Ptolemy's knowledge. Mercator's version of the coast-line, based largely on the reports he decried, follows broadly the lines that we know today to be accurate. In the same way that he embraced religious reform without ever explicitly rejecting the traditional role of the Catholic Church, so he revolutionized the picture of the world without once denying the authority of the classical geographers.

WHATEVER THE DECLARED INTENTIONS of its title, "intended for the use of navigators," the world map of 1569 was more than a seaman's chart. Mercator was a landsman, with no firsthand knowledge of the cramped conditions of the navigator's table on board a ship. As far as we know, the only time he ever stepped off dry land was to board the barge going up the Rhine to the Frankfurt fairs. The deceptively simple alteration to the cylindrical projection that had served since Ptolemy's time presented a system that would enable sailors to plot a straight course on the map and steer the same straight course on the sea, but his map had developed far beyond his initial intentions. The detailed legends—fifteen of them, all in scholarly Latin—were never intended for sailors; the towns with which the interior of Europe, Asia, and North Africa were so closely packed, the rivers and mountains, would have had little relevance for a shipboard navigator.

Some of Mercator's work, like the maps of Lorraine and England, or the map of Ghent presented to Emperor Charles V, had a steely political edge to it. The map of 1569, on the other hand, was created from the reconciliation of different ideas from Spain, Portugal, France, Germany, and even from beyond Europe. It was intended for sailors pushing back the boundaries of trade and knowledge, and for the peaceful contemplation of scholars. In that sense, it ran completely counter to the militaristic spirit of the times.

Chapter Nineteen

Presenting Ptolemy
to the World

WHEN CHARLES V handed over control of the Netherlands to his son Philip in 1555,* he instructed him to hold fast to the Catholic religion of his forefathers and show no toleration of heresy within his dominions. Protestantism and anti-Spanish feeling were gaining strength side by side, and Philip followed his father's advice with a policy of blood and fire. At his shoulder to deal with the heretics, as he had been at Charles's, was his most mighty subject, Mercator's former classmate Antoine de Granvelle, who took the lead in a renewed policy of judicial slaughter that lasted for years. One of Granvelle's purges had sent Jan Vermeulen scurrying for his life in 1553. There was a brief moment of hope in 1564: Hated, mocked, and lampooned by the people he oppressed, Granvelle himself was sent into exile by the king, who suggested that he should pay a lengthy visit to his mother in Besançon. Nationalists and Protestants, delighted at his disgrace, rose in revolt against the Catholic power of the king of Spain, and tens of thousands of people flocked out of the towns to take part in open-air religious services at which Catholic priests and rituals were mocked and lampooned; but, like the brief celebration of freedom in Ghent nearly thirty years earlier, it could not last. The killing in the Low Countries continued.

*Charles handed over his possessions in the Netherlands to Philip one year before his formal abdication as king of Spain.

Simple figures are hopelessly unreliable, twisted and inflated over the centuries by biased accounts and Protestant propagandists; but the laws passed during this bloodthirsty time give some idea of the atmosphere of fear. Shortly after Granvelle's departure, Philip's privy councillors in the Netherlands announced what they called a "moderation" of his decrees.

The new laws, described by the Netherlanders as "murderation" rather than moderation,* were even more fierce than those that had swept up Mercator and the other forty-two suspects in the purge of 1543. Under this supposedly moderate policy, anyone who discussed religious matters might be executed. So might anyone who interpreted the Bible without having studied theology at a "renowned university," anyone whose house was used by heretics, or who protected illegal ministers or teachers of religion. The popular rejoicing that had greeted the departure of the hated Granvelle was premature—the people had not yet heard of Fernando Álvarez de Toledo, duke of Alva.

Alva arrived in the Netherlands (in 1567) at the head of ten thousand highly disciplined and professional Italian soldiers as effective ruler on the king's behalf, to instigate a reign of military terror that sent thousands more to the executioner's block. Alva was Philip's most loyal adviser, the snarling guard dog that he would unleash upon his enemies,[1] and his record in the Netherlands speaks for itself: Over the next two years, he put down the Protestant revolt in a welter of blood and smoke. In January 1568, just five months after his arrival, 84 leading rebels died on the scaffold in a single day; the following month another 37 were condemned; in March, fifteen hundred people were arrested and charged with treason. There were secret accusations, midnight arrests, bodies hanging from trees to terrify the population, and even a new court to hurry through the rudimentary trials that preceded many of the killings. Alva named it the Council of Troubles, but it rapidly became known, more evocatively, as the Council of Blood.

---

*The wordplay, "Moorderatie, niet moderatie," works better in Flemish than it does in English.

Antoine de Granvelle

By 1569, the land of Mercator's birth had endured two of the bloodiest years it had known. Groups of refugees, their possessions piled onto carts or just bundled on their backs, began the long trek toward the cities of northwest Germany. Recent estimates suggest that as many as sixty thousand Protestants and reformists moved to the towns of Emden, Hamburg, Cologne, Bremen, Frankfurt, and Duisburg. They were safe enough there for the present, but there was a new atmosphere of unease, a sense that the fighting and brutality might still spread east and engulf the Rhinelands. The same forces that had blighted Mercator's youth were stirring again.

THE BLOODLETTING in the Netherlands was still on the distant horizons of Mercator's life. Behind Duisburg's city walls, he was updating and redrawing the map of Europe he had published in 1564, getting it ready for a second edition that was to appear in 1572. Above all, he was anxious to press ahead with the mammoth task he had set himself in the *Cosmographia*.

This remained his overarching ambition, to such an extent that for the rest of his life he hardly even mentioned the world map from the day that it left his desk. Of the five individual volumes he had planned for the *Cosmographia*, the *Chronologia* was completed, and he had writings from earlier in his life that he would develop into another book describing the universe and the science of astronomy. The works on astrology and on the creation of the elements were important to him, but the geography of the world was closest to his heart. The information he had gathered together in producing the map of 1569 would form the basis of his description of the world as the explorers of the last hundred years had proved it to be. This would be the crowning glory of the *Cosmographia*— the work that would put him alongside Ptolemy as the undisputed geographer of his age.

The globes that were still being turned out from his workshop for Christopher Plantin and other dealers all over Europe had brought the world into the library, while the world map of 1569 had hung it on the wall and spread it across the navigator's bench. The new project would present a collection of individual maps, bound together to show how the conception of the world had changed since Ptolemy's time, and place it in all its detail on the scholar's bookshelf, accessible to the reader. "Finally, I shall produce all the regions of the world, keeping repetition to a minimum, lest he who buys the book should be overloaded with too many maps," he wrote later.[2]

That work had to wait. To show how the world had changed, he had first to show how it had been seen by the scholars of ancient times. Ptolemy had left projections, directions, and coordinates, and practically every map drawn in the sixteenth century owed some debt to his *Geographia*, but there were no maps in his own hand. Mercator's aim was to strip away the later additions and interpretations and base his version as closely as he could on the master's original writings, to produce a vision not of the world as he knew it to be, but of the world that

Ptolemy had envisaged. Paradoxically, at a time when explorers from Portugal, Spain, Italy, and England were frantically extending the known limits of geography, Europe's leading cartographer concentrated on the best way of presenting knowledge that dated from fifteen hundred years earlier.

MERCATOR WAS NOT the only one to have thought of producing a modern collection of maps. As his new map of the world was coming off the press in 1569, his friend Abraham Ortelius in Antwerp was about to make the change from colorist, map seller, and collector with a modest reputation to one of the most successful publishers of the century. He had also hit on the idea of a book of maps, but he considered it with the eyes of a businessman rather than those of a scholar. As a craftsman and salesman, he had few equals; while Mercator turned to maps as a way of understanding the world, Ortelius saw them as merchandise to be sold as quickly and as profitably as possible.

Born in 1527, he was fifteen years younger than Mercator, and at the age of seven he, too, had been orphaned and brought up by an uncle. The experience left him, like Mercator, with a lifelong appreciation of the value of money and a keen sense of the need for security. While still in his teens, he became a map seller and *afsetter van caerten,* or illuminator, to support his two sisters and later gathered influential friends of his own in the worlds of business and cartography in Antwerp and Leuven. He also made dangerous acquaintances, whose friendship brought him to the attention of the Inquisition; he is believed to have spent several months in England in his youth to avoid arrest. It is possible that Mercator met him in Leuven or Antwerp, but their close friendship developed after their meeting at the Frankfurt fair in 1554. Six years later, they traveled to Poitiers together, and the language they used in the letters they exchanged demonstrates how relaxed they felt in each other's company. These letters had a familiarity that was unique among Mercator's correspondence. In one of them, Mercator thanked Ortelius for some small

Abraham Ortelius

gift,* which he said he "embrace[d] lovingly,"[3] and in another he observed almost bashfully, after praising his friend's work and talents,
"I can babble on like this to you, my dear Ortelius."[4]

Compared with Mercator, Ortelius did little original work as a geographer,[5] and had none of Mercator's theoretical interest in the relevance
of Ptolemy in the modern world to distract him from the more pressing
business of making money. In the mid-1560s, one of his Antwerp business contacts, a successful merchant named Gilles Hooftman, gave him
the idea for a collection of small, portable maps designed to be bound together as a book.

---

*Van Durme, in his edition of Mercator's letters, suggests that the gift may have been an
account of a journey through France and the Low Countries made by Ortelius and his
friend, an Antwerp merchant named Jean Vivianus.

Hooftman owned more than a hundred ships that traded in the Baltic and North Africa, dealing in timber and various imports and exports. Like Ortelius, Christopher Plantin, and Mercator himself, he had his troubles with the religious authorities—in 1566 he appeared on a list of *riches calvinistes* to be investigated—but he managed to avoid arrest and imprisonment. He was sufficiently rich and educated to share in the fashionable obsession with maps, and also astute enough to see how it could be turned to his advantage. At sea, Hooftman's merchant vessels might be delayed by winds, currents, and coastlines, while by land, shifting religious conflicts might make one road or another more or less hazardous from one day to the next. The ability to switch to alternate routes could pay significant dividends.

Since the only copies of the maps he needed were huge and unwieldy, he suggested to Ortelius that they would be much more convenient if printed in some uniform way and bound as a single book. Hooftman was a good customer, and Ortelius made up a collection of some thirty maps that he had bound specially for him. They covered the Low Countries, Germany, France, and Italy, and each was printed on a single sheet of paper. As he worked, the idea formed in his head that a similar project might appeal to a wide range of potential customers.

Books of maps had been sold before. In Italy, map sellers had bound together various items from their stock to make haphazard collections,* and innumerable editions of Ptolemy's *Geographia* had been issued, both with and without illustrations. Yet no one had hit on the simple idea of publishing a collection of contemporary maps drawn specifically to be bound in book form.

The advantages of such a collection were clear enough. Sheet maps were bulky and inconvenient when rolled up for storage, and likely to be damaged however carefully they were handled. When the eighteen

---

*Antonio Lafreri in Rome and Paolo Forlani in Venice are two of several Italian map sellers and publishers known to have produced collections of their wares in the 1560s. Such books were generally designed for individual customers rather than compiled for publication. Portuguese discoveries of the fourteenth and fifteenth centuries had also been recorded in collections of manuscript charts bound together as books.

sheets of Mercator's world map were pasted together, they formed a map of around thirty square feet, while Waldseemüller's giant map earlier in the century had been a full thirty-six square feet. Impressive as they might have been—Ptolemy himself had said that a map should be as big as possible—the new maps were impossible to use. Few houses, except for those of the very wealthy, could provide the space to unroll them or the light by which to consult them. They were too big to frame, constant rolling and unrolling damaged them, and hanging them on the wall left them vulnerable to accidental tears, dirt, and fire, so they could not be stored safely even in the most meticulously ordered library. For merchants and travelers trying to find their way from town to town across Europe, all the problems were compounded: The maps that were big enough to include the details they needed were too big to be carried or unrolled. In any case, as Mercator had found out for himself, the advance of regional cartography across Europe had produced more information than could easily be incorporated on a single map of the entire continent.

As he started work on the new venture that Hooftman's project had inspired, Ortelius had published only two or three maps of his own, although he had embellished and colored hundreds of printed maps for sale. His plan was to collect the work of other cartographers, not to produce the maps himself. He was an unlikely rival for Mercator, known rather as a student of classical history and a collector of books and old coins than as a geographer, and it is clear from the surviving letters between them[6] that they exchanged suggestions and ideas freely, helping each other where they could. New maps were found more easily in the busy shops of Antwerp than in Duisburg, and in one letter Mercator asked Ortelius to buy him a copy of the latest work on the Holy Land.

From the start, Mercator allowed his own maps to be used in the new collection, and he also recommended the work of Wolfgang Lazius, an Austrian professor of medicine who was official historian at the court of Emperor Ferdinand. "I could wish that you add the most recent works of Lazius, who described the area subject to the King of Hungary, which Johannes Maior of Vienna sells, and certain other works," he suggested[7] after looking through the first edition of Ortelius's atlas.

Ortelius expected that his new book would attract more customers and bring maps within reach of those who might not otherwise be able to afford them. "There are many that are much delighted with Geography or Chorography, and especially with Mappes or Tables contayning the plottes and descriptions of Countreys, [who] . . . would willlingly lay out the money [for them] were it not, by reason of the narrowness of the roomes and places, broad and large Mappes cannot be opened and spread, that everything on them may easily and well be seene and discerned," he wrote in the introduction to the English edition.[8] His book, the *Theatrum Orbis Terrarum*, would solve these problems, he said. It would be a "well-furnished shoppe,"[9] so arranged that geographer, scholar, or dilettante could find whatever map he wanted quickly and easily.

When the book appeared in 1570, Ortelius made no claims of originality. It was made up of seventy maps on fifty-three sheets, all of them copied or adapted from the work of other cartographers, and accompanied by a detailed explanatory text. At least eight plates, including a magnificent representation of Southeast Asia, were based on Mercator's world map, and his map of Europe was also used. Ortelius's contribution was to collect and select the maps, and redraw them to fit the 22½-by-16½-inch size of his pages. Authors and others in the sixteenth century rarely acknowledged sources or references, but Ortelius's first edition included a *Catalogus Áuctorum* listing a total of eighty-seven leading geographers who were known to him, including thirty-three cartographers whose maps he had consulted.[10] Among them were Mercator's friends from years ago, Gemma Frisius and Franciscus Monachus. Humfrey Lhuyd, a Welsh physician and amateur cartographer, provided maps of England and Wales, and there were contributions from the Nuremberg engraver Christopher Zell and from Jacob Van Deventer, the Flemish cartographer who worked exclusively on maps of the Netherlands.[11]

The *Theatrum* was a compendium of the new mapmaking, the first serious work to turn its back on Ptolemy as the ultimate geographic authority. It made Ortelius's name and his fortune, enabling him to move into a palatial new house in Antwerp. He was appointed royal geographer to King Philip II of Spain three years after its publication, and the massive success of his book began to eclipse even Mercator's reputation.

As it went through its successive editions, Ortelius began to be seen by his contemporaries as the most successful geographer of the age.

The *Theatrum* was an improbable success, reversing the trend of the previous century toward ever-bigger, more detailed maps, and sparking a demand for similar collections which could be taken from the shelf and consulted at one's desk. Such collections offered more than just convenience; they encouraged the reader both to concentrate on a single geographic area and to compare the maps one with another. Their effect was immense: Comparative geography, once the preserve of the specialist and the scholar, was available to everyone. "You have made the earth portable," one delighted owner wrote to him.

There was cordiality rather than rivalry between Ortelius and his old friend Mercator—at least on the surface. Mercator had inspired and encouraged Ortelius's project from the start, and he wrote to congratulate him on the appearance of the *Theatrum*. The pair corresponded as professional colleagues, secure in their mutual regard and in their contempt for the efforts of other mapmakers who, Mercator said, merely entangled and obscured the whole of geography.[12] In the *Theatrum*, Ortelius described him as "the Ptolemy of our days," and in his letter, Mercator responded in kind. He declared the book to be a triumph, but his praise had an edge to it: "[The *Theatrum*] may be bought for a low price, kept in a small place, and even carried about wherever we wish. . . . I am certain that this work of yours will be saleable whatever maps may in the course of time be reprinted by others."[13]

The *Theatrum* was not a work of original scholarship, and in that word *saleable,* there is a very human mixture of admiration and something a little less generous—a recognition by the scholar painstakingly creating his own maps that Ortelius's project was both less and more than his own. It had called for no judicious weighing of contrasting claims of accuracy, no balancing of probabilities, and certainly no mathematical wrestling with the multiple dilemmas of projection. Mercator was well aware of the need to produce what people wanted to buy, but his own maps had always gone beyond what was merely "saleable." He praised the shrewdness of Ortelius's business sense as much as his book. The *Theatrum* was a compendium of other men's maps that had added very little to the sum of knowledge about the world, though it made its publisher a very rich and well-respected man.

As ORTELIUS LUXURIATED in the plaudits he was receiving and counted the profits of successive editions of the *Theatrum* in English, Latin, Dutch, German, French, and Spanish, Mercator struggled solemnly on in Duisburg with his scholarly edition of Ptolemy's maps. He had been unstinting in his encouragement of Ortelius's efforts at gathering the best maps of his generation, but he intended to produce a collection of his own work, feeling that only original cartography would be worthy of a place in the *Cosmographia*. Walter Ghim, loyal to a fault, insisted, "Since this Ortelius was an intimate friend of his, he purposely held up the enterprise he had begun until Ortelius had sold a large quantity of his *Theatrum Orbis Terrarum* and had substantially increased his fortune with the profits from it."[14] Truthfully, Mercator's own projected book was simply not ready: Another eight years elapsed before his edition of Ptolemy's maps was printed, and seven years after that before the initial collection of his own, original maps, bound together as the first volume of his atlas, was completed. He was constantly struggling to meet the orders for his terrestrial and celestial globes, the mainstay of his business, and all the time he could spare from his workbench was taken up with his work on Ptolemy. From one year to the next, he struggled through the *Geographia,* painstakingly constructing maps based on Ptolemy's own instructions. Details of the sources he consulted took up five pages in the book when it was eventually published.

He labored at it with urgency, resenting anything that called him from his desk: "I am so distracted by business that I am slow in finishing Ptolemy, but I do what I can," he told Ortelius in 1575,[15] five years after he started. Age and interruptions appeared to conspire against him: In another letter that same year, he wrote wearily: "As I toil alone, I get on very slowly. Other occupations keep cropping up to interrupt this work, but I hope to be able to finish it by the end of the year."[16] His timetable was slow, but still overambitious: The book would not be finished for another two and a half years from the date of his letter.

The work took its toll on his health. Some years after the appearance of the *Theatrum*, Mercator's portrait was engraved by his friend Frans Hogenberg.* Ortelius had asked for the picture, to be included in his *Album amicorum*, or book of friends. Mercator had been reluctant to supply it—not through any lack of friendship, but because, he explained, "I feel ashamed to parade myself among famous men, as if I were of any importance."[17] The picture has become the image by which he is remembered, and his diffidence is reflected in its worn and weary features. One hand is laid across a globe, half covering America, the continent that was still, more than eighty years after Columbus's arrival, largely hidden and unexplored, while the other holds a pair of dividers, symbols of the meticulous measurement and calculation that he had brought to the art of mapmaking. Yet his eyes are the most memorable feature of the portrait. Heavy lidded, surrounded by deeply etched wrinkles, they gaze into the middle distance, ignoring the globe in front of him, the eyes of a tired and aging man.

In a letter of 1578 to the emperor's physician, Johannes Crato von Krafftheim,[18] Mercator referred to a "serious illness" he had suffered some six years earlier. Worse than that, it was already becoming clear that he had set himself an impossible task. Before he could even start work on the next phase of his *Cosmographia,* he still had to finish his edition of Ptolemy.

The actual research remained his own, as he sifted patiently through the hundreds of different versions, revisions, and improvements of Ptolemy's maps that had been produced over the preceding hundred years; but Mercator was in his sixties and could no longer trust his own hand to carve the delicate lines across the wax-coated copper plates. Not only his surviving sons but also his grandsons, Arnold's children Gerard and Jean—the latter would become official geographer himself at the court of the duke of Cleves—helped him with the engraving. His was truly a family business, almost a dynasty, with Mercator himself at the

---

*The engraving, dated 1574, was later used as the frontispiece for Mercator's atlas.

head of three generations of scholars, but there were never enough workmen at the benches to produce copies of the globes ordered from his workshop, which had to be carefully packed in straw and shipped off. Mercator worked with some of the best craftsmen in Europe, but there were too few skilled engravers to be found in Duisburg, and the growing backlog of work preyed on his mind.

Even the tragic news from Wesel, thirty miles farther down the river, that his daughter Dorothée had died could not distract him. His friends were alarmed at how hard he was driving himself—"You are so deep in your studies that you can't enjoy life, never mind your friends," Vermeulen wrote to him reproachfully.[19] He ignored their pleas, just as he had ignored the warning breakdown that followed his efforts in Lorraine six years before. "I am continually overburdened with a crowd of different occupations. . . . For three years, I had hoped each term to be able to finish, but as I pressed on, I found more difficulties and problems which I hadn't seen at first," he wrote to a friend, in a letter marking the completion of the edition of Ptolemy in the autumn of 1578, a full nine years after the publication of the map of the world.[20] Mercator was sixty-six years old when the new book was published, presenting readers with the most accurate representation of Ptolemy's work that had ever been produced. The maps were precisely drawn according to Ptolemy's coordinates—indeed, if the *Geographia* had included maps, they would have looked like the ones in Mercator's edition. Camels, elephants, and strange beasts that Herodotus might have described prowled through the interior of Africa, while a winged dragon roared in the Libyan desert. The creator of a new, objective, and mathematical system of geography was demonstrating his skill as a medieval cartographer.

The great atlas that Mercator planned needed these maps to put the modern view of the world into universal context. He acknowledged that the maps showed the way the world had been imagined, not the way it was—the huge island of Taprobane dominated an Indian Ocean with no India; Africa disappeared off the bottom of the map; there was no America, and no Pacific Ocean—but just as he had traced the story of the Earth from its very beginning in the *Chronologia,* so in his *Ptolemy's Geographia* he showed the origin of geographic thought. The maps of Ptolemy were the maps of Mercator's own intellectual history. For the rest of his life, he would concentrate on mapping the world as he knew it to be.

Chapter Twenty

A "Thick Myste
of Ignorance" Dispelled

Because of his intense focus on Ptolemy, Mercator had published no new contemporary maps for almost a decade. Ortelius's *Theatrum* reflected the scholarly regard in which his world map was held—Mercator was by far the most prolific contributor to the collection—but he had made no significant progress on his *Cosmographia* or on the atlas of modern maps that was to be its crowning glory.

The maps that Ortelius had borrowed were drawn in the *Theatrum*, as on the original wall map from which they were taken, according to Mercator's projection, but there was no sign that any cartographers appreciated or even understood what he had achieved. Among sailors—who were specifically mentioned in the title—there was even less comprehension.

In 1576, seven years after publication, the financial accounts for Martin Frobisher's first expedition to the Far Northwest included a provision for the purchase of a printed copy of Mercator's world map—"a great mappe universal of Mercator in prente." It was one of a very few copies to be sold for such use, rather than hung on the wall of a library. Frobisher's accounts were precise about its price—one pound, six shillings, and eight pence[1]—but the journals are infuriatingly silent about its value at sea. Even though John Dee gave rudimentary instructions in the latest techniques of navigation before the voyage, it is unlikely that any of Frobisher's seamen understood properly how to use Mercator's map.

They were not alone. Four years later, the expert chart maker William Burrough was called in by the backers of yet another English expedition to the North. His role, like John Dee's before him, was to train the shipmasters in modern navigational techniques, but he advised them to stick meticulously to the methods that had been employed by Columbus nearly a century before. They should keep a careful note of their latitude, he said, and do their best to establish their longitude by dead reckoning, with the conscientious use of the hourglass to measure the time—"one, two, three or four glasses at most" between readings. He provided the sailors with simple charts, or plats, and instructions on how they could mark down and map the observations they made, but he warned them of the difficulties they would meet in the polar regions, where traditional charts were so distorted by the failure of mapmakers to allow for the problems of projection.

Burrough, younger brother of Stephen Burrough, who had looked in vain for the people of Cathay along those same frozen coastlines years before, knew Mercator's world map well; he liked to claim that part of it had been based on a map of Russia he had drawn himself. The problem of projection, he said later, had been solved. "These defects of the latitudes have been very well reformed by . . . Gerard Mercator (whom I honour and esteem as the Chief Cosmographer of the World) in his universall mappe."[2]

Burrough had finally hit upon the way in which the map was truly revolutionary. The new projection of "the famous and learned Gerardus Mercator," he said later, and "the streight lines in sea cardes" which it provided, had given navigators a new way to plot a course. "Such as condemne them for false, and speak most against their use, cannot give other that should serve for navigation to better purpose and effect. Experience (one of the keyes of knowledge) hath taught mee to say it."[3]

Significantly, Mercator's map had made use of the sailors' portolan charts, dismissed contemptuously by many other scholarly cartographers, as important source material, but his second and greatest innovation tackled the problem that had defeated not just Ptolemy but every cartographer who had followed him. Thanks to his new projection, a navigator could plot a straight course on the map and follow that same compass bearing across the sea.

The problem was that sailors would not use it. Intellectuals like Burrough might appreciate its creator's ingenuity, but there is no evidence that Mercator's map was actually consulted by the navigators Burrough advised in 1580 or by anyone else at sea. As a tool of navigation, which is what Mercator thought he was designing, the map of 1569 was an initial failure. For several reasons, only after another sixty years did maps based on the new projection become standard equipment on ocean-going expeditions.

For all Mercator's stated intention to produce a map fit for sailors to use, the 1569 world map has the look of an academic document, rather than a practical aid to navigation at sea. Its cartouches, notes, and explanations are all in Latin, rather than the vernacular, while the accounts of famous explorers and the allegorical representations of Peace, Justice, and Piety all seem more suitable for a library, not a ship's chart room. In short, the projection worked, but the map didn't.

The lack of interest among professional seamen may have been due partly to their own instinctive resistance to change, and partly to a crucial weakness of the map: Despite the fact that direction could be calculated easily, the distortion of distance that resulted from the projection made it difficult to work out the exact position of a ship. Chart makers, too, were reluctant to incur the trouble and expense of reengraving their plates unless a clear and immediate profit was to be made.

In a triple irony, the map was largely ignored by ships that were pushing deep into the very latitudes where it would have been most useful; designed to be easy to use, it was rejected because it was too complicated; and although aimed at seamen, it was purchased overwhelmingly by intellectuals. Even so, Mercator, remembering his days in the studio of Gemma Frisius, realized he needed to protect his work. He wrote to the emperor Maximilian, who had succeeded to the imperial crown five years earlier, asking for a fourteen-year ban on any copies being made—effectively, the granting of an exclusive copyright—and showed no false modesty about the extent of his achievement. "I omitted nothing by which I could emend geographical knowledge, but I restored everything to its true state . . . not only in regard to the arrangement of meridians, parallels, and compass points (in which our nautical tables have so far been erroneous) but also in the descriptions of shorelines and seas, which have been erroneous in existing maps," he declared.[4]

Apart from this businesslike concern, he did nothing actively to promote his invention; on the contrary, he never made any detailed attempt even to explain the theory behind it. According to a comment made by Walter Ghim, after Mercator's death, the great geographer could offer no mathematical formula to prove that his projection worked. He simply knew that it did. The projection, said Ghim, was "a new and convenient device, which corresponded so closely to the squaring of the circle that nothing, as I have often heard from his own mouth, seemed to be lacking except formal proof."[5]

The words were precise—Mercator had indeed transformed a circular world into a rectangle—but from the moment he took the map from his printing press, it appears as though he simply forgot about what would prove to be one of the greatest technical advances in mapmaking, never writing about it further, never even numbering it among his achievements. Only Ghim's comment survives to suggest that he even talked about it with his friends. He had other priorities; as he aged, his great medieval synthesis of knowledge, not his "squaring of the circle," was what inspired him.

Nearly thirty years after the map appeared, the English geographer William Barlowe, one of the tutors of the young son of James VI of Scotland,[6] Prince Henry, described Mercator's projection in his book *The Navigator's Supply*. The imperfections of other charts, he said, were well-known, but there existed a forgotten alternative, "set forth by the excellent cosmographer Gerardus Mercator," that solved all those problems—one which had been kept from widespread appreciation only by the jealousy of other cartographers. "A cloude (as it were) and thick myste of ignorance doth keep (this chart) hitherto concealed; and so much the more, because some who were reckoned for men of good knowledge, have by glauncing speeches (but never by any one reason of moment) gone about what they coulde to disgrace it," he said. Navigators on long voyages, he went on, would find that traditional charts, or cards, could not show places in their correct position, "being yet the very principal point that the navigator desireth." Mercator's map had solved the problem. "No card hitherto invented was ever comparable unto it, neither (as I think) any that shall be hereafter, will in all respects surpass it."[7]

In the same year that Barlowe invoked Mercator's projection, an English mathematician, Edward Wright, finally dispelled the "thick myste of ignorance," explained the new system, and produced a series of tables to enable navigators to correct the distortions of distance that it produced.* Wright's book of 1599, confidently titled *Certaine Errors in Navigation Detected and Corrected*, explained Mercator's achievement for both layman and sailor in a masterpiece of clarity and simplicity. The Earth, he suggested, might be imagined as a partially inflated round balloon, with latitudes and meridians equally spaced around it. If the balloon were placed inside a cylinder so that its equator just touched the cylinder's walls, and then more air were pumped in, its curved meridians would be flattened against the walls of the cylinder. If each line then left an imprint, simply unrolling the cylinder would reveal the impression of a Mercator-projection map on the inside.

More important for navigators, he went farther and worked out how much distortion of distance there would be at each individual line of latitude on the map. All a navigator had to do was measure the latitude of his ship and find the equivalent figure in Wright's tables. With the map alone, a vessel might be almost anywhere on the compass bearing it was following; using Wright's mathematical tables, its position could be calculated with remarkable accuracy. Where Mercator seemed to have lost interest in his own masterpiece, Wright had seen its potential.

Wright admitted he was inspired by Mercator's map; only after viewing it had he spotted the "gross errors and absurdities" of common, non-Mercator, sea charts. *Certaine Errors* had a map of the world drawn

---

*Wright had been first a student and then a lecturer at Cambridge University, and was considered one of the leading mathematicians of his age. He made several trips to sea and became navigational adviser to the East India Company, the challenge and profit of exploration tempting another mathematician to put his skills to profitable use. He was, according to one contemporary, Mark Ridley (in his book, *A short treatise of magnetical bodies and motions*, 1613, cited in Taylor, *Late Tudor and Early Stuart Geography* [London: Methuen, 1934]), "a very skilful and painful man in the Mathematics, a worthy reader of the art of Navigation for the East India Company."

according to Mercator's projection for its title page. At the same time, Wright was jealous of his own achievement in showing how it could be made easier to use. "The way how this should be done, I learned neither from Mercator nor any man els," he added defiantly in the preface to the book, staking out his own claim to mathematical excellence. He had made his own calculations, the mathematician following in the direction that the cartographer had indicated.

The Geography
of the World

THE COPY OF THE "great mappe universal" of 1569 that accompanied the Yorkshire-born explorer Sir Martin Frobisher on his 1576
expedition to the Far North was not Mercator's only contribution to the
search for a northern route to the Spice Islands; his name, adroitly
manipulated by John Dee at Queen Elizabeth's court, was largely responsible for the official backing Frobisher received for two further
expeditions.

From that first expedition, Frobisher brought back to England a captured Inuit fisherman, whose "oriental" appearance seemed to offer exciting new evidence for the existence of a northwest passage. Frobisher's
pilot, Christopher Hall, declared excitedly that the people of the northern Americas were "like to Tartars, with long black hair, broad faces,
and flat noses."[1] To add to the excitement, Frobisher also brought back
samples of a black rock that seemed to be threaded with veins of gold.

In England, John Dee put not just his arguments but also twenty-five
pounds of his own money behind Frobisher's efforts to raise funds for a
second expedition in 1577. Apart from the lure of gold in the frozen soil,
Dee and other investors were tempted by the potential for profitable new
trade routes, while Elizabeth herself saw the possibility of new foreign
possessions, which, scholars declared, would bring not only international
esteem but also great riches. "Without sword drawn, we shall cut the
comb of the French, of the Spanish, of the Portingal, and of enemies, and

of doubtful friends, to the abating of their wealth and force, and to the great saving of the wealth of the realm," she was told by the clergyman and geographer Richard Hakluyt.[2]

To support the case for another expedition, Dee turned to Mercator. Just as the Portuguese had established their dominance by building coastal settlements on the way to the Indies, so the English could set up way stations in the Far North, ran the argument Dee and others put forward before Queen Elizabeth at Windsor Castle in 1577. Pope Alexander's decree and the Treaty of Tordesillas meant that such settlements west of his line would infringe on the rights of the king of Spain—except, Dee declared triumphantly, that the English had established their right of occupation hundreds of years before. That was the considered opinion of his esteemed friend, the famous Gerard Mercator.

In 1577, he produced a letter from Duisburg in which Mercator repeated stories of an ancient expedition led by the great King Arthur himself, which had set out into the northern seas during the sixth century.[3] Four thousand men had traveled with King Arthur, the letter said, though none returned. Mercator's letter maintained that Arthur had "conquered the Northern Islands and made them subject to him."[4] Dee told the queen excitedly that these English colonists had established a prior claim to several territories that the pope had awarded to the Spanish and Portuguese. Inconveniently, he admitted, no trace had ever been found of their settlements on the islands in the Far Northwest; but according to ancient sources that Mercator had consulted, their descendants had visited the court of the king of Norway more than eight centuries later.

As history, Mercator's letter is less than convincing, but it allowed Dee to use his name as evidence to persuade a willing queen of the justice of British claims to establish an empire of their own. Mercator was interested in what the accounts of Arthur's expedition told him about the geography of the northern seas and the people who had sailed them, but Dee had a clear political motive, and on the basis of these accounts and similar stories he constructed a series of proposals for a new and adventurous English foreign policy. Even though England was overshadowed by the great military and mercantile strength of Spain, Portugal, and France, Elizabeth could build a navy, which would enable her mariners and explorers to create a "Brytish Impire" abroad, he said.[5] It seemed a far-fetched idea, but with Francis Drake already preparing his flotilla of five ships for their voyage to America and around the world, Dee's impassioned optimism and Mercator's more measured encouragement were exactly what the queen wanted to hear.

Her hopes, and Dee's, were doomed to disappointment. Three expeditions in successive years headed by Frobisher ended in disappointment and financial scandal; in the end, there was no northwest passage to be found,[6] and no easily won empire either. Not until the seventeenth century was a sustained effort made to establish English settlements on the American mainland.

Amid the disillusionment that followed Frobisher's failure, attention shifted once again to the Northeast and the possibility of battling through the ice floes north of Russia. An expedition was prepared in

Martin Frobisher

London under the leadership of Arthur Pet, an experienced captain on the Muscovy trading routes that had been established after the early expeditions of the 1550s. Mercator was almost certainly aware of the plans from an early stage. His son Rumold, still in England, had struck up a friendship with the geographer Richard Hakluyt. Investors had asked Hakluyt for any information he could gather to improve the expedition's chances of success, and he eventually wrote to his friend's father in Duisburg.

The letter, though, was almost certainly written, and certainly received, after the expedition sailed in May 1580.[7] It was hardly a genuine request for information; perhaps Hakluyt simply wanted to show the investors that he had left no stone unturned in his inquiries, and was writing to Mercator to reassure the investors rather than to guide the sailors; or perhaps his letter was simply an afterthought.

Whatever the reason, there is no mistaking the tartness of Mercator's reply. "Sir," he wrote, with unaccustomed directness, "I felt great displeasure. . . . I would greatly have wished that your Arthur Pet should have been warned of many important matters before his departure." He went on to demonstrate exactly what firm information he could have provided, describing in detail the island of Nova Zembla,* which earlier expeditions had sighted, and the promontory of Cape Tabin beyond, which ancient accounts described as jutting far out into the frozen sea. Around the cape, he warned, lay "many rocks, which make navigation very difficult and dangerous." Even so, he declared, "The voyage to Cathaio by the east is doubtless very easy and short." In return for his advice, Mercator said, as he always did, that he would welcome information about the coastlines and tides in that region; perhaps Frobisher could give him information also about his voyages in the Northwest, he added hopefully.[8]

What little hope of cooperation he had would vanish over the following weeks, and not only because of the lateness of the letter he had

---

*Nova Zembla, which separates the Barents Sea from the Kara Sea, is now known by its Russian name of Novaya Zemlya (New Land). It is actually an archipelago rather than a single island, with two main islands and a number of smaller ones.

been sent. He was convinced that important new discoveries were being kept from him. News of Pet's expedition had thrown him into a frenzy of frustrated suspicion, and in December he wrote to Ortelius, who was in London, that he believed its secret aim had been to meet Drake's flotilla as it returned from the East by a secret northern route. There had been many rumors about Drake, who had been away for three years, and it was widely believed that his expedition must have been lost, but Mercator believed a journey around Russia's northern coastline was perfectly possible, despite the savage, icy conditions previous explorers had faced.

He said he had received a secret tip-off months before about Drake's returning fleet, which was indeed making its way back toward Plymouth, completing the first circumnavigation of the world since Magellan's ill-fated voyage fifty-five years before, as Pet's ships set sail on their speculative trip north. Perhaps Hakluyt or John Dee had given him this information, or one of Rumold's acquaintances—Mercator's youngest son was assiduous in maintaining his contacts in the geographic world of London. With the same discretion that had marked his dealings with the mysterious figure who had commissioned the map of Britain sixteen years before, Mercator told Ortelius simply that "someone wrote to me from England." The information had come, he said, under an oath of secrecy, but this time it was an oath he was prepared to break if doing so might bring him new information.[9]

Pet had left in May, and Drake arrived in September, his ships groaning with plundered Spanish bullion. Mercator urged Ortelius to do all he could to ferret out the truth. "Hide that you know anything, but meanwhile, fish around among your friends to see what you can find out," he told him. "If there are many people asking questions, they cannot lie so splendidly that the truth won't leak out." The English, he added with some justification, had always concealed the routes of their expeditions for as long as they could because they made such huge profits from them. The vast amounts of gold and silver that Drake had brought back seemed to Mercator to put the matter beyond question: "They have concealed the route of this voyage with such zeal, and they have talked about the expedition in such different ways, that I believe they have found the greatest riches that have ever been discovered by Europeans, not to mention the Indians who have sailed the oceans. A great proof to me of this point is that huge treasure of silver and precious stones, which they pretend, as I suspect, to have seized as booty."[10]

His suspicions were unfounded; in fact, Drake had taken the traditional route home around the southern tip of Africa. But though Mercator was mistaken to suggest that the journey would be easy and short—such words would not have been recognized by the explorers in the northern seas and hardly fitted with his own warnings about Cape Tabin—his information about Pet's expedition and its objectives had been startlingly close to the truth. Pet had indeed been given details of what was known of Drake's position in the hope he might meet the flotilla somewhere in the Pacific Ocean.[11]

It was a disappointing outcome for everyone. Of the two ships of Pet's expedition, one went down with all hands off the coast of Norway, while the other limped back to England with its crew almost dead from exposure and exhaustion. The expedition marked the end of English interest in the search for a northern passage and dashed Mercator's hopes for obtaining exciting information to be incorporated into his new geography of the world.

What he saw as duplicity on the part of the "lying" English must have been frustrating for him as he continued to gather material for the atlas. The work was all-consuming. The same letter that urged Ortelius to spy out details of Pet's expedition included a description of Mercator's efforts to acquire a newly printed map of France and also his account of a world map he had managed to borrow. It was, he said, "big, but crudely drawn," yet included parts of the Far East that had clearly been "described from information from merchants."

ARNOLD HAD TAKEN OVER many of the responsibilities of overseeing his father's workshop, producing and packing up the globes that remained the mainstay of the business—Christopher Plantin, in Antwerp, was paying some thirty-six florins for a pair—but Mercator had little time on his hands. The correspondence with Dee, the researches described in his letter to Ortelius, and the daunting timetable he had set himself—only one of the five books of the planned *Cosmographia* was complete, and he was nearly seventy years old—all suggest a man desperately concentrating on his studies. Little wonder, then, that Mercator should apologize to an English correspondent for his delay in writing to him: "I have had so many different matters to deal with."[12]

With Ptolemy's maps finally off his desk, he turned his attention to his ultimate priority, the new geography of the world, which would bring together the current state of geographic knowledge in a collection of maps drawn by his own hand, designed to fit together as a coherent image of the entire world. In a letter written in 1578, around the time of the publication of Ptolemy's maps, he estimated that such a project would comprise a total of around a hundred maps—nearly four times as many as had appeared in the edition of Ptolemy.[13]

The engraving was beyond him, because of his weakening hands and eyes—he told a friend in a letter of 1583 that he was unable to make out individual characters even in broad daylight[14]—but the researching, designing, and drawing of the maps themselves were all his own work. They were the product of years of checking and cross-checking, reconciling the different regional maps from various hands that Mercator had collected in his study.

As he worked, the task grew bigger, not smaller. All his life, in his promises to clients and sponsors, he had underestimated how long his various projects would take him to complete, and in this one, each new map he consulted brought more details to be incorporated into his finished collection. By 1583, he was estimating that covering Germany alone would require about twenty separate maps; after those were completed, he would turn to "Italy, Spain, England, and other lands."[15]

By this time, he had decided that the collection would have to be brought out piecemeal. Money may have been a factor in his decision, but there was also the implicit realization that he was getting older, and his time was limited. When the first set of maps appeared, in 1585, covering France, Germany, and Mercator's own homeland in the Low Countries, a note in the introduction left no doubt how the work was weighing down the aging cartographer: "The entire work is upon my shoulders alone, and there is no one to help me, except for the engravers of the plates."[16]

The whole appearance of the collection was different from the edition of Ptolemy he had published seven years before. The dragons and monsters that had decorated Ptolemy's maps were gone, replaced by a sober, realistic view of the Earth. France, in particular, covered by seven separate maps, had a thriving tradition of its own regional cartography, but it had never been so thoroughly represented. In the *Theatrum*, Ortelius had provided a collection of maps by different hands and without a single theme, but Mercator's were drawn in a consistent style, in such a way that readers could move easily from one to another. "All those places that lie closest to the edges of each map are found again in the next map . . . so that the voyages and journeys from one to another can be easily seen as if there were a single map with both places," he explained in the dedication. Just as his world map had been intended for navigators as well as scholars, so this collection was practical as well as decorative.

This first volume contained fifty-one maps—more than he had drawn in his life until then, but only half of what he had to do. The geography of the world, which had been planned as just one part of the great *Cosmographia,* was taking on a life of its own. Sixteen years after he had first set out his ideas for a five-part synthesis of knowledge, he had changed his scheme for the work; but far from trimming back his ambitions to a more manageable scale, he had added an extra book. A sixth volume, he said, would deal with the history of humankind on Earth, from the first biblical inhabitants, by studying "the genealogies of princes from the creation of the world."[17]

Over the next few years, he started his detailed researches for this book alongside the work he was doing in drawing together the maps for the next volume of his modern geography. In his seventies, he was working more frenziedly than ever before. Within days of finishing his first volume of maps, he wrote to Henry of Rantzau, the aristocratic governor of the province of Holstein (some two hundred miles to the northeast of Duisburg),[18] to ask for help with the next. Henry had promised him advice on the borders of Sweden, presumably from maps in his own extensive collection, and Mercator took the opportunity to spell out his new

World map from Mercator's edition of Ptolemy's Geography

plan. "Your Illustrious Dignity will see how I propose to describe king-doms, dukedoms, principalities and dominions not only geographically but also politically, so that the order and power of the ruling nobility, the governance of the dominions, and the civic status should be visible," he wrote. There was also a personal note for Henry: "In the maps of Den-mark, I hope that by the help of my work, the glory of your name will soon be celebrated as someone who has had a large part in the gover-nance of the kingdom."[19]

The egregious flattery did not miss its mark. A few months later, he wrote again to thank Henry not just for the two maps of Sweden that he had sent, but also for a "golden gift" that had accompanied them: "I give and will give eternal thanks to your generosity and, God willing, I will show this to your honour and will preserve the memory and testimony of your kindness to me."[20]

The accuracy and precision of the maps he had drawn so far were not in doubt, but in one sense they gave a misleading impression of the lands they represented. Spread out on the page, the Netherlands and Germany had an air of stability and calm; there was no hint of the bloody violence that had swept across Mercator's homeland, and which was soon to threaten to engulf him.

Chapter Twenty-two

The Gathering Dark

THE NEWS FROM the Netherlands, where the duke of Alva's reign of terror had brought no lasting peace, had been bad for years. Over the last two decades, there had been repeated uprisings against the Spanish repression and massacres. King Philip, horrified not just by the bloodshed of Alva's warfare and executions, but also by the staggering cost to his treasury,* had removed the duke from the Netherlands in 1573, and tried to engage the nationalist rebels in negotiation, but it was too late. The Protestant revolt, under the charismatic prince of Orange, swept across the northern and eastern areas of the Low Countries. Towns that had been brutalized and cowed by Alva's soldiers declared their allegiance to the Protestant cause once more, and the bloodletting continued throughout the 1570s, often without any clear strategic pattern. In Antwerp, pillaged by mutinous Spanish troops in November of 1576 in what became known as the Spanish Fury, thousands of citizens were put to the sword in four days.[1] In a letter to Ortelius, who had managed to avoid the slaughter, John Dee observed from London that the Netherlands were being "torn to pieces" by the fighting,[2] and in 1578, a new governor-general was installed—Alexander Farnese, the future duke of Parma,[3] a man whose brutality would eas-

---

*Edward Grierson, in *The Fatal Inheritance—Philip II and the Spanish Netherlands* (London: Victor Gollancz, 1969), estimates that by the 1570s, the wars in the Netherlands were eating up some 2 million ducats a year, or nearly twice the revenue from Spain's South American possessions.

ily match that of Alva or Granvelle. He was about to make Dee's observation come true.

At Gembloux, near Namur, he routed an army of twenty thousand men and then set about the towns of eastern Brabant. At Sichem, he massacred the garrison after it had surrendered, and hanged its commander from the town walls; after the fall of Maastricht, according to a later account, "the pavement ran red with blood. . . . eight thousand heretics lay unburied in the streets."[4]

For Mercator, reports of these and similar atrocities had an apocalyptic resonance, for his *Chronologia* had set his own time firmly in the third and final age of God's Creation. In a letter to the Swiss pastor Wolfgang Haller, he struggled to find an optimistic response: "I am convinced that the current war is that of the armies of the Lord, mentioned towards the end of Revelation 17, in which the Lamb and the elect will win the victory, and the church will flourish as never before." It was all far from the Rhine, but Mercator clearly felt some premonition that Duisburg was no longer the safe haven it once had been. "I fear that the nearby disturbances in Belgium will cause us grief," he admitted in the same letter.[5]

Nine months later, in December of 1582, Gebhard Truchsess von Waldburg, who was elector and archbishop of Cologne, renounced his allegiance to the papacy and turned to the Dutch rebels for help in establishing the Protestant Reformation within his lands—a fresh challenge to the forces of Spain and Catholicism that brought the fighting perilously close to Duisburg. Once the rebellious cities of the Low Countries had been taken—Ghent in 1584, Brussels a few months later, and then Antwerp, after a siege of thirteen months, during which Mercator's hometown of Rupelmonde was laid waste—Parma turned to Cologne and the German Protestant towns.

Cologne, the wealthiest and most beautiful city on the Rhine, held fond memories for Mercator. He had passed through it often on his way to Frankfurt and had spent time there with a naturalist and humanist named Ludgerus Heresbachius, a councillor to Duke William. "My mind often turns to Cologne, where I delighted in . . . exploring the libraries," he wrote to him wistfully in 1583. "Sadly, my studies keep me away, as well as my age and sickness and the dangers of war."[6]

Boxes of globes were still being shipped upriver past the city. Mercator told Heresbachius that he was sending all the globes from his workshop to the Frankfurt fair, but traveling was riskier than it had ever been. For the next six years, Cologne and the area around it were ravaged by ill-disciplined and brutal troops as the Spanish forces lived off the land. Towns were sacked, defeated soldiers butchered, peasants plundered, killed, or forced to flee.

As the threat of war drew closer in the summer of 1586, Barbe, Mercator's wife of fifty years, died. She was an old woman,[7] and there is no record of what killed her, but conditions in Duisburg were becoming impossible. Business and trade were in turmoil, and the simplest foods were in short supply. When Mercator wrote to Henry of Rantzau a couple of months after her death, there is no mention of his grief, only a brief apology for his "long silence," but there is no hint, either, of the religious optimism of his earlier correspondence. "Everything is sad, in a place where there has usually been peace and tranquillity. It is a cruel war, in which no one is spared. Friend and neutral are treated the same—hunger and lack of bread are everywhere. Unless God shortens the war, we fear that many will die of famine. . . . May God grant an end to this war," he wrote.[8]

Rumors of impending disaster were rife. "We are pressed by armies, with Neuss besieged and captured. . . . everything is in disorder, and there is no safe road anywhere," he reported in the same letter. Neuss was less than twenty miles up the Rhine, and no one knew whether Duisburg might be next. Horrific stories were told of the collapse of Neuss's defenses, of Spanish soldiers running riot through the streets, of women and children massacred in their homes. Parma's forces began to move down the Rhine in earnest for what promised to be a bloody settling of accounts with the towns that had for years provided such a welcome shelter for Calvinists, Lutherans, and Protestants. As rumors spread through Duisburg, Mercator began packing up the contents of his study and workshop, getting ready to flee. Thirty-six years of security were at an end.

Even amid the chaos of an expected siege, neither the death of his wife nor the threat of conflict had distracted him from the task of gathering cartographic information. In his letter to Henry of Rantzau, he reported that the maps of Italy and Greece for the next collection of his maps were almost finished. "While these are being engraved for the press, I will attack the Sarmatian regions* and the northern kingdoms, and I have the Danish kingdom already drawn and prepared for the engraver. I am awaiting full descriptions of Poland and Livonia from a noble Pole at Cologne, and when I have received them, I will gird up my loins to start their accurate measurement," he wrote.[9]

The Spanish advance was slow and deliberate, and by 1588 Duisburg was surrounded, with the soldiers drawing slowly closer. Passage down the Rhine was blocked by the troops who had plundered Neuss, and upstream, more Spanish troops were besieging the town of Berck. Little knots of people gathered in the empty market, passing stories of torture, killings, and bloodshed from one to another. There were outbreaks of disease in the town as the population, weakened with hunger, waited for the inevitable catastrophe. Outlying fortifications, well within sight of the town walls, were besieged and taken by Spanish troops. For the first time in a century and a half, Duisburg was under siege.

And then, inexplicably, the soldiers marched away. There was no assault, no surrender, no massacre.

Duisburg was saved by the ambition of King Philip. His eyes had turned toward a different conquest, and Parma's troops left the Rhine to return to the Netherlands, ready to join the great Spanish Armada in its ill-fated invasion of England. Thanks to Sir Francis Drake and his fellow sea captains, they never boarded the ships of the Armada, which was broken up and scattered in the Channel storms. But for the next five years, the threat of France and the rebellion of the Netherland provinces would keep Parma away from Germany.

While the Spanish troops were still rampaging through Neuss, Mercator had received another personal blow. In July of 1587, his son Arnold died at the age of forty-nine after an attack of pleurisy. If Bartholomew

---

*This region of central Europe stretched east from the Vistula and the Danube.

had been Mercator's intellectual heir, Arnold was the consummate crafts-man, the surveyor and instrument maker, the engraver who had worked with his father on the map of Europe. Ghim said he "excelled his contemporaries with his keen intellect and good powers of judgement in mathematics. . . . If heaven had granted him a longer life, he would have won distinction as an architect of public buildings."[10] For the last seven years, Arnold had taken day-to-day control of his father's workshop; he had been a member of the town council in Duisburg and a father to nine sons and four daughters. With his death, only Mercator's youngest son, Rumold, was left of the three young men he had hoped might continue his work, and Rumold was often away in London still working for the Antwerp-based bookseller and publisher Arnold Birckman, and presumably still sending back to his father whatever geographic information he could glean. Perhaps Mercator's third daughter, Catherine, was still alive; there is no record of her death, and no mention of her in Mercator's correspondence. Mercator's grandsons, Arnold's boys Gerard and Jean, who were in their twenties, still worked as engravers in the workshop, but for a man who had taken such a delight in his family, he must have felt the losses keenly.

Nonetheless, infirm and aged as he was, Mercator took the practical advice for his own well-being that he had offered to his son-in-law more than twenty years before, and found himself a new wife. In 1589, he married Gertrude Vierlings, the widow of a prosperous friend of his. It was a family occasion—Rumold married Gertrude's daughter at the same time. Mercator was seventy-seven years old, and like most of the major decisions of his life, this one was based on good sense rather than passion: Gertrude was another hardworking woman on whom he would be able to rely. Neither one needed financial security; Gertrude's husband, who had been mayor of Duisburg, had left her comfortably enough provided for, and Mercator himself certainly had no need to marry for money. Presumably, they each wanted companionship.

There were few celebrations. Mercator shrank increasingly into his inner life; what Ghim had earlier referred to as periods of "profound meditation" became more and more frequent, attacks of depression from which neither his new wife nor his family could rouse him. There were constant worries about sickness and ill health—he began to be troubled by gout, the same affliction that had crippled Charles V—but overshadowing everything else was a growing and morbid terror of imminent death and judgment. His letters made frequent mention of sickness getting in the way of his work, and that remained by far his greatest fear. If he were to die, his great projected masterpiece would die with him. William Tyndale, Pierre du Fief's victim more than fifty years before, had died with his translation of the Bible unfinished; the same thing might happen to the grand scheme of the *Cosmographia*, the crown and justification of Mercator's own life's work.

His friends were dead or dying. Gemma Frisius, his teacher, mentor, friend, and contemporary, had been gone for nearly forty years. His book on the design and use of the astrolabe, *De Astrolabio*, was published after his death. Vermeulen had died in Bremen ten years before. Christopher Plantin went home to Antwerp to die in 1589. John Dee was still alive in England, but he was a sick man.

Within a few months of his marriage, in 1589 Mercator published the second volume of his maps of the modern world. Perhaps Henry of Rantzau's maps of Sweden had arrived too late, or perhaps they had been unsatisfactory; in any case, the collection of twenty-two maps that appeared was limited to Greece, Italy, and the Balkans. This was the book in which Mercator seized on the name of Atlas—not after the mythical Titan whose bent figure, carrying the world on his shoulders as a punishment from the gods, was already a commonplace among geographers and cartographers, but in memory of another ancient and equally mythical figure.

The word *atlas* would not be used to describe a collection of maps until the entire set of volumes was published after Mercator's death, but in the preface to this collection, Mercator told the story of another Atlas, a great philosopher-king from Phoenicia who ruled in North Africa and was reputed to be the first man to design a globe. "My purpose is to follow this Atlas, a man so excelling in erudition, humanity, and wisdom, as from a lofty watchtower to contemplate Cosmography, as much as my strength and ability will permit me, to see if peradventure, by my diligence, I may find out some truths in things yet unknown, which may serve to the study of wisdom," he declared.[11] It is as close as he came to offering a description of himself and his own talents and aspirations, and the old man's reservations about his strength and ability reflected his anxieties about his ebbing powers.

Included in this latest volume of maps was a promise to the reader that Mercator would not fail to complete his task: "Finally, we will present all the regions of the world."[12] He was still working on twenty-nine maps that would cover the northern lands, and the maps that were planned for Spain and Portugal were still unstarted. Piled about his desk were maps of England, northern Europe, and the Arctic regions. A few, such as the map of England and Wales drawn by the Welsh physician, antiquarian, and cartographer Humfrey Lhuyd, were the same sources as those Ortelius had used in the first edition of the *Theatrum* nearly twenty years earlier, but many had been researched and drawn within the last few years. A Danish historian named Anders Sørensen Vedel[13] had published a new map of Iceland in 1585 with more than two hundred place-names, all of which were carefully transcribed onto Mercator's version. The hopes of startling new private information from the English explorations in the Far North had been largely disappointed, but there were many changes to be compared, reconciled one with another, and incorporated into the new maps. The coastline of northern Scandinavia and Russia was radically different both from Mercator's earlier map of Europe and from his world map of 1569, with rivers, inlets, and peninsulas newly marked and named. Mercator was making no concessions to age or infirmity in his determination to produce the most up-to-date version possible.[14]

Then, on May 5, 1590, came the blow that made the threat of failure real and imminent: A stroke left him paralyzed on his left side. Not even Ghim could miss the anguish in his soul. "Often he complained with great sorrow in his heart that his illness would prevent him from finishing the works which . . . he had conceived in his mind, and in a sense had at his fingertips," Ghim wrote later.[15] For several weeks he was not only paralyzed but also unable to speak. His new daughter-in-law massaged his arms and legs, and he slept for hours at a time during the day, trying to recover his strength.

Reiner Solenander, one of the team of personal physicians who were treating Duke William at the ducal court in Düsseldorf, sent his advice and prescriptions in a last gesture of respect from the court to the old duke's faithful servant, but he could neither cure him nor ease the ultimate dread Mercator shared with so many of his contemporaries: the fear of hell and eternal damnation. He had feared this for his daughter Emerance, and he feared it for himself. Even the mercy he hoped for from his religion took on a brutal edge. Ghim could only look on in horror. "When the full use of speech had been restored to him, I saw him weep and strike his breast two or three times with his fist, saying 'Hit, burn, cut your servant, O Lord, and if you have not hit him hard enough, strike harder and sharper according to your will, so that I may be spared in the life to come!'"[16]

There was a fresh desperation about his studies: Unable to walk, and with his left arm useless, he had his family carry him, chair and all, into the study, where his books awaited him. He worked, Ghim said, with "his small store of strength," struggling to complete not only the final maps of his modern collection but also a commentary that would place his geographic work in the context of eternity. He wrote of "the beautiful order, the harmonious proportion, and the singular beauty" of Creation with the dignified wonder that had marked his writings about religion since he was a young man, and he also set out his justification for his life's work in geography. The title of this book, finally published after his death as the preface to the final volume of his atlas, was *Cosmographical Meditations Upon the Creation of the Universe, and the Universe as Created*. It is a phrase that could have been applied to the Hereford *mappamundi* more than three centuries earlier, or to any of the hundreds of maps that preceded it—a view of mapmaking as a subjective, impressionistic, and imaginative art rather than the precise, scientific operation to which Mercator actually aspired in his work.

His fingers trembled, his hands were weak, and his eyes were sometimes struck blind, he explained to Haller, apologizing for writing that was occasionally illegible—but his words could have come from the days of his clear-eyed strength and confidence. His work, he declared, was intended for the world, for navigators, explorers, merchants, and great princes. Scholarship was a matter for the study, but the man of the world should look to politics and trade, he wrote. Maps were the eyewitness of empire, and without them, not just trade but also good government would be impossible. "Without geographical maps," he declared in his atlas, "merchants could not journey to the greatest and richest countries to trade with their inhabitants and make all the world the partners of Europe. Without maps, princes would know only with difficulty and through unreliable reports how they could best govern their domains with unwavering confidence."

Maybe those words would have had some resonance in the court of Charles V, the first emperor of an empire on which the Sun literally never set, but Charles had been dead for nearly forty years, and there was little grandeur left at the court of Mercator's protector and patron, Duke William. He had been reduced by a series of strokes to a pathetic, shambling figure, slumped awkwardly in his chair and slurring his words—a bitter parallel to Mercator's own situation. His son and heir, John William, suffered from bouts of madness that were becoming steadily more frequent and more serious.[17] The noble house that had promised so much, that had planned the university on which the young scholar from Leuven had built his unrewarded hopes, that had stood by him and supported him, seemed to be collapsing in madness and disgrace.

He was working on the final volume of the Atlas that would bring all his geographic work together, but his friends could tell that he had not long to live. "When I delight myself with reading your meditations, it is as if I heard the song of the swan," wrote Reiner Solenander from the ducal court in Dusseldorf—the swan, that is, that was reputed to sing before it died. "I wish that I could depart from my decrepit and unhealthy prince, and run to you for the sake of your health," he said.[18]

Solenander did come to treat his friend, but it was too late. A sudden and overwhelming cerebral hemorrhage finally killed him on December 2, 1594, blood gushing from his mouth. A Lutheran priest was called, and the dying man struggled through the night, begging his family to arrange for public prayers to be said for him in the Salvatorkirche where he was to be buried. In death, as in life, he was thinking both of his religion and his place in society. When the end came, it was peaceful. The bookseller

Arnold Mylius, who had heard the news in Cologne, described the moment of his death to Abraham Ortelius in a short, simple, and somber letter: "Dr Gerard Mercator died on 2nd of December. . . . Thus, little by little we all move on." He died about midday, "sitting in his chair before the hearth, as though dropping off to sleep."[19]

Mercator's writings on the Creation, at least, were finished. It was his final intellectual testament, in which he expressed the belief that had been unshaken since his days as an earnest young student in Leuven: that the study of cosmography, of the heavens and Earth, was directed solely toward the understanding of God's wisdom and goodness. The work in which he had planned to demonstrate the extent of the "marvellous harmony of all things towards God's sole purpose," however, was still incomplete. The Atlas in which he had invested all the hopes of his last years lay unfinished on his desk.

The church bell tolled, and word began to spread across Duisburg and across Europe that the great man was dead. For his contemporaries, it was a somber but fitting end to a life of scholarly achievement, religious devotion, and civic probity. In his eighty-third year, he had lived to see his children grow and make successes of their lives; he had seen his grandchildren establish themselves as geographers and scholars in the tradition he had started, and even lived to see the birth of his great-grandchildren. Despite his part in the new age of learning that was dawning, he was revered at his death as a scholar in the most ancient traditions. Ironically, the man Ortelius called the Ptolemy of his age had practically forgotten his projection, his great achievement, as a thing of no importance.

Afterword

WITHIN A FEW MONTHS of his funeral, Mercator's sole surviving son, Rumold, had brought out the final part of his father's three-volume atlas, with its twenty-eight separate maps of England and the Far North. A complete version came out the same year, incorporating the seventy-three maps of the previous two volumes, along with additional ones prepared by Rumold and by Mercator's grandsons Gerard and Michael.[1] Jean, the third of the grandsons who had worked in Mercator's studio, wrote a personal dedication to his "aged and saintly grandfather." Spain and Portugal were still unmapped, but the book also contained Walter Ghim's reverential biography and the thirty-six-thousand-word commentary on the Creation on which Mercator had been working in his last days.[2]

Rumold died before the second edition appeared in 1602, but when the Flemish engraver Jodocus Hondius bought the plates and started to publish his own editions of the atlas with new and updated maps added to the original ones, Mercator's lasting reputation was ensured. Twenty years after he died, the Mercator atlas was still selling across Europe, completely overshadowing the *Theatrum Orbis Terrarum*.[3]

The first edition had also contained a eulogy to Mercator by the Flemish humanist and cartographer Bernardus Furmerius, in which he demonstrated in passing that the achievement of 1569 had not been forgotten. Mercator, he noted, had "gathered together the wide globe of the earth into a map." By the time the second edition was printed, Edward Wright's *Certaine Errors* had provided the mathematical tables

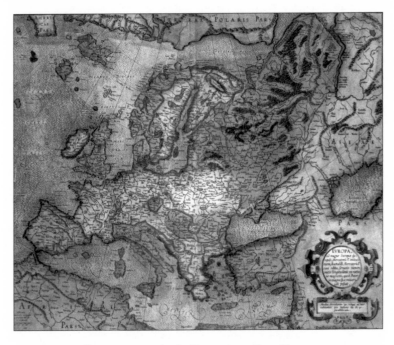

Europe, an engraving by Mercator's son, Rumold, 1595

that simplified the use of Mercator's projection for navigators, and it gradually became the most popular projection for marine charts. Contemporary records in Dieppe, the busiest market of the time for charts and navigational equipment, show that by 1630, most of the marine maps on sale there were drawn on the Mercator projection.

This was what Mercator had wanted; he had designed the projection specifically with the needs of navigation in mind. It has remained the standard for marine navigators for more than four hundred years, and when the spaceship Mariner 9 mapped the surface of Mars in the early 1970s, a Mercator projection was used.[4] The Ordnance Survey issues maps of the British Isles constructed on the Mercator projection; a version of it was used in the first satellite map of the United States in 1974.

There was scholarly recognition, too, in the years following Mercator's death. When Oxford University's newly established Bodleian Library was decorated with a frieze of portraits of learned men early in the seventeenth century, reflecting Protestant England's view of the whole field of learning and literature down the ages, Mercator was there among them. A later, less deferential age covered the paintings in plaster and whitewash, but when they were rediscovered by chance in 1949, his face emerged from behind its covering, gazing rather mournfully out into the room. His academic cap, his high lace collar, and his long flowing beard all spoke of intellectual distinction—the archetype of the scholar and wise philosopher. The portrait is still there, high on a wall in one of the world's great libraries. It is the memorial and the place he might have chosen for himself.

In the years that followed its painting, though, Mercator's face was not an uncontroversial choice. He was known as a scholar and as the author of the great world atlas, but during the next two centuries some claimed that he had stolen the idea for his projection. Writers of the Enlightenment were unwilling to believe that the projection could have been constructed without the supporting mathematical calculations, and they said that the real credit should go to Wright, the English mathematician who refined and explained it. Edmond Halley, the discoverer of the famous comet and a mathematician and cosmographer himself, declared that the projection, "though it generally be called Mercator's[,] was yet undoubtedly Mr Wright's invention."[5] In 1717, the writer, geographer, and cartographer Bradock Mead said that Mercator, having heard from a too-talkative Wright about the new projection, "Batillus-like, took the invention of it to himself." Batillus was a mediocre Roman versifier who claimed to have written much of Virgil's poetry, until exposed before the emperor Augustus; Mead was accusing Mercator of theft and deceit.[6] Unjust as they were, there were good nationalistic reasons for such claims; how much more satisfactory it would have been for Halley, Mead, and the London intellectuals of the eighteenth century that the honor should go to a good English mathematician, rather than to a Flemish engraver working in Germany.

Just as Filippo Brunelleschi had ignored the theoretical explanation of his technique of perspective in the early fifteenth century, so Mercator

*Detail of Mercator from
the portraits of* The Frieze *at
the Bodleian Library, Oxford*

had turned his back on his projection by failing to provide any theoretical background for it. In explaining it, Wright had performed for him the same service that Leon Battista Alberti had done for the Florentine artist—and in doing so, had nearly cost him the immortality of which he had dreamed.

One may question whether Mercator's or any map projection can be truly "objective," but there can be no doubting the change of philosophy between the maps Mercator drew and the subjective, impressionistic efforts of the Middle Ages. Only in the mid–nineteenth century did the word *scientist* begin to have any meaning—more than 250 years after Mercator began concentrating on a cartography based on precise measurement that could be reproduced and relied upon.* He was a scientist before he or anyone else had heard of such a calling; for all the short-

*The *Oxford English Dictionary* lists the first use of *scientist* in 1840.

comings caused by a lack of knowledge, his maps sought to represent what was, not what might have been.

Whether the projection succeeds in doing that is a question about which experts still argue. The supporters of different map projections can be blindly partisan, yet no projection can be ideal for every type of map; it is a compromise, not a solution to a problem. Mercator's world map distorts distances and sizes to the north and south, so that, for example, the polar regions appear out of all proportion, and Europe, too, is much bigger than it should be compared with the equatorial regions. Cartographers and mathematicians periodically demand that its use should be abandoned, or at least restricted, in much the same way that linguistic scholars want spelling to be modified and made more logical. It is not only specialists who launch these campaigns; the *New York Times* on February 21, 1943 even declared grandly, "We cannot forever mislead children and even college students with grossly inaccurate pictures of the world."

Such criticisms were partly a reaction to maps of the British Empire, which were produced almost exclusively according to the Mercator projection, and on which the distortions of size in the higher latitudes produced gratifyingly large expanses of imperial pink. Objectors also point to the layout of the map, which they say enshrines Pope Alexander's high-handed division of the world into two spheres of influence by presenting a clear split between the Americas in the West and Asia in the East. It has even been argued[7] that the map of 1569 was influential in marginalizing Asia in contrast to the overwhelming power of the West—and Mercator was certainly happy to please Philip of Spain by demonstrating the immensity of his domain in the Americas.

Such a layout, with Europe as the focus of the map, was probably inevitable. Mercator was working within a tradition of European mapmaking that had started when the known world was centered on the Mediterranean. In his day, there was little certainty about the areas most distant from Europe, and even today, the vast spread of the Pacific Ocean is a natural place for cartographers to make the cut that is necessary to lay the world out flat. Other cartographers, from Ptolemy through Martin Waldseemüller, had depicted the world as they knew it from a similar viewpoint. It would have been perverse for Mercator to have done differently.

In any case, the other projections that have been suggested in place of his have their own failings and their own distortions. They, too, can be no more than compromises. In the eighteenth century, for instance, a French hydrographic engineer named Rigobert Bonne developed a projection based on concentric, equally spaced arcs as parallel lines of latitude. There was one central perpendicular meridian, with other lines of longitude becoming increasingly curved to the west and east. All areas on the map were in the correct proportion, but the distortion of shape and direction increased with the distance from the central meridian and central parallel.

In 1963, an academic geographer from the University of Wisconsin, Arthur Robinson, was asked to solve the crucial problem of Mercator's projection by creating a system of mapping the world that kept the distortion of the size of continents to a minimum. His design, known as the orthophanic* projection, had curved meridians and straight parallels that were equally spaced between the latitudes of thirty-eight degrees north and thirty-eight degrees south, after which spacing was gradually reduced. It was used in various atlases and a wall map in the United States and elsewhere. The relative sizes of landmasses were accurately portrayed, but their shapes were seriously distorted in the North and South, and as a result the wall map was withdrawn from popular distribution.

Ten years later, a German historian named Arno Peters offered his own solution, which he claimed produced a more balanced image of the world than the "Euro-centered" Mercator projection, showing the sizes of the continents in the correct proportion to one another. It was not original,[8] and the claims made on its behalf were hugely inflated, but it won the backing of the Vatican, the World Council of Churches, and the United Nations. They saw it as a representation of the world that was somehow fairer to developing countries—even though it distorted the shape of all the equatorial regions, stretching them along a north-south axis. Far from being more accurately depicted, many of the developing countries were among the most seriously affected.

Even so, such an alliance of the great and the good, coupled with the

---

Orthophanic means "correct-appearing."

natural enthusiasm of the specialists for change, might have seemed irresistible—and yet, in the twenty-first century, the Mercator projection remains the accepted image of the world. Other projections of the past one hundred years have been based on circles, triangles, torus ring segments that have the appearance of a piece cut from a doughnut, and flattened icosahedrons.* None, perhaps, had the bizarre appeal of the Cahill butterfly map of the world patented in 1913 by a California architect,[9] and none challenged the popularity of Mercator's original proposals. Any map projection depends on a suspension of disbelief: Everyone knows that the world is round, not flat, and that it does not really look like the map, and yet Mercator's rectangular image remains in the mind. His map of the world has caught the imagination of the world. Over map projections, as over proposals for spelling reform, argument is futile; the experts may say what they like, but people hold on to what they find attractive, convincing, and familiar. It is Mercator's map that appears on schoolroom walls, in diaries and magazines, and, most important of all, in people's minds. Their approval is the ultimate democracy.

A modern age may be unwilling to follow Walter Ghim and see Mercator as a saintly figure of scholastic probity. There are questions to be asked today about the genuine objectivity of his vision, and there is no doubt that his desire to please his patrons and to make money for himself sometimes affected his judgment. He might comment tartly on the "saleability" of Ortelius's *Theatrum*, but he himself deliberately chose the Holy Land as the subject for his first map because it would sell well. He was eager to secure the favor of those who were butchering his coreligionists without mercy, and more than ready to join in the flattery of Charles V, with his map of Flanders, his surveying instruments, and his tiny crystal globe. Throughout his life, Mercator had a keen eye for profit and personal advantage, and he was shameless in seeking out and pleasing the rich and mighty. "Golden gifts" were the currency of his life—some of them from people like Antoine Perrenot de Granvelle, whose hands dripped with innocent blood.

---

*An icosahedron is a twenty-faced three-dimensional figure.

Such criticisms, though, would have been barely understood in the times in which he lived. The astonishing achievement of Gerard Mercator is that, living in the sixteenth century, he defined the world for ordinary people in a way that remains current in the twenty-first. His projection was a triumph of modern thought in a world still concentrating on the wisdom of ancient times—and it survived. Modern mapmaking began with Mercator of Rupelmonde; today, more than four centuries later, his vision remains the prevailing worldview. It has its limitations, but if any moderately educated person at the start of the third millennium is asked to imagine a world map, the picture in his or her mind, allowing for the geographic discoveries of four hundred years, will be that of Mercator's projection.

Columbus, Vasco da Gama, and scores of other daring mariners of spirit and imagination pushed back the shadows and found new lands for their countrymen to conquer. Gerard Mercator, hunched over his desk in Duisburg, redrew the world and hung it on the wall.

NOTES

CHAPTER ONE. *Pushing Back Shadows*

1. The *Saga of Erik the Red* records an expedition led by Leif Eriksson around the year AD 1000 that landed on a warm, wooded coast far to the west, which he called Vinland. It is now believed to have been somewhere along the Atlantic coast of eastern or northeastern Canada.

2. Alexandrian merchants traded with the people of Taprobane, and although Ptolemy believed the island was several times larger than it really is, and mistakenly positioned it on the equator, he was able to include the positions of five rivers and nineteen towns in his detailed description.

3. Ezekiel 27: 12–14.

4. Claudius Ptolemy, *Geographia,* book 1, chapter 5.

5. Ibid., book 2, chapter 1.

6. Abu al-Qasim Muhammad ibn Haukal, *The Book of Roads and Kingdoms,* cited in *The Oriental Geography of Ibn Haukal,* ed. Sir William Ousley (London, 1800), p. 4.

7. Al Idrisi, *Opus Geographicum,* cited in Bernard Lewis, *The Muslim Discovery of Europe* (London: Weidenfield and Nicholson, 1982), pp. 147–48.

8. "Thus saith the Lord God; This is Jerusalem: I have set it in the midst of the nations and countries that are round about her." (Ezekiel, 5.5)

9. The map was probably drawn by an obscure churchman, Richard of Haldingham, sometime around 1280. It is on permanent display now on the wall of a specially built exhibition room at the cathedral, protected, as befits an irreplaceable treasure, behind the glass front of a stone cabinet and under subdued lighting.

CHAPTER TWO. *Forgotten Wisdom*

1. Eratosthenes noted that in Syene, or Aswan, the Sun was directly overhead at the summer solstice. At Alexandria, which he assumed to be five hundred miles due north, a vertical stake in the ground cast a shadow at an angle of 7.2 degrees, or one-fiftieth of a circle. From that, he deduced that the distance between the two cities—which he knew to be five hundred miles—was one-fiftieth of the circumference of the world. That gave him an answer of twenty-five thousand miles. He mistakenly took the Earth to be a perfect sphere, and his other assumptions were slightly inaccurate—Alexandria is not due

north of Aswan, and the distance between the two is slightly less than five hundred miles—but his answer was remarkably close to the accepted figure of 24,899 miles.

2. Ptolemy, *Geographia,* book 1, chapter 22.

3. Recent historical study suggests that the Royal Observatory could actually have been based in the nearby port of Lagos.

4. The globe has never left the town, although in the 1930s Behaim's descendants were about to sell it to a private buyer in America—until Adolf Hitler intervened. Hitler ordered that it should be sold instead to the museum as a monument to German skill, artistry, and ingenuity. Cruella de Ville has a replica of it in Walt Disney's version of *The Hundred and One Dalmatians,* and another appears in the 2001 film *Harry Potter and the Sorceror's Stone.*

5. Christopher Columbus, Prologue to *Journal of the First Voyage,* cited in S. E. Morison, *Journals and Other Documents on the Life and Voyages of Christopher Columbus* (New York: Heritage, 1963), pp. 47–48.

6. Columbus, *Journal,* cited in ibid., p. 54.

7. Christopher Columbus, letter of October 1498, cited in ibid., p. 287.

8. Christopher Columbus, entry for Wednesday, October 24, 1492, *Journal*, cited in ibid.

9. Cited in Donald Weinstein, ed., *Ambassador from Venice* (Minneapolis: University of Minnesota Press, 1960). Priuli, who died in 1512, was a nephew of the ninety-fourth doge of Venice, Antonio Priuli. His diaries were republished by Citta de Castello, Bologna, in 1912.

10. Cabral spent ten days exploring the South American coastline and rivers, and then sailed on to India, having claimed the land for Portugal and named it Isla da Santa Cruz, or Island of the Holy Cross—a name which demonstrates that he had no idea that it was part of a continent. Some historians believe that Cabral sailed intentionally to Brazil, following earlier sightings of the land. Columbus, on his third voyage across the Atlantic in 1498, had sighted the northern coastline of South America.

11. The phrase occurs in a pamphlet, *Mundus Novus (The New World),* which Vespucci published in 1503 or 1504, after his second expedition to the Americas.

12. Keats's reference to "stout Cortez" in his sonnet was the poet's mistake.

13. Martin Waldseemüller, *Cosmographia,* 1507, cited in John Noble Wilford, *The Mapmakers* (New York: Vintage, 1982), p. 84.

14. There has been considerable controversy over recent suggestions that a Chinese fleet circumnavigated the world, and also landed on the American mainland, as early as 1421.

15. George Beste, *A True Discourse of the Late Voyages of Discoverie ... Under the Conduct of Martin Frobisher* (1578), cited in James McDermott, *Martin Frobisher, Elizabethan Privateer* (New Haven, Conn.: Yale University Press, 2001), p. 242.

16. From the Italian *portolano,* meaning "pilot-book," derived from the word *porto,* or *port.*

17. Michiel Coignet, "Instruction nouvelle ... touchant l'art de naviguer" (Antwerp, 1581), cited in Lloyd A. Brown, *The Story of Maps* (London: Cresset Press, 1951).

18. Traditional seaman's saying, quoted in William Galvani, *Mainsail to the Wind* (New York: Sheridan House, 1999), p. 71.

CHAPTER FOUR. *Among the Brethren of the Common Life*

1. Albrecht Dürer, *Diary of a Journey in the Netherlands* (1520–21).

2. The twentieth-century psychologist Carl Jung described Bosch as "master of monsters, discoverer of the unconscious."

3. Lynda Harris, in her book *The Secret Heresy of Hieronymus Bosch* (London: Floris Books, 1995), argues intriguingly that Bosch was a secret adherent of the heretical sect, the Cathars, who rejected the entire physical world as the kingdom of Satan, and the Roman Church as his embassy on Earth. They had been cruelly persecuted by the Inquisition for hundreds of years, so if Bosch had any connection with them, he would have been at pains to keep it hidden.

4. The painting is now in Madrid's Prado Museum.

5. Now in the Louvre, Paris.

6. Quoted in R. B. Drummond, *Erasmus, His Life and Character* (London: Smith, Elder, 1873), p. 7.

7. Some universities could be more demanding than others: Lynn Thorndike, in *University Records and Life in the Middle Ages* (New York: Columbia University Press, 1944), p. 353, quotes a fifteenth-century decree of the University of Heidelberg warning a student that "if he does not know how to read, he shall pay careful attention in other respects lest he annoy or impede the master or masters or scholars by clamour or insolence." Leuven, which already enjoyed a reputation as one of the most academically distinguished seats of learning of Europe, would have been less relaxed in its demands.

CHAPTER FIVE. *At the College of the Castle*

1. Nicolas Vernulaeus, *Academia Lovaniesis* (1667), cited in H. Rashdall, *The Universities of Europe in the Middle Ages* (Oxford: Oxford University Press, 1936), pp. 263–68.

2. Erasmus to Guillaume Taleus, August 3, 1521, cited in J. Van Raemdonck, *Gerard Mercator, sa vie et ses oeuvres* (Saint Nicolas, 1869), p. 19.

3. Léon van der Essen, in *Une institution d'enseignement superiéur* (Brussels: University of Leuven Press, 1921), says no student was allowed to take part in any official activity unless he was wearing a long, sober gown that reached to his ankles.

4. Pope Adrian VI, as he became known, started a process of reform in the Catholic Church but died in September 1523 after only eighteen months. He was the last non-Italian pope for over 450 years.

5. Gemma Frisius, *De usu globi,* in *De principiis astronomiae et cosmographiae* (Antwerp, 1530).

6. Mercator to Wolfgang Haller, March 3, 1581. Mercator's surviving correspondence is edited by M. Van Durme in *Correspondance Mercatorienne* (Antwerp: De Nederlandsche Boekhandel, 1959), from which all his letters are quoted.

7. Ibid.

8. Mercator, dedication to *Evangelicae historiae quadriparta Monas . . . ,* (1592).

9. Martin Luther to John Lang, May 1517, in Preserved Smith, *Life and Letters of Martin Luther* (Boston: Houghton Mifflin, 1911), p. 26.

10. Mercator, dedication to *Evangelicae historiae quadriparta Monas . . .*

11. Ibid.

CHAPTER SIX. *Doubts and Dangers*

1. There are no detailed records of Mercator's visit to Antwerp and Mechelen. Walter Ghim says it lasted for "some years." J. Van Raemdonck, in his authoritative biography *Gérard Mercator, sa vie et ses oeuvres,* suggests that 1534 is the most likely date for his return, making his stay in Antwerp and Mechelen about two years. All that can be certain is that Mercator was back in Leuven before starting work with Gemma Frisius in 1535.

2. Walter Ghim, *Vita Mercatoris,* translation in A. S. Osley, *Mercator: A Monograph on the Lettering of Maps, etc, in the 16th Century* (London: Faber, 1969), p. 185.

CHAPTER SEVEN. *Gemma's Globe*

1. Granvelle left his paintings behind when he was sent away from Antwerp by Charles V in 1564. They were eventually looted by rioting Spanish troops in 1572.

2. Niclaes Jonghelinck was the brother of the successful sculptor and artist Jacob Jonghelinck.

CHAPTER EIGHT. *Craftsman and Cartographer*

1. Ghim, *Vita Mercatoris.*

2. Macropedius, *The Rebels,* chorus to act 3, 1535, in Yehudi Lindeman, *Two Comedies of Macropedius* (Nieuwkoop: De Graaf, 1983), pp. 64–65.

3. Molanus (Jan Vermeulen) to Mercator, March 24, 1566. Vermeulen used his Latinized name, Molanus, in his correspondence.

4. Reuwich printed the first three editions of the *Peregrinatio* at his own house in Mainz between 1486 and 1488.

5. Ziegler's book, *Quae Intus Continentur,* was published in 1532. It relied largely on Old Testament sources.

6. Mercator to Andreas Masius, May 22, 1567.

7. Ghim, *Vita Mercatoris.*

8. Van Maes's commentary controversially suggested that although Moses had been the author of the Pentateuch, later editors had added to his work.

9. Andreas Van Maes to Georges Cassander, 1563.

10. William Prescott's classic *History of the Conquest of Peru* (1847) explains: "The distance was so great, and opportunities for communication so rare, that the tidings were usually very long behind the occurrence of the events to which they related."

11. Werner's *Libellus de quattuor terrarum orbis in plano figurationibus* was published in 1514.

CHAPTER NINE. *The Greatest Globe in the World*

1. Mercator to Antoine Perrenot de Granvelle, August 4, 1540.

2. Ibid.

3. One of the gores carried the inscription "Edebat Gerardus Mercator Rupelmundanus cum privilegio Ces Maiestatis as an sex Lovanii an 1541" (Published by Gerard Mercator of Rupemonde under the license of His Majesty for six years at Leuven in the year 1541).

4. During the 1540s, he also manufactured a pair of globes to fill an order from Charles V. The globes are lost, but it seems likely that the celestial globe would have been a prototype for the one he produced for sale in 1551.

5. "I think we do know the sweet Roman hand . . ."—*Twelfth Night,* act 3, scene 4.

6. Mercator, *Literarum latinarum, quas italicas . . .* (1539–40).

7. His pictures showing how to hold a quill pen were shamelessly plagiarized in another writing manual published in Zurich a few years later.

8. Benito Arias Montano oversaw the publication of Bibles in the Netherlands on behalf of the king. He later became royal librarian.

CHAPTER TEN. *In the Hands of the Inquisition*

1. In later official documents concerning his arrest, he is referred to as M. Gerard Mercatoris.

2. Pierre de Corte to Mary of Hungary, February 1543.

3. Pierre de Corte to Mary of Hungary, February 23, 1543.

4. Francisco de Enzinas, *La chasse aux Lutheriéns des Pays-Bas,* ed. Albert Savine (Paris: Louis Michaud, 1910).

5. Francisco de Enzinas, *La chasse aux Lutheriéns des Pays Bas,* ed. Albert Savine (Paris: Louis Michaud, 1910), p. 127.

6. The note was interpreted four centuries later by the Belgian historian Antoine de Smet, a former map curator at the Royal Library of Belgium.

7. Mercator to Antoine Perrenot de Granvelle, October 9, 1544.

CHAPTER ELEVEN. *Two New Arrivals*

1. John Dee to Mercator, July 20, 1558.

2. Quoted in W. H. Sherman, *John Dee* (Amherst: University of Massachusetts Press, 1995).

3. John Dee to Mercator, July 20, 1558.

4. John Dee, *The Compendious Rehearsal . . . ,* 1592, cited in E. G. R. Taylor, *Tudor Geography, 1485–1583* (London: Methuen, 1930).

5. Ibid.

6. *Acts of Privy Council NS 5, no. 261,* cited in Benjamin Woolley, *The Queen's Conjuror* (London: HarperCollins, 2001), p. 310.

7. Christopher Marlowe, *The Tragical History of the Life and Death of Dr Faustus,* prologue to scene 1, 120.

8. John Aubrey, *Brief Lives,* ed. Oliver Lawson Dick (London: Secker and Warburg, 1971), p. 90.

9. All personal correspondence between the two men has been lost to history.

10. Colin Clair, in *Christopher Plantin* (London: Cassell, 1960), p. 12, quotes an entry in the register of the burgesses of Antwerp that notes the arrival of "Christoffel Plantyn . . . van Tours en Franche" in that year.

11. When the Spanish left Antwerp in 1576 Plantin changed sides again. The same presses that had been printing Bibles turned out virulent nationalist pamphlets for the States General that ruled the city. The man who had kept King Philip so well supplied with Catholic prayer-books and hymnals then dedicated one of his books to William of Orange, the leader of the nationalist cause and the king's bitterest enemy, and he became the most loyal supporter of the new regime. In 1579, with the Spanish beginning the systematic task of reconquering the lowland cities they had left, he finally slipped out of the town where he had made his home and his fortune in thirty-five years of shifting al-

liances, friendships, and loyalties. Thirteen months of siege, in which the River Scheldt was blockaded by the Spanish, saw Antwerp starved into surrender, while Plantin stayed safely in Leyden, some seventy miles to the north. Three years later, the danger past, he returned quietly to Antwerp, where he died in 1589 at the age of seventy-five.

12. Mercator, dedication to *Evangelicae historiae quadripartita Monas . . .*

1. The massive, square blocks of the new church with its high, arched Gothic windows, its steep pitched roof, and its intricate carved pinnacles, stained today with the grime of a heavy industrial past, still look over the carefully preserved ruins of the ancient town square in Duisburg. Twin steel frameworks mark the position of the fourteenth-century market-hall, its foundations revealed by modern archaeologists exactly where Corputius depicted them. But the spire of the church, which is the focal point of his view of the town, is missing; only a curiously stumplike tower remains. The church, a triumph of the sixteenth century, was a victim of the twentieth, targeted by Allied bombers during World War II.

2. Mercator, "Dedicatory Letter to John William the Younger, Duke of Jülich, Cleves, and Berg," *Atlas, sive cosmographicae meditationes de fabrica mundi et fabricati figura* (1594).

3. Ghim, *Vita Mercatoris,* p. 192.

4. Ibid., p. 193.

5. Ibid., p. 192.

6. It is not clear how much of this plan was ever completed. Mercator's dedication to his atlas of 1595 suggests that the work went on for years.

7. In Van Durme's *Correspondance Mercatorienne,* the first letter to Vermeulen is dated May 1559 and the last October 1577, but the tone of the first letter suggests they had already been corresponding for some time.

8. Molanus to Mercator, September 1, 1575.

9. Molanus to Mercator, March 24, 1566.

10. Mercator to Wolfgang Haller, March 23, 1582.

11. Molanus to Mercator, September 1, 1575.

12. Molanus to Mercator, April 8, 1575.

13. Mercator to Molanus, July 27, 1576.

14. Ibid.

15. Charles had probably read references to similar globes owned by Archimedes in the third century BC and by the mathematician and inventor Hero of Alexandria in the first century.

16. Ghim, *Vita Mercatoris,* pp. 186–87.

1. The *Dictionary of Belgian Biography* notes that Vermeulen left the Neatherlands for Bremen in 1553. It is not clear whether he was banished or simply fled to escape the threat of arrest.

2. Mercator to Antoine Perrenot de Granvelle, August 4, 1540.

3. Mercator to Abraham Ortelius, November 22, 1570.

4. Ghim, *Vita Mercatoris,* p. 187.

5. John Dee and Christopher Plantin were also important contacts of Ortelius.

6. Ghim, *Vita Mercatoris,* p. 187.

7. The second edition of the map was also believed to have vanished completely until a single copy was discovered in 1898 in the library of Basle University. Another was found some years later in the library of the grand duke of Weimar, and a third in 1936 in the Italian city of Perugia. These are now believed to be the only surviving copies.

CHAPTER FOURTEEN. *A Mysterious Commission*

1. Mercator to Wolfgang Haller, March 23, 1582. Haller had a reputation of his own for his avid collecting of details of weather patterns in his native Switzerland.

2. Molanus to Mercator, August 10, 1559.

3. Molanus to Bartholomew Mercator, 1560. Like his father, Bartholomew used the name Mercator in his correspondence.

4. Molanus to Mercator, August 10, 1559.

5. Peter Barber, in *The Mercator Atlas of Europe,* ed. M. Watelet (Pleasant Hill, Oregon: Walking Tree Press, 1998), suggests that the map was probably delivered to Mercator during 1561.

6. The only printed maps of Britain to be had were a twenty-year-old version drawn in Italy by a Catholic exile named George Lily and various unsatisfactory copies of an anonymous and unfinished map drawn on two parchment skins in the mid–fourteenth century.

7. Letter to Sir William Cecil, 1559. Quoted by Barber in *The Mercator Atlas of Europe,* p. 70.

8. Letter from Thomas Byschop to Sir William Cecil (1561 or 1562), quoted in D. G. Moir et al., *The Early Maps of Scotland to 1850* (Edinburgh: Scottish Geographical Society, 1973), vol. 1, p. 13.

9. The pope's line was moved westward to the meridian 46°37′ W by agreement between the two nations a few months later in the Treaty of Tordesillas—a change that gave the newly discovered land of Brazil to Portugal just six years later. There was bitter argument over the effect of extending the line to the other side of the world, where it proved impossible to agree on which side of it the Spice Islands were situated. Modern explorers, ancient geographers, and travelers' tales were all called in evidence by the Spanish and Portuguese claimants, but in the end, politics and hard cash ended the dispute. Charles V, Holy Roman emperor and also king of Spain, desperately needed funds for his wars with the French and sold his claim to the islands in 1529 for 350,000 ducats. It was not a high price—twenty-four years later, still chronically short of money, Charles spent six times that sum on the disastrous siege of Metz alone—but a modern atlas shows that the islands did in fact lie comfortably on the Portuguese side.

10. Attributed in German Arciniegas, *Caribbean Sea of the New World,* trans. Harriet de Onis (New York: Knopf, 1946), p. 118.

11. Quoted in Taylor, *Tudor Geography,* p. 121.

12. Quoted in Richard Hakluyt, *Divers Voyages* (1582).

13. In Mercator's later world map of 1569, he followed other cartographers in naming this passage the Strait of Anian, after a kingdom called Anan by Marco Polo. Modern research suggests that this may be the island of Hainan, off the southern coast of China.

Efforts to find the mythical strait, which Jonathan Swift placed close to his equally mythical kingdom of Brobdingnag, continued well into the nineteenth century.

CHAPTER FIFTEEN. *In the Forests of Lorraine*

1. Duke Charles's maternal grandmother, Isabella Habsburg, was Charles V's sister.
2. Ghim, *Vita Mercatoris,* p. 187.
3. Ibid., p. 192.
4. Ibid., p. 187.
5. The French poet and storyteller Jean La Fontaine, in 1633.
6. Georg Hoefnagel's *Civitates orbis terrarum* (1561) quotes an anonymous author,
writing in 1532.
7. The story is mentioned in the edition of Mercator's atlas published by Jodocus
Hondius in 1606. The prefect of Poitiers was fascinated enough by the story in the late
nineteenth century to mount an unsuccessful search for the inscriptions.
8. Gerard Mercator, *Ptolemy's Geographia* (1584).
9. Gerard Mercator, *Chronologia* (1569).

CHAPTER SIXTEEN. *Tragedy*

1. Van Raemdonck, *Gerard Mercator, sa vie et ses oeuvres,* p. 92.
2. Juvenal, *Satires,* 4, l. 110.
3. Martin Dorpius complained in 1515 about a Greek edition of the New Testament
that Erasmus had prepared, and later challenged him to speak out against Luther. Sir
Thomas More later wrote to him in Erasmus's defense. *Dorpius* is a Latin word meaning
"from Dusseldorf."
4. Mercator, preface to the *Chronologia.*
5. Molanus to Mercator, February 8, 1575.
6. Mercator, preface to the *Chronologia.*
7. Molanus to Mercator, April 8, 1575.
8. Three hundred years later, when Robert Browning wrote about the town of
Hamelin, a few score miles upriver, where "The River Weser, deep and wide, / Washes
its walls on the southern side," the terror was just a memory; he could afford to tell a
lighthearted tale about the Pied Piper and the rats. In the sixteenth century, nothing was
feared more than the plague.
9. Molanus to Mercator, May 19, 1567.
10. Ibid. It is uncertain whether the reference to "brothers and sisters" means that
any of Mercator's children in addition to Arnold were there, or whether she was accompanied by her spiritual "brothers and sisters" in the Church.
11. Boccaccio's account of the plague is included in the introduction to the *De-
cameron* (1349–51).
12. Molanus to Mercator, July 15, 1567.
13. Ibid.

CHAPTER SEVENTEEN. *The Sum of Human Knowledge*

1. The question of dates was particularly topical: A slight underestimate of the
length of the solar year when Julius Caesar instituted the Julian Calendar throughout the
Roman Empire sixteen hundred years earlier had left the calendar and the solar year
gradually slipping out of step by just under eleven minutes a year. While Mercator was

working on his book, preparations were being made for the great reform of 1582 by which Pope Gregory XIII brought them back into line by the simple expedient of skipping ten days in October. It was a radical change, which left many people complaining bitterly that they had been robbed of ten days of their lives.

2. Ghim, *Vita Mercatoris,* p. 190.

3. Ibid.

4. Twenty years later, the German cartographer Sebastian Münster had followed his edition of Ptolemy with a *Cosmographia universalis,* drawing on the researches of over 120 collaborators, which went into some forty editions over the next eighty years.

5. The dome of the cathedral was completed in 1436, following a design by Brunelleschi himself. A wooden model that he made is still on display in the museum of the Opera del Duomo, Florence.

6. The remark appears in da Vinci's *Notebooks,* quoted in Edwin Panofsky's *Perspective as Symbolic Form* (New York: Zone Books, 1997), p. 66.

7. Antonio di Tuccio Manetti, *The Life of Brunelleschi,* ed. H. Saalman, trans. C. Enggass (University Park: Pennsylvania State University Press, 1970), p. 44. The original book was written during the 1490s.

8. Marcus Vitruvius Pollio, *De Architectura libri decem.*

9. During Mercator's lifetime, craftsmen were producing perspective machines on the same principle as a pinhole camera to produce a correct image of a scene that could be copied from a translucent sheet. In 1558, the Neapolitan scholar Giovanni Battista della Porta described in his *Magiae Naturalis* (Natural Magic) how such a device could be made and used.

10. In the second century BC, the astronomer Hipparchus of Nicaea suggested that lines of latitude, or *climata,* parallel to the equator could be fixed at regular intervals by making observations of the stars. Lines of longitude at right angles to them could be calculated by measuring the variation in the time of sunrise or sunset at different points, based on the fact that one hour of time difference would indicate 15 degrees of longitude, being one twenty-fourth of 360 degrees. His contemporary Eratosthenes of Cyrene made a similar suggestion but pointed out that the question was largely academic as there was no reliable way to take all the necessary observations. Ptolemy, working in the second century AD, devised more reliable instruments for taking astronomical observations but was still limited by the lack of reported figures from outside the eastern Mediterranean region. Many of the coordinates in his *Geographia* were necessarily estimated.

11. Martin Waldseemüller used a version of the cylindrical projection for his world map of 1507, as did the Bristol merchant Robert Thorne when he constructed a map twenty years later to support his plea to King Henry VIII for an expedition to the Far North. Araham Ortelius and Mercator himself produced regional maps on a similar model.

12. Claudius Ptolemy, *Geographia* book 1, chapter xxiv, cited in Lloyd A. Brown, *The Story of Maps* (London: Cresset Press, 1951), p. 70.

CHAPTER EIGHTEEN. *The World Hung on the Wall: The Projection*

1. Ghim, *Vita Mercatoris,* p. 187.

2. Mercator to Antoine Perrenot de Granvelle, February 23, 1546.

3. Similar maps in northern Europe were referred to as *rutters,* from the French word *routier,* meaning "something that finds a way."

4. Taylor, in *Tudor Geography*, p. 88, suggests that Rumold worked at the London office of the Cologne publisher and bookseller Arnold Birckman "between 1569 and 1575, and possibly for a longer period," but it is likely that he made frequent trips to London before he moved there to live.

5. The scale of this exaggeration is larger than one might expect: The sixtieth parallel on a Mercator map is twice as long as it should be, the seventy-fifth parallel fifteen times as long, and the eightieth parallel thirty-three times as long.

6. Mercator, legend to world map of 1569.

7. At various times from the end of the twelfth century the mysterious Christian kingdom of Presbyter, or Prester, John was reputed to be in the Far East, central Asia, India, or Africa. Marco Polo identified him as a prince of a Mongolian tribe, and two centuries later, Vasco da Gama carried letters of introduction to Prester John with him on his voyages up the eastern African coastline.

8. Mercator, legend to world map of 1569.

9. Diego Gutierrez, a cartographer from Spain's Casa de la Contratacion, the government ministry dealing with the possessions in the Americas, cooperated with the Antwerp engraver Hieronymus Cock in producing the map, which comprised six sheets pasted together to form a map of about thirty-six inches by thirty-four inches. Despite its limitations, it was the largest and most authoritative map of America of its time.

10. This was an exaggeration; modern maps show the continent to be some 110 degrees at its widest point.

11. This argument continued to carry weight until Captain Cook's voyages in the eighteenth century established the true empty vastness of the southern seas.

12. He took this image almost entirely from Jacob Cnoyen, a fourteenth-century traveler from 's Hertogenbosch who claimed to have visited Asia and Africa as well as the Far North. Cnoyen also described four strong currents running north before disappearing into the Earth at the North Pole.

13. Several of the rivers in South America were clearly borrowed from Gutierrez's map.

CHAPTER NINETEEN. *Presenting Ptolemy to the World*

1. J. L. Motley, *The Rise of the Dutch Republic* (London: Dean and Son, 1906), pp. 555–56.

2. Mercator, preface to first volume of *Atlas* (1589).

3. Mercator to Abraham Ortelius, March 26, 1575.

4. Mercator to Abraham Ortelius, November 22, 1570.

5. Ortelius produced a world map in 1564 and a map of Egypt in 1565. Maps of Asia and Spain followed in 1567 and 1570.

6. Van Durme's edition of Mercator's letters shows the two men writing to each other between 1570 and 1580, but they were clearly in touch before and after those dates. The first surviving letter from Mercator refers to earlier correspondence, and Ortelius was in touch with Mercator's son Rumold in 1596.

7. Mercator to Abraham Ortelius, November 22, 1570. This was good advice, well taken—Lazius's map of Hungary appears in later editions of the book.

8. Abraham Ortelius, "To the Courteous Reader," in *Theatrum Orbis Terrarum*.

9. Ibid.

10. There was little formal copyright protection for authors or artists in the sixteenth century, although Mercator was always at pains to obtain licenses for his maps from the emperor.

11. Apart from maps at Brabant, Holland, Zeeland, Geldria, and Friesland, Van Deventer completed more than two hundred hand-drawn plans of various towns in the Netherlands, which are preserved in atlases in Brussels and Madrid.

12. Mercator made clear in his letter of November 22, 1570, that his criticisms did not refer to the maps included in the *Theatrum* for which, he said, Ortelius had "selected the best descriptions of each region." Ortelius, in turn, declared in the book that he believed Mercator was preeminent among the geographers of the time.

13. Mercator to Abraham Ortelius, November 22, 1570.

14. Ghim, *Vita Mercatoris,* p. 188.

15. Mercator to Abraham Ortelius, March 26, 1575.

16. Mercator to Camerarius, August 20, 1575.

17. Mercator to Abraham Ortelius, May 9, 1572.

18. Mercator to Johannes Crato von Krafftheim, October 23, 1578.

19. Molanus to Mercator, February 8, 1575.

20. Mercator to Johannes Crato von Krafftheim, October 23, 1578.

CHAPTER TWENTY. *A "Thick Myste of Ignorance" Dispelled*

1. Approximately £1.33.

2. William Burrough, *Instructions to Arthur Pet and Charles Jackman,* in Richard Hakluyt's *Principal Navigations, Voyages, Traffiques, and Discoveries of the English Nation* (1589 edition).

3. William Burrough, *A Dedicatory Epistle . . . unto his exact and notable mappe of Russia,* published in Richard Hakluyt's *Principal Navigations.*

4. Mercator to Emperor Maximilian II, February 1569.

5. Ghim, *Vita Mercatoris,* p. 187.

6. King James would succeed Elizabeth I as James I of England in 1603.

7. William Barlowe, *The Navigator's Supply* (1597).

CHAPTER TWENTY-ONE. *The Geography of the World*

1. Christopher Hall, in Richard Hakluyt's *Principal Navigations.*

2. Hakluyt's advice was later published in his book *A Discourse Concerning Western Planting* (1584).

3. The story Mercator told came originally from Jacob Cnoyen, the fourteenth-century traveler whose description of the North Pole he had incorporated into his world map of 1569. Cnoyen claimed to have heard about Arthur's expedition from a priest who had served in the court of the king of Norway.

4. Mercator to John Dee, April 1577. Quoted in E. G. R. Taylor, *A Letter Dated 1577 from Mercator to John Dee,* in *Imago Mundi,* vol. 13, 1955, pp. 55–68.

5. John Dee, *General and Rare Memorials Pertayning to the Perfect Arte of Navigation* (London, 1577).

6. A glance at a modern atlas shows why: The only possible way through the great islands north of Canada goes as far north as seventy-four degrees, the fringes of the permanent ice cap, while Russia's Taymyr Peninsula, known to Mercator as Cape Tabin, reaches almost to seventy-eight degrees. Not until the end of the nineteenth

century did a Swedish vessel, Baron Nils Nordensköld's *Vega,* fight a way around it, and a few years after that the Norwegian explorer Roald Amundsen spent three years struggling through the winding passage to the northwest.

7. Hakluyt's original letter to Mercator is lost and could conceivably have been written during May. In any event, it was too late for any reply to be received in London before the expedition departed.

8. Mercator to Richard Hakluyt, July 28, 1580.

9. Mercator to Abraham Ortelius, December 12, 1580.

10. Ibid. In fact, Drake paid off investors in his expedition at a rate of £47 for every pound. The English court, anxious to play down reports of his piracy and attacks on Spanish settlements in the Americas, would have been keen to encourage rumors of mysterious new trading routes.

11. Taylor, in *Tudor Geography,* p. 44, notes that reports about Drake's exploits off the coast of Central America—then the most recent reports about his position—were transcribed in the same document as the instructions for the masters of Pet's fleet.

12. Mercator to William Camden, January 31, 1579.

13. Mercator to Werner von Gymnich, July 14, 1578.

14. Mercator to Ludgerus Heresbachius, March 24, 1583.

15. Ibid.

16. Mercator, "Dedicatory Letter," *Atlas.*

17. Ibid.

18. Henry of Rantzau was well-known as an openhanded patron of scholars and artists across northern Europe, among them the astronomer Tycho Brahe. He was a noted writer and bibliophile in his own right, whose works on astrology featured in John Dee's famous library.

19. Mercator to Henry of Rantzau, December 12, 1585.

20. Mercator to Henry of Rantzau, September 7, 1586.

CHAPTER TWENTY-TWO. *The Gathering Dark*

1. Jerome de Roda, one of Philip's Council of State in the Netherlands, estimated in a letter to the king that over eight thousand citizens were killed.

2. John Dee to Abraham Ortelius, January 16, 1577.

3. He inherited the dukedom on the death of his father in 1586.

4. J. L. Motley, *The Rise of the Dutch Republic* AMS, 1973. (Originally published in 1856.)

5. Mercator to Wolfgang Haller, March 23, 1582.

6. Mercator to Ludgerus Heresbachius, March 24, 1583.

7. Barbe's birth date is unknown.

8. Mercator to Henry of Rantzau, September 7, 1586.

9. Ibid.

10. Ghim, *Vita Mercatoris,* p. 191.

11. Mercator, preface to *Atlas.*

12. Ibid.

13. Vedel was a Danish historian and ballad collector, who had also published a collection of over a hundred Danish folk songs from oral and manuscript sources. The map of Iceland had probably been drawn by Gubrandur Thorlaksson, bishop of Holar.

14. At the Arctic, where there were neither maps nor reliable reports from travelers on which to rely, he was forced to fall back on tradition and mythology. The curiously symmetrical inset from the world map of 1569 was enlarged and amended, with its four islands surrounding the great black rock at the pole. Between the islands, with deltas on the outer coastline, four channels carried the "indrawing seas" to the great whirlpool around the rock in which they were sucked into the earth.

15. Ghim, *Vita Mercatoris,* p. 194.

16. Ibid., p. 188.

17. John William succeeded to the dukedom in 1592.

18. Reiner Solenander to Mercator, July 1, 1954.

19. Arnold Mylius to Ortelius, December 26, 1594.

AFTERWORD

1. Michael, Arnold's third son, had been working in London with Rumold.

2. A copy of the 1595 edition of the atlas, measuring just over seventeen inches by eleven inches, is held at the Lessing J. Rosenwald Collection in the Library of Congress, Washington, D.C.

3. The commercial success of the atlas was at least partly due to Hondius's business sense. Apart from adding his own text, and maps to cover Spain, Africa, Asia, and America, he supervised the production of editions in Dutch, French, German, English, and Latin, and also produced a small-size version, which he named the *Atlas Minor.*

4. Venus and Jupiter have also been mapped by Mercator's projection.

5. Mercator's authorship of the projection did not prevent him from employing it on his own chart of the Atlantic in 1701. In a legend to the chart, he observed that "from its particular use in navigation [it] ought rather to be named the Nautical, as being the only true and sufficient chart for the sea." Halley's quote, and Mead's immediately following it, are both cited in John P. Snyder, *Flattening the Earth* (Chicago: University of Chicago Press, 1993), p. 293.

6. There is some irony in such accusations of dishonesty from a man with a record like Mead's of dishonesty, trickery, and deception: As a young man, he spent time in prison following the failure of a plot to cheat a twelve-year-old heiress of her property with a fake marriage, and after that he lived under several aliases as he swindled his way around London. Despite his gambling, womanizing, and chicanery, though, he was responsible for ten or more books, maps, and collections of travels for a variety of publishers. And for all his colorful background, his accusation reflected a widespread feeling at the time that Mercator had been wrongly credited with the discovery.

7. Particularly by Jerry Brotton, in his cogent and incisive book *Trading Territories* (London: Reaktion Books, 1997). He suggests on p. 169, "It could be viewed as the first map to signify, geographically and politically, the triumph of the west."

8. The projection was strikingly similar to one constructed by James Gall, an Edinburgh clergyman, in the mid–nineteenth century, although Peters always denied having seen the earlier version.

9. The map, designed by Bernard J. Cahill, was constructed on eight triangles arranged in the shape of a butterfly with its wings spread.

BIBLIOGRAPHY

Alvarez, Manuel Fernandez. *Charles V*. London: Thames and Hudson, 1975.

Arciniegas, German. *Caribbean: Sea of the New World*. Trans. Harriet De Onis. New York: Knopf, 1946.

Aston, Margaret. *The Fifteenth Century—the Prospect of Europe*. London: Harcourt, Brace and World, 1968.

Aubert, R. *The University of Louvain, 1425–1975*. Trans. Norman Stone. Antwerp: University of Louvain Press, 1976.

Aubrey, John. *Brief Lives*. Ed. Oliver Lawson Dick. London: Secker and Warburg, 1971.

Best, Thomas W. *Macropedius*. New York: Twayne, 1972.

Birch, T. W. *Maps Topographical and Statistical*. London: Oxford University Press, 1964.

Blockmans, W., and W. Prevenier. *The Promised Land: The Low Countries Under Burgundian Rule*. Philadelphia: University of Pennsylvania Press, 1999.

Blondeau, Roger A. *Mercator van Rupelmonde*. Tielt: Lanoo, 1993.

Brotton, Jerry. *Trading Territories*. London: Reaktion Books, 1997.

Brown, Lloyd A. *The Story of Maps*. London: Cresset Press, 1951.

Buisseret, David. *The Mapmakers' Quest*. Oxford: Oxford University Press, 2003.

Cam, G. A. *Gerhard Mercator: His Orbis Imago of 1538*. New York: vol. 41 Bulletin of the New York Public Library, 1937.

Clair, Colin. *Christopher Plantin*. London: Cassell, 1960.

———. *History of European Printing*. London: Academic Press, 1976.

Collinson, Rear Admiral Richard. *Frobisher's Three Voyages*. London: Hakluyt Society, 1897.

Crane, Nicholas. *Mercator, the Man Who Mapped the Planet*. London: Weidenfield and Nicholson, 2002.

de Enzinas, Francisco. *La chasse aux Luthériens des Pays-Bas*. Ed. Albert Savine. Paris: Louis Michaud, 1910.

De Smet, Antoine. *Mercator à Louvain*. Vol. 6: Duisburger Forschungen, 1962.

Deacon, R. *John Dee, Scientist, Geographer, Astrologer and Secret Agent to Elizabeth I*. London: Frederick Muller, 1968.

Dekker, Elly. *Globes at Greenwich*. London: Oxford University Press, 1999.

Dekker, Elly, and Peter van der Krogt. *Globes from the Western World*. London: Zwemmer, 1993.

Dekker, Thomas. *The Wonderful Year 1603*. Ed. A. L. Rowse. London: Folio Press, 1989.

Delevoy, Robert L. *Bosch, Biography and Critical Study*. Paris: Albert Skira, 1972.

Dickens, A. G. *The Counter Reformation*. London: Thames and Hudson, 1968.

Dickens, A. G., and W. R. D. Jones. *Erasmus the Reformer*. London: Methuen, 1994.

Drummond, R. B. *Erasmus, His Life and Character*. London: Smith, Elder, 1873.

Edson, E. *Mapping Time and Space*. London: British Library, 1999.

Elton, G. R., ed. *Cambridge Modern History—Reformation, 1520–59*. Cambridge: Cambridge University Press, 1956.

Erasmus, Desiderius. *Collected Works of Erasmus*. Toronto: Toronto University Press, 1974.

Eyck, Frank. *Religion and Politics in German History*. Houndmills: Macmillan, 1998.

Fenton, Edward, ed. *The Diaries of John Dee*. Charlbury: Day Books, 1998.

Ghim, Walter. *Vita Mercatoris*. See Osley, A. S.

Grierson, Edward. *The Fatal Inheritance—Philip II and the Spanish Netherlands*. London: Victor Gollancz, 1969.

Haasbroek, N. D. *Gemma Frisius, Tycho Brahe, Snellius and Their Triangulations*. Delft: Rijkscommissie voor Geodesie, 1968.

Hakluyt, Richard. *Principal Navigations, Voyages, Traffiques, and Discoveries of the English Nation*. London: Dent, 1907. (Originally published in 1598.)

Hale, John Rigby. *The Civilisation of Europe in the Renaissance*. London: HarperCollins, 1993.

Hardt, R. *The Globe of Gemma Frisius*. London: vol. 9, Imago Mundi, 1952.

Harris, Lynda. *The Secret Heresy of Hieronymus Bosch*. London: Floris Books, 1995.

Hyma, Albert. *The Youth of Erasmus*. Ann Arbor: University of Michigan Publications, 1930.

Karrow, Robert W. *Mapmakers of the 16th Century and Their Maps*. Chicago: Speculum Orbis Press, 1993.

Kish, George. *Life and Works of Gemma Frisius*. Minneapolis: University of Minnesota Press, 1967.

Koenigsburger, H. G. *Early Modern Europe*. London: Longman, 1987.

Lewis, Bernard. *The Muslim Discovery of Europe*. London: Weidenfeld and Nicholson, 1982.

Lindeman, Yehudi, ed. *Two Comedies of Macropedius*. Nieuwkoop: De Graaf, 1983.

McDermott, James. *Martin Frobisher, Elizabethan Privateer*. New Haven, Conn.: Yale University Press, 2001.

Manetti, Antonio di Tuccio. *Life of Brunelleschi*. Ed. H. Saalman, trans. C. Enggass. University Park: Pennsylvania State University Press, 1970.

Mead, Bradock. *The Construction of Maps and Globes*. London, 1717.

Menzies, Gavin. *1421—the Year China Discovered the World*. London: Bantam Press, 2002.

Mercator, Gerard. *Atlas, sive cosmographicae meditationes de fabrica mundi et fabricati figura*. Dusseldorf, 1595.

———. *Chronologia*. Cologne, 1569.

———. *Evangelicae historiae quadripartita Monas . . .* Duisburg, 1592.

———. *Literarum latinarum, quas italicas . . .* Leuven, 1539–40.

Midelfort, H. C. E. *The Mad Princes of Renaissance Germany*. Charlottesville: Virginia University Press, 1994.

Moir, D. G., et al. *The Early Maps of Scotland to 1850*. Edinburgh: Scottish Geographical Society, 1973.

Morrison, S. E. *Journals and Other Documents on the Life and Voyages of Christopher Columbus*. New York: Heritage, 1963.

Motley, J. L. *The Rise of the Dutch Republic*. London: Dean and Son, 1906 (originally published in 1856.)

Murray, John J. *Flanders and England—a Cultural Bridge*. Antwerp: Fond Mercator, 1985.

Ortelius, Abraham. *Theatrum Orbis Terrarum*. London, 1606.

Osley, A. S. *Mercator: A Monograph of the Lettering of Maps in the 16th Century*. London: Faber, 1969. (Includes a translation of Walter Ghim's *Vita Mercatoris*.)

Ousley, Sir William, ed. *The Oriental Geography of Ibn Haukal*. London, 1800.

Panofsky, Erwin. *Perspective as Symbolic Form*. New York: Zone Books, 1991.

Parker, G. *The Dutch Revolt*. London: Allen Lane, 1977.

Pelletier, Monique, ed. *Geographie du monde au Moyen Age et à la Renaissance*. Paris: Comité des Travaux Historiques et Scientifiques, 1989.

Porter, Steven. *The Great Plague*. Stroud: Sutton, 1999.

Rashdall, H. *The Universities of Europe in the Middle Ages*. Oxford: Oxford University Press, 1936.

Roach, Susan, ed. *Across the Narrow Seas—Studies in the History and Bibliography of Britain and the Low Countries*. London: British Library, 1991.

Rudolph Hirsch. *Printing, Selling, and Reading, 1450–1550*. Weisbaden: Harrassovitch, 1974.

Sherman, W. H. *John Dee*. Amherst: University of Massachusetts Press, 1995.

Skelton, R. A. *History of Cartography*. Cambridge, Mass.: Harvard University Press, 1964.

———. *Mercator and English Geography in the 16th Century*. Vol. 6. Duisberg-Ruhrort: Duisburger Forschungen, 1962.

Snyder, John P. *Flattening the Earth—2000 Years of Map Projections*. Chicago: University of Chicago Press, 1993.

Taylor, E. G. R. *Late Tudor and Early Stuart Geography, 1583–1650*. London: Methuen, 1934.

———. *Tudor Geography, 1485–1583*. London: Methuen, 1930.

Thorndike, Lynn. *University Records and Life in the Middle Ages*. New York: Columbia University Press, 1944.

Thrower, Norman J. W. *Maps and Civilization*. Chicago: University of Chicago Press, 1996.

Tracy, James D. *Holland Under Habsburg Rule, 1506–1566*. Berkeley: University of California Press, 1990.

Van der Essen, Leon. *Une institution d'enseignement supérieur.... L'université de Louvain 1425–1797*. Brussels; Paris: University of Leuven Press, 1921.

Van Durme, M., ed. *Correspondance Mercatorienne*. Antwerp: De Nederlandsche Boekhandel, 1959.

Van Macklenbergh, E., and J. Van Ouhesden. *The Cathedral of St. Jan, 's Hertogenbosch*. Zwolle: Boekhandel Adr. Heinen, 1985.

Van Raemdonck, J. *Gerard Mercator, sa vie et ses oeuvres*. Saint Nicolas, 1869.

Voet, L. *Les relations commerciales entre Gerard Mercator et la maison Plantinienne*. Duisburg-Ruhrort: vol. 6, Duisburger Forschungen, 1962.

Watelet, M, ed. *The Mercator Atlas of Europe*. Pleasant Hill, Oregon: Walking Tree Press, 1998.

Waters, D. W. *Art of Navigation in England in Elizabethan and Early Stuart Times*. London: Hollis and Carter, 1958.

————. *The Art of Navigation in Tudor and Stuart Times*. New Haven, Conn.: Yale University Press, 1958.

Weinstein, Donald, ed. *Ambassador from Venice*. Minneapolis: University of Minnesota Press, 1960.

Wernham, R. B., ed. *Cambridge Modern History—Counter-Reformation and Price Revolution, 1559–1610*. Cambridge: Cambridge University Press, 1968.

Wilford, John Noble. *The Mapmakers*. New York: Vintage, 1982.

Woolley, Benjamin. *The Queen's Conjuror*. London: HarperCollins, 2001.

Wyndham-Lewis, D. B. *Emperor of the West*. London: Eyre and Spottiswoode, 1932.

INDEX